Studies in Diversity Linguistics

Chief Editor: Martin Haspelmath
Consulting Editors: Fernando Zúñiga, Peter Arkadiev, Ruth Singer, Pilar Valenzuela

In this series:

1. Handschuh, Corinna. A typology of marked-S languages.

2. Rießler, Michael. Adjective attribution.

3. Klamer, Marian (ed.). The Alor-Pantar languages: History and typology.

4. Berghäll, Liisa. A grammar of Mauwake (Papua New Guinea).

5. Wilbur, Joshua. A grammar of Pite Saami.

6. Dahl, Östen. Grammaticalization in the North: Noun phrase morphosyntax in Scandinavian vernaculars.

7. Schackow, Diana. A grammar of Yakkha.

8. Liljegren, Henrik. A grammar of Palula.

9. Shimelman, Aviva. A grammar of Yauyos Quechua.

10. Rudin, Catherine & Bryan James Gordon (eds.). Advances in the study of Siouan languages and linguistics.

11. Kluge, Angela. A grammar of Papuan Malay.

12. Kieviet, Paulus. A grammar of Rapa Nui.

13. Michaud, Alexis. Tone in Yongning Na: Lexical tones and morphotonology.

14. Enfield, N. J (ed.). Dependencies in language: On the causal ontology of linguistic systems .

15. Gutman, Ariel. Attributive constructions in North-Eastern Neo-Aramaic.

16. Bisang, Walter & Andrej Malchukov (eds.). Unity and diversity in grammaticalization scenarios.

ISSN: 2363-5568

Dependencies in language

On the causal ontology of linguistic systems

Edited by

N. J. Enfield

N. J. Enfield (ed.). 2017. *Dependencies in language: On the causal ontology of linguistic systems* (Studies in Diversity Linguistics 14). Berlin: Language Science Press.

This title can be downloaded at:
http://langsci-press.org/catalog/book/96
© 2017, the authors
Published under the Creative Commons Attribution 4.0 Licence (CC BY 4.0):
http://creativecommons.org/licenses/by/4.0/
ISBN: 978-3-946234-88-3 (Digital)
   978-3-946234-74-6 (Hardcover)
   978-3-946234-66-1 (Softcover)
ISSN: 2363-5568
DOI:10.5281/zenodo.573773

Cover and concept of design: Ulrike Harbort
Typesetting: Sebastian Nordhoff, Gus Wheeler
Illustration: Felix Kopecky
Proofreading: Martin Haspelmath
Fonts: Linux Libertine, Arimo, DejaVu Sans Mono
Typesetting software: XᴇLATEX

Language Science Press
Habelschwerdter Allee 45
14195 Berlin, Germany
langsci-press.org

Storage and cataloguing done by FU Berlin

Language Science Press has no responsibility for the persistence or accuracy of URLs for external or third-party Internet websites referred to in this publication, and does not guarantee that any content on such websites is, or will remain, accurate or appropriate.

Contents

1 Dependencies in language
   N. J. Enfield   1

2 Implicational universals and dependencies
   Sonia Cristofaro   9

3 New approaches to Greenbergian word order dependencies
   Jennifer Culbertson   23

4 From biology to language change and diversity
   Dan Dediu   39

5 Language intertwined across multiple timescales: Processing,
   acquisition and evolution
   Morten H. Christiansen   53

6 What comes first in language emergence?
   Wendy Sandler   63

7 Is language development dependent on early communicative
   development?
   Elena Lieven   85

8 Dependency and relative determination in language acquisition: The
   case of Ku Waru
   Alan Rumsey   97

9 Beyond binary dependencies in language structure
   Damián E. Blasi & Seán G. Roberts   117

10 Real and spurious correlations involving tonal languages
   Jeremy Collins   129

Contents

11 What (else) depends on phonology?
    Larry M. Hyman   141

12 Dependencies in phonology: hierarchies and variation
    Keren Rice   159

13 Understanding intra-system dependencies: Classifiers in Lao
    Sebastian Fedden & Greville G. Corbett   171

14 Structural and semantic dependencies in word class
    William A. Foley   179

15 On the margins of language: Ideophones, interjections and
    dependencies in linguistic theory
    Mark Dingemanse   195

Index   203

Chapter 1

Dependencies in language

N. J. Enfield
University of Sydney

Consider the if-then statements about language listed in Table 1 (overleaf).
 Each of these statements implies a kind of dependency between systems or structures in language (and sometimes with systems or structures outside of language), though the statements invoke different timescales, and imply different types of causal relation. Do these statements – and the many more that exist like them – belie a unified notion of dependency in language? Or do they merely point to family resemblances among loosely related concepts? Here are some of the (non-exclusive) ways in which we might mean that A is dependent on B:

- To state a rule concerning A one must refer to B
- When a process affects B, it will necessarily affect A
- The existence of B is a condition for the existence of A
- The existence of B is a cause of the existence of A
- A cannot be expressed without also expressing B
- If B is the case, A is also likely to be the case

 It is important to define dependency clearly, because the notion of dependency in language is central to our understanding of key questions in our discipline. These questions include: How are linguistic sub-systems related? Are there constraints on language change? How are languages learned by infants? How is language processed in the brain? What is the relation between language and social context?
 This book explores the question of dependency in language with case studies and reviews from across the language sciences. Despite the importance of the concept of dependency in our work, its nature is seldom defined or made explicit. What kinds of dependencies exist among language-related systems, and how do we define and explain them in natural, causal terms?

Table 1: Some of the *if-then* statements found in language

If the verb comes before the object in a language, then that language probably has prepositions and not postpositions	Greenberg (1966)
If a speaker has just heard a passive construction, then they are more likely to produce one now	Pickering & Ferreira (2008)
In Estonian, if the verb 'to be' is negated, then no distinctions in person or number may be marked	Aikhenvald & Dixon (1998: 63)
If a conceptual theme is expressed in multiple different semantic systems of a language, then that theme will be of cultural importance to speakers of the language	Hale (1986)
If a language has three places of articulation in fricatives, then it has at least three places of articulation in stops	Lass (1984: 154)
If a transitive clause in Hindi is not in perfective aspect, then no ergative marking may occur	Kellogg (1893: 239)
If a language expresses manner and path of motion separately in its lexical semantics, then speakers of the language will express manner and path separately in their gestures	Özyürek et al. (2007)
If there is a voicing contrast in stops, then /t/ and /k/ are present	Sherman (1975)
If a child has not yet learned to produce and comprehend pointing gestures, then she will not acquire language	Tomasello (2008)
If a specific structure is highly embedded in language-specific grammatical structures, then it is less likely to be borrowed into an unrelated language	Thomason (2001: 69)

1 Condition

One important kind of relation that can define a dependency between co-occurring features is the relation of condition. This is where the existence of B is a condition for the existence of A. It is where A would not be observed were B not also observed. Clear examples are when B is a medium for A. For instance, without phonation, there can be no pitch contrast. Pitch contrast depends on phonation, because the existence of phonation is what makes pitch contrast possible. Similarly, in turn, without pitch contrast, there can be no systems of lexical tone. Note that conditional dependency cannot be paraphrased in terms of cause. We can say that if Thai speakers did not have phonation they would not have lexical tone. We cannot say that Thai speakers have lexical tone because they have phonation. Dependence in this conditional sense defines the relations between nested framings of language as a form of human action, as in Austin's ladder that links all types of linguistic act from the phonetic to the perlocutionary (Austin 1962; see also Clark 1996: 146; Enfield 2013: 91-92).

Conditional dependency introduces collateral effects (Enfield & Sidnell 2012). If A is conditionally dependent on B, then A cannot be expressed without also expressing, implying, or revealing B, regardless of whether this was wanted; thus the expression of B is a collateral effect of the intention to express A. An example comes from the expressive use of the hands in sign language (or co-speech hand gesture). If a person wants to use their hands to show the speed at which something moved, they are forced to show movement *in a certain direction* (e.g., North, South, North-Northeast, etc.), regardless of any intention to depict or reveal directional information. In this case, the depiction of direction of motion is a collateral effect of the depiction of speed of motion.

2 Cause

A second important kind of relation underlying dependency is that of cause. A problem with positing dependency relations among synchronic structures in language is that often no causal link between the two synchronic structures is posited at all (Clark & Malt 1984: 201). We are familiar with proposals of connections between language, culture, and thought, but explicit causal paths are seldom posited. What would it take to establish that there is a causal relation between a linguistic feature and a cultural value (in either direction)? First, consider how a grammatical feature comes to exist in a language in the first place. Grammatical properties of languages mostly come about by means of invisible hand processes (Smith 1776: Bk 4 Ch 2). This means that the causes of these effects are distributed through tiny steps in a massive process of diffusion of innovation in populations, a process that no person can directly guide. The outcomes of the process need not bear any direct relation to the beliefs, goals, or intentions that individuals have had in producing the original behaviour.

But this does not mean those things were not caused by people's behaviour. To discover and define those causes, one needs the microgenetic and enchronic and historical frames together, and one needs to allow that those frames be independent. This is not to say that such a relation of direct link between individuals' internal behavior and linguistic structures is impossible. It is merely to say that if a pattern is observed in language, it is not necessarily the case that it is there or like that because people wanted it to be there or like that. What I have just described is a type of causal disconnect between individual intentions and aggregate outcomes that is inherent to the causality involved in diachronic processes. These diachronic processes are, at base, actuated by the contributions of individuals. But they cannot be consummated by individuals. Rather they accumulate at the population level in ways that are beyond individuals' reach.

There is a further type of causal disconnect that should be pointed out here, which concerns the distinction between diachronic and ontogenetic framings of causal explanation of a linguistic structure. If I observe that a person has conventionalized a certain linguistic structure, and if I ask why this has happened, one explanation is ontogenetic: she speaks like that because her peers and elders spoke like that when she was learning her language. Her reasons for speaking that way might simply be "this is how we speak": when learning a language, infants apply a kind of docility principle (Simon 1990) by which they follow the practices of their community without questioning why things are done in the way that they are done. This strategy is efficient and adaptive. In this way one person's reasons for speaking in a certain way may have ontogenetic explanations (and of course with relation to specific instances of speaking, they may have enchronic and microgenetic explanations), yet they may be completely disconnected from the diachronic explanations for why those structures came to be used in that infant's community in the first place. Simpson (2002) argues that if innovations and extensions of meaning can be generated out of cultural values, they will not spring directly into grammar. Rather they will spring from patterns of inference, and patterns of discourse usage, and it is these patterns, in turn, that may later lead to a grammatical "structuration" of cultural ideas (see also Evans 2003; Blythe 2013). But importantly, we see here how there is a chain from microgenetic and enchronic processes to diachronic processes, and then to ontogenetic processes, through which the kinds of individual beliefs, goals, and motivations that we typically associate with cultural values get delinked from higher-level/cultural systems such as languages. In this way, a correlation between a grammatical structure in my language and a set of beliefs or values in my culture does not entail a causal relation in the sense that is usually understood, namely a direct causal relation.

3 Frames and biases

If we are going to understand dependency, we need to focus on the underlying dynamics of causal/conditional relations. One reason dependency is understudied in linguistics is that most of our questions begin with statements in a synchronic frame. But this is the one frame that fails to draw our attention to causes and conditions, because it is the one frame that brackets out time. Analyses of synchronically framed facts are accountable to a transmission criterion (Enfield 2014; 2015): if a trait is there, it has survived, in the sense that it has successfully passed through all the filters that might otherwise have blocked its diffusion and maintenance in a speech community.

To provide a natural, causal account for dependencies in language systems, we need to be explicit about the ontology of the transmission biases that define the causes and conditions we invoke. We need to specify how the abstract notion of a synchronic system has come to be instantiated in reality. It is not enough to describe a piece of language structure, a linguistic (sub)system, or a pattern of variance in language. We must ask why it is that way. One way to answer this is to find what has shaped it. "Everything is the way it is because it got that way", as biologist D'Arcy Thompson is supposed to have said (cf. Thompson 1917; see Bybee 2010: 1). The aim is to explain structure by asking how structure is created through use (Croft & Cruse 2004). If we are going to do this systematically and with clarity, a central conceptual task is to define the temporal-causal frames within which we articulate our usage-based accounts (see Enfield 2014: 9-21). Some of those frames are well established: in a diachronic frame, population-level dynamics of variation and social diffusion provide biases in a community's conventionalization of structure; in a microgenetic frame, sub-second dynamics of psychological processing, including heuristics of economy and efficiency, provide biases in the emergence of structure in utterances; in an ontogenetic frame, principles of learning, whether social, statistical, or otherwise, provide biases in the individual's construction of a repertoire of linguistic competence in the lifespan; and in an enchronic frame, the interlocking of goal-directed, linguistically-constructed actions and responses in structured sequences in social interaction. These frames vary widely in kind and in scale, but we need to keep them all in the picture at once. It is only by looking at the broader ecology of causal/conditional frames in language that we will we have any hope of solving the puzzles of dependency in language.

4 Questions

Here are some of the fundamental questions about dependency that kicked off the agenda for the collaboration that led to this book:[1]

- Some have tried to explain Greenbergian dependencies with reference to microgenetic or cognitive processes (appealing to ideas such as ease, economy, and harmony); To what extent have they succeeded? Why hasn't this work in psychology made a greater impact in linguistic typology?

- Others have tried to explain dependencies with reference to diachronic processes (where, to be sure, microgenetic processes are often causally implied); To what extent have they succeeded? Are these accounts different from pure processing accounts (given that there must be a causal account of linkage between individual processing biases and the emergence of community conventions)?

- Dependencies can be shown to hold in the application of rules and operations in different grammatical subsystems – e.g., the presence or absence of negation will often determine whether marking will be made in other systems, such as person/number/transitivity-related marking; what is the causal nature of such dependencies? How are they explained?

- There are numerous interfaces between lexical, grammatical, and perceptual/cognitive systems. What dependencies are implied?

- What are the knowns and unknowns of causal dependency in language? What is the state of the art? In what ways are the different notions of

---

[1] The project that produced this book began with a retreat titled "Dependencies among Systems of Language", held on June 4-7, 2014 in the Ardennes, at Château de la Poste, Maillen, Belgium. I gratefully acknowledge funding from the European Research Council through grant 240853 "Human Sociality and Systems of Language Use". I also thank the participants, including the authors, as well as Balthasar Bickel, Claire Bowern, and Martin Haspelmath for their contribution.

dependency related? Can we best make progress with these questions by taking an interdisciplinary approach?

Many further questions arose in the collaborations and discussions that ensued. Each of the chapters of the book addresses these questions in one way or another. None of the questions receives a final answer. It is hoped that this book makes some progress, and helps to sharpen these questions for further consideration as our knowledge, methods, and understanding of language develop.

References

Aikhenvald, Alexandra Y. & R. M. W. Dixon. 1998. Dependencies between grammatical systems. *Language* 74(1). 56–80.

Austin, J. L. 1962. *How to do things with words*. Cambridge, MA: Harvard University Press.

Blythe, Joe. 2013. Preference organization driving structuration: Evidence from Australian Aboriginal interaction for pragmatically motivated grammaticalization. *Language* 89(4). 883–919.

Bybee, Joan. 2010. *Language, usage and cognition*. Cambridge: Cambridge University Press.

Clark, Herbert H. 1996. *Using language*. Cambridge: Cambridge University Press.

Clark, Herbert H. & Barbara C. Malt. 1984. Psychological constraints on language: A commentary on Bresnan and Kaplan and on Givón. In Walter Kintsch, James R. Miller & Peter G. Polson (eds.), *Methods and tactics in cognitive science*, 191–214. Hillsdale, NJ: Lawrence Erlbaum.

Croft, William & D. Alan Cruse. 2004. *Cognitive linguistics*. Cambridge: Cambridge University Press.

Enfield, N. J. 2013. *Relationship thinking: Agency, enchrony, and human sociality*. New York: Oxford University Press.

Enfield, N. J. 2014. *Natural causes of language: Frames, biases, and cultural transmission*. Berlin: Language Science Press.

Enfield, N. J. 2015. *The utility of meaning: What words mean and why*. Oxford: Oxford University Press.

Enfield, N. J. & Jack Sidnell. 2012. Collateral effects, agency, and systems of language use. *Current Anthropology* 53(3). 327–329.

Evans, Nicholas D. 2003. Context, culture, and structuration in the languages of Australia. *Annual Review of Anthropology* 32. 13–40.

Greenberg, Joseph H. 1966. Some universals of grammar with particular reference to the order of meaningful elements. In Joseph H. Greenberg (ed.), *Universals of language (second edition)*, 73–113. Cambridge, MA: MIT Press.

Hale, Kenneth L. 1986. Notes on world view and semantic categories: Some Warlpiri examples. In Pieter Muysken & Henk van Riemsdijk (eds.), *Features and projections*, 233–254. Dordrecht: Foris.

Kellogg, S. H. 1893. *A grammar of the Hindí language*. London: Routledge & Kegan Paul.

Lass, Roger. 1984. *Phonology: An introduction to basic concepts*. Cambridge: Cambridge University Press.

Özyürek, Aslı, Roel M. Willems, Sotaro Kita & Peter Hagoort. 2007. On-line integration of semantic information from speech and gesture: Insights from event-related brain potentials. *Journal of Cognitive Neuroscience* 19(4). 605–616.

Pickering, Martin J. & Victor S. Ferreira. 2008. Structural priming: A critical review. *Psychological bulletin* 134.3. 427–459.

Sherman, Donald. 1975. Stop and fricative systems: A discussion of paradigmatic gaps and the question of language sampling. *Working Papers in Language Universals* 17. 1–32.

Simon, Herbert A. 1990. A mechanism for social selection and successful altruism. *Science* 250. 1665–1668.

Simpson, Jane. 2002. From common ground to syntactic construction: Associated path in Warlpiri. In N. J. Enfield (ed.), *Ethnosyntax*, 287–308. Oxford: Oxford University Press.

Smith, Adam. 1776. *An inquiry into the nature and causes of the wealth of nations*. London: W. Strahan.

Thomason, Sarah Grey. 2001. *Language contact: An introduction*. Edinburgh: Edinburgh University Press.

Thompson, D'Arcy Wentworth. 1917. *On growth and form*. Cambridge: Cambridge University Press.

Tomasello, Michael. 2008. *Origins of human communication*. Cambridge, MA: MIT Press.

Chapter 2

Implicational universals and dependencies

Sonia Cristofaro
University of Pavia

1 Introduction

In the typological approach that originated from the work of Joseph Greenberg, implicational universals of the form X → Y capture recurrent cross-linguistic correlations between different grammatical phenomena X (the antecedent of the universal) and Y (the consequent of the universal), such that X only occurs when Y also occurs. Y, on the other hand, can also occur in the absence of X.

Classical typological explanations for these correlations often invoke functional principles that favor Y and disfavor X. For example, a number of implicational universals describe the distribution of overt marking for different grammatical categories. If overt marking is used for nominal, inanimate or indefinite direct objects, then it is used for pronominal, animate or definite ones. If it is used for inalienable possession ('John's mother', 'John's hand'), then it is used for alienable possession ('John's book'). If it is used for singular, then it is used for plural. These universals have been accounted for by postulating an economy principle whereby the use of overt marking is favored for the categories in the consequent of the universal (pronominal, animate, or definite objects, alienable possession, plural) and disfavored for those in the antecedent (nominal, inanimate, or indefinite direct objects, inalienable possession, singular). This is assumed to be due to the former categories being less frequent and therefore more in need of disambiguation (Greenberg 1966; Nichols 1988; Comrie 1989; Dixon 1994; Croft 2003; Haspelmath 2006 and Haspelmath 2008, among others).

This type of explanation accounts for the fact that there are cases where Y occurs while X does not, rather than the implicational correlation between the occurrence of X and that of Y. To the extent that they are offered as explanations for the implicational universal as a whole, however, the relevant functional principles are meant to account also for this correlation. In this respect, there is an (often implicit) assumption that the phenomena disfavored by some functional principle, for example overt marking for a more frequent category, can only take place if the phenomena favored by that principle, for example overt marking for a less frequent category, also occur. This presupposes that the occurrence of the latter phenomena is a precondition for the occurrence of the former, hence there is a dependency relationship between the two.[1]

These explanations, however, have mainly been proposed based on the synchronic distribution of the relevant grammatical phenomena, not the actual diachronic processes that give rise to this distribution in individual languages. In what follows, it will be argued that many such processes do not provide evidence for the postulated dependencies between grammatical phenomena, and suggest alternative ways to look at implicational universals in general.

2 The diachrony of implicational universals

2.1 No functional principles leading to dependency

A first problem with assuming a dependency relationship between different grammatical phenomena X and Y in an implicational universal is that, in many cases, the actual diachronic processes leading to configurations where Y occurs while X does not do not appear to be related to principles that favor Y as opposed to X. A a result, there is no evidence that there should be a dependency relationship between X and Y due to these principles.

This is illustrated precisely by a number of processes leading to the use of zero vs. overt marking for different grammatical categories. Sometimes, the initial situation is one where all of these categories are marked overtly, and the marker for the less frequent category is eliminated as a result of regular phonological changes. In English, for example, the current configuration with zero marked

---

[1] An alternative possibility would be that particular principles that favor Y and disfavor X lead to the former being present in most languages an the latter being absent in many languages. In this case, the languages that have X would most likely also have Y, but there would be no dependency between X and Y. This implies, however, that Y should be found in most of the world's languages, which is often not the case. For example, while languages usually do not have overtly marked inanimate direct objects and zero marked animate ones, they often use zero marking for both. Zero marking for animate direct objects, then, is not infrequent, so in principle it would be perfectly possible for a language to have overtly marked inanimate direct objects and zero marked animate ones.

singulars and -s marked plurals resulted from a series of phonological changes that led to the elimination of all inflectional endings except genitive singular -s and plural -es (Mossé 1949). As phonological changes are arguably independent of the categories encoded by the affected forms, such cases provide no evidence that the presence of overt marking is related to the need to disambiguate the relevant categories, and hence that this should lead to a dependency between these categories in regard to their ability to receive overt marking. In fact, cross-linguistically, such processes can also affect the less frequent category. In Sinhala, for example, some inanimate nouns have overtly marked singulars and zero marked plurals (e.g. *pot-a/ pot* 'book-SG/ book.PL'). This was a result of phonological changes leading to the loss of the plural ending of a specific inflectional class (Nitz & Nordhoff 2010).

In other cases, all of the relevant categories are originally zero marked, and overt markers for the less frequent category arise as a result of the reinterpretation of pre-existing elements. For example, as illustrated in (1) below for Kanuri, markers for pronominal, animate or definite direct objects are often structurally identical to, and diachronically derived from topic markers.

(1) Kanuri (Nilo-Saharan)
   a. *Músa shí-**ga** cúro*
      Musa 3SG-OBJ saw
      'Musa saw him' (Cyffer 1998: 52)
   b. *wú-**ga***
      1SG-as.for
      'as for me' (Cyffer 1998: 52)

Markers for alienable possession arise from locative expressions, e.g. 'at the home of' and the like, as illustrated in (2) for Ngiti.

(2) Ngiti (Nilo-Saharan)
   a. *ma m-ìngyè   àba   bhà idzalí-nga*
      1SG sc-be.in.the.habit.PFPR father POSS courtyard-NOMLZR
      'I normally stay at the courtyard of my father' (Kutsch Lojenga 1994: 322)
   b. ***bhà:***
      at.home
      'at home' (Kutsch Lojenga 1994: 154)

Plural markers can arise from a variety of sources, for example distributive expressions, as in Southern Paiute, illustrated in (3). Another source are partitive expressions of the type 'many of us' and the like, in which the quantifier is dropped and the plural meaning associated with it is transferred to a co-occurring element, for example a genitive case inflection originally indicating partitivity, as illustrated in (4) for Bengali, or a verbal form, as illustrated in (5) for Assamese. In this language, the plural marker was originally a participial form of the verb 'to be' used in expressions such as 'both of them' (literally, '(they) being two').

(3) Southern Paiute (Uto-Aztecan)
qa'nɪ / qaŋqa'nɪ
house / house.DISTR

'house, houses' (Sapir 1930: 258)

(4) Bengali (Indo-European)

a. *chēlē-rā*
child-GEN

'children' (15th century: Chatterji 1926: 736)

b. *āmhā-rā*
we-GEN

'of us' (14th century: Chatterji 1926: 735)

(5) Assamese (Indo-European)

a. *chātar-**hãt***
student-PL

'Students' (Modern Assamese: Kakati 1962: 295)

b. *dui-**hanta***
two-be.PTCPL

'Both of them' (Early Assamese: Kakati 1962: 282)

These processes are plausibly context-driven, either in the sense that some element becomes associated with a meaning that can be inferred from the context or in the sense that it takes on a meaning originally associated with a co-occurring element. Any restrictions in the distribution of the resulting markers are directly related to the properties of the source construction. For example, topic markers can become direct object markers when they are used with topicalized direct objects (Iemmolo 2010, among others). As topics are usually pronominal, animate, and definite, it is natural that the resulting markers should be restricted to these types of direct objects, at least initially. Possession can be inferred in many contexts involving locative expressions (e.g., 'the courtyard in my father's house' > 'my father's courtyard': Claudi & Heine 1986; Heine, Claudi & Hünnemeyer 1991: chapter 6), so these expressions can easily develop a possessive meaning. As they are not usually used to refer to inalienably possessed items (? 'The mother in John's house', ? 'The hand in John's house'), the resulting possessive markers will be restricted in the same way. Distributives can develop a plural meaning because, when applied to individuated items, they always involve the notion of plurality (Mithun 1999: 90). Partitive expressions with plural quantifiers also involve the notion of plurality, so this notion is easily transferred from one component of the expression to another.

This type of process has long been described in classical historical linguistics and grammaticalization studies (see, for example, Heine, Claudi & Hünnemeyer 1991, Bybee, Perkins & Pagliuca 1994, or Traugott & Dasher 2005). In all of the cases just discussed, the use of overt marking for particular categories is a result of contextually dependent associations that speakers establish between those categories and highly specific source elements. The categories not involved in this process retain zero marking, which was the strategy originally used for all categories. In such cases too, then, there is no obvious evidence that the distribution of overt marking reflects some principle that favors overt marking for particular categories as opposed to others, nor that such a principle should determine a dependency between the use of overt marking for some category and its use for some other category. This is further confirmed by the fact that, depending on the source construction, some of these processes can also give rise to markers for more frequent categories, even if less frequent categories are zero marked in the language. In Imonda, for example, a partitive case ending took on a meaning component originally associated with a co-occurring quantifier. As this process took place in expressions involving singular quantifiers (e.g. 'one of the women'), the result was the creation of a singular marker, leading to a situation where singular is overtly marked and plural is zero marked. This is illustrated in (6) (the marker is also used to indicate dual, and is therefore called "nonplural" in the source)[2].

---

[2] Evidence that the distribution of overt markers is directly related to the properties of the source construction is also provided by the fact that, cross-linguistically, overt markers derived from sources compatible with different categories usually apply to all of these categories regardless of their relative frequency. This is discussed in detail in Cristofaro (2013) and (2014) with regard to the development of direct object markers applying to all types of direct objects.

(6) Imonda (Border)

    a. *agõ-ianèi-m   ainam fa-i-kõhõ*
       women-NONPL-GL quickly EL-LNK-go
       'He grabbed the woman' (Seiler 1985: 194)

    b. *mag-m ad-ianèi-m*
       one-GL boys-SRC-GL
       'To one of the boys' (Seiler 1985: 219)

2.2 Co-occurrence patterns are not dependency patterns

Another problem for the idea of a dependency between X and Y in implicational universals of the form X → Y is that, in several cases where X and Y co-occur, the two are not actually distinct phenomena, hence there is no evidence that one of the two is a precondition for the other.

When overt marking for singular co-occurs with overt marking for plural, for example, the relevant markers are actually sometimes gender markers that evolved from demonstratives or personal pronouns, as is often the case with gender markers (Greenberg 1978). As the source elements had distinct singular and plural forms, the resulting gender markers end up indicating singular and plural in addition to gender. This process, for instance, has been reconstructed by Heine for Kxoe, where a series of gender markers with distinct singular and plural forms are structurally similar to the forms of the third person pronoun, as can be seen from Table 1.

Table 1: Gender/number markers and third person pronouns in Kxoe (Khoisan: Heine 1982: 211)

		Nouns		Pronouns	
SG	M	/õa-mà	'boy'	xà-má, á-mà, i-mà	'he'
	F	/õa-hḛ̀	'girl'	xà-hḛ̀, á-hḛ̀, i-hḛ̀	'she'
	C	/õa-('à), /õa-djì	'child'	(xa-'à)	'it'
PL	M	/õa-//uʻa	'boys'	xà-//u̩á, á-//u̩á, í-//u̩á	'they'
	F	/õa-djì	'girls'	xà-djí, á-djí, í-djí	'they'
	C	õa-nà	'children'	xà-nà, á-nà, í-nà	'they'

As the singular and plural markers are originally different paradigmatic forms of the same source element (one not specifically used to indicate number), cases like this provide no evidence that there is a dependency between overt marking for singular and overt marking for plural in themselves. To prove this, one would need cases where singular and plural markers develop through distinct processes. It is not clear, however, how many of the cases where singular and plural markers co-occur synchronically are actually of this type.

A similar example is provided by a word order universal discussed by Hawkins (1983; 2004). In prepositional languages, if the relative clause precedes the noun, then so does the possessive phrase. Hawkins accounts for this by assuming that, since relative clauses are structurally more complex than possessive phrases, the insertion of the former between the preposition and the noun creates a configuration more difficult to process than the insertion of the latter. Thus, a language will permit the more difficult configuration only if it also permits the easier one.

Aristar (1991) shows, however, that relative clauses and possessive phrases sometimes represent an evolution of the same construction, one where an expression involving a demonstrative is in apposition to a head noun, e.g. 'That (who) Verbed, X' or 'That (of) Y, X', which give rise, respectively, to 'The X who Verbed' and 'The X of Y', with the demonstrative evolving into a genitive and a relative marker. Evidence of this process is provided for example by Amharic (one of the languages considered by Hawkins), where the same element, derived from a demonstrative, is used both as a relative and as a possessive marker (Cohen 1936; Leslau 1995).

(7) Amharic (Semitic)

a. *yä-mäṭṭa   säw*
   REL-come.PERF.3SG person
   'a person who came' (Leslau 1995: 81)

b. *yä-tämari   mäṣaf*
   POSS-student book
   'a student's book' (Leslau 1995: 81)

In such cases too, there is no evidence of a dependency between preposed relatives and preposed possessive phrases in themselves, because the reason why both the relative clause and the possessive phrase precede the noun is that this was the order of the demonstrative phrase from which they both derive. Evidence for the correlation could be provided by cases where preposed relative clauses and preposed possessive phrases develop independently, but, once again, it is not clear how many of the synchronic cases where the two co-occur are actually of this type.

Sonia Cristofaro

3 Accounting for unattested configurations: goal-oriented vs. source-oriented explanations

The idea that the configurations described by an implicational universal X → Y reflect the properties of particular source constructions and developmental processes provides no specific explanation for why X does not usually occur in the absence of Y. In theory, this could still be viewed as evidence that there must be some general functional principle that disfavors X as opposed to Y, leading to a dependency relationship between the two. In this case, however, it is necessary to explain how such a principle could interact with the actual, apparently unrelated diachronic processes leading to the configurations described by the universal.

One possibility would be to suppose that the principle provides the ultimate motivation for individual diachronic processes. For example, overt markers for less frequent categories develop through several processes of reinterpretation of different source elements, but these processes could all somehow be triggered by the relative need to give overt expression to those categories. Likewise, phonological erosion of markers used for more frequent categories could ultimately be related to the lower need to give overt expression to those categories.

These assumptions, however, are not part of any standard account of the relevant processes in historical linguistics, and they are not supported by any kind of direct evidence (see Cristofaro 2013 and 2014 for further discussion). Rather, some processes provide evidence to the contrary. For example, when markers for particular categories develop through the reinterpretation of pre-existing elements, the language often already has other markers for those categories. This supports the idea that such processes are a result of context-driven inferences, not the relative need to give overt expression to particular categories. Also, some of the processes that give rise to configurations where Y occurs while X does not can also give rise to the opposite configuration. For example, as mentioned above, phonological erosion can target both markers for more frequent categories and markers for less frequent categories, leading to configurations where more frequent categories are overtly marked and less frequent categories are zero marked. Likewise, depending on the source construction, some processes of context-driven reinterpretation can give rise both to markers for less frequent categories and markers for more frequent categories, leading to configurations where less frequent categories are zero marked and more frequent categories are overtly marked. This suggests that whether or not X can occur without Y actually depends on particular processes and source constructions that give rise to X, rather than any principle specifically pertaining to X or Y in themselves.

2 Implicational universals and dependencies

Another possibility would be that particular functional principles that favor Y as opposed to X are responsible for differential transmission rates for X and Y within a speech community, ultimately leading to the loss or maintenance of different configurations involving X and Y. For example, it could be the case that, while the development of overt marking for particular categories is independent of the relative frequency of those categories, overt marking for less frequent categories is more easily transmitted than overt marking for more frequent categories because the latter are less in need of disambiguation. This could eventually lead to the loss of configurations where more frequent categories are overtly marked[3].

As suggested by a referee, this would be the equivalent of the technical distinction between proximate vs. ultimate explanations in evolutionary biology (Scott-Phillips, Dickins & West 2011, among many others): the development of particular traits is independent of the fact that those traits confer an evolutionary advantage to the organisms carrying them, but this provides the ultimate explanation for their distribution in a population. In evolutionary biology, however, this idea is based on the fact that particular traits are demonstrably adaptive to the environment, in the sense that they make it more likely for the organisms carrying them to survive and pass them on to their descendants. For languages, there is generally no evidence that particular functional properties of grammatical constructions (e.g. the fact that they conform to a principle of economy) are adaptive, in the sense of these properties making it demonstrably more likely for the construction to be transmitted from one speaker to another. This is a crucial difference between linguistic evolution and biological evolution, and there is a long tradition of linguistic thought in which the transmission of individual constructions within a speech community is entirely determined by social factors independent of particular functional properties of the construction (see, for example, McMahon 1994 and Croft 2000 for reviews of the relevant issues and literature).

In general, diachronic evidence suggests a different way to tackle the problem of why certain configurations are unattested or rare. Classical explanations of this phenomenon are goal-oriented, in the sense that they assume that particular configurations arise or do not arise in a language depending on whether the properties of the configuration conform to particular principles, for example economy or processing ease. To the extent that individual configurations are a result of specific developmental processes involving pre-existing constructions, however, the issue of why certain configurations arise or do not arise should

---

[3] Note, however, that this predicts that configurations where more frequent and less frequent categories are both overtly marked should not occur, or should be relatively rare, which is not the case.

rather be addressed by taking a source-oriented approach, that is, by looking at what source constructions, contexts and developmental processes could give rise to those configurations, and how frequent these are. This need not be related to any principle pertaining to the resulting configurations in themselves, and should therefore be assessed independently.

4 Concluding remarks

Ever since Greenberg's work, implicational universals have been regarded as one of the most important results of typological research because it is generally assumed that they capture some type of dependency between logically distinct grammatical phenomena. The fact that diachronic data often provide no evidence either for the principles assumed to motivate the dependency or for the dependency in the first place suggests that this view is at least partly biased by the adoption of an exclusively synchronic perspective. In general, this supports the point raised by some typologists that explanations for language universals should always be tested against the diachronic processes that give rise to the relevant grammatical phenomena in individual languages (Bybee 1988, 2006 and 2008, among others; see also Cristofaro 2013 and 2014 for a recent elaboration on this view and Blevins 2004 for a similar approach in phonology).

There also is, however, a more fundamental sense in which diachronic evidence challenges current views of implicational universals The use of implicational universals to describe the attested distributional configurations for two grammatical phenomena X and Y (that is, given X → Y, X and Y both present or both absent, or X absent and Y present) is usually associated with an assumption that these configurations are manifestations of some overarching pattern captured by the universal. This is apparent from the fact that the various configurations are usually accounted for in terms of a single principle, for example economy or processing ease. Diachronic evidence shows, however, not only that individual principles that can be postulated on synchronic grounds may play no role in the actual diachronic processes that give rise to the relevant configurations, but also that different configurations described by a universal can be a result of very different processes.

For example, the use of overt marking for both singular and plural and its use just for plural can be a result of different grammaticalization processes involving different source constructions, such as demonstratives or personal pronouns evolving into gender markers on the one hand and distributives evolving into plural markers on the other. Different instances of the same configuration can also be a result of very different processes. For example, phonological erosion, meaning transfer from a quantifier to an accompanying element, and the grammaticalization of distributives into plural markers can all give rise to a configuration with zero marking for singular and overt marking for plural, yet they do not obviously have anything in common. In fact, at least some of these processes may also sometimes have the opposite outcome (zero marking for a more frequent category and overt marking for a less frequent one).

These facts suggest that implicational universals might actually just be schemas that are general enough to capture the outputs of several particularized diachronic processes, rather than theoretically significant generalizations capturing an overarching pattern. In domains such as biological evolution, the distribution of some trait in a population is demonstrably related to particular properties of that trait that are independent of its origin. Even if the trait develops through different mechanisms in different cases, then, its distribution will reflect some general underlying pattern. There is no evidence, however, that this is the case in linguistic evolution. In order to obtain a full understanding of implicational universals, then, we should focus on qualitative and quantitative data on different source constructions and developmental processes that can give rise to the distributional configurations described by individual universals, rather than the configurations in themselves.

Acknowledgements

I wish to thank Joan Bybee, Bill Croft, Matthew Dryer, Spike Gildea, Martin Haspelmath, Elena Lieven, and Seán Roberts for their feedback on previous versions of this paper. Seán Roberts, in particular, provided extremely detailed and stimulating comments, not all of which could be addressed here due to space constraints. The usual disclaimers apply.

Abbreviations

ART	article	NOMLZ	nominalizer
C	common	NONPL	non-plural
DEP.FUT	dependent future	OBJ	object
DISTR	distributive	PFPR	perfective present
GEN	genitive	PTCPL	participle
GL	goal	REL	relative
IMPF	imperfect	SG	singular
INAL	inalienable		

References

Aristar, Anthony R. 1991. On diachronic sources and synchronic patterns: An investigation into the origin of linguistic universals. *Language* 67. 1–33.

Blevins, Juliette. 2004. *Evolutionary phonology: The emergence of sound patterns.* Cambridge: Cambridge University Press.

Bybee, Joan. 1988. The diachronic dimension in explanation. In John A. Hawkins (ed.), *Explaining language universals*, 350–379. Oxford: Basil Blackwell.

Bybee, Joan. 2006. Language change and universals. In R. Mairal & J. Gil (eds.), *Linguistic universals*, 179–194. Cambridge: Cambridge University Press.

Bybee, Joan. 2008. Formal universals as emergent phenomena: The origins of structure preservation. In J. Good (ed.), *Linguistic universals and language change*, 108–121. Oxford: Oxford University Press.

Bybee, Joan, Revere Perkins & William Pagliuca. 1994. *The evolution of grammar.* Chicago & London: The University of Chicago Press.

Chatterji, Suniti Kumar. 1926. *The origin and development of the Bengali language.* Calcutta: Calcutta University Press.

Claudi, Ulrike & Bernd Heine. 1986. On the metaphorical base of grammar. *Studies in Language* 10. 297–335.

Cohen, Marcel. 1936. *Traité de langue amharique (abyssinie).* Paris: Institut d'Ethnologie.

Comrie, Bernard. 1989. *Language universals and linguistic typology.* 2nd edition. Oxford: Basil Blackwell.

Cristofaro, Sonia. 2013. The referential hierarchy: Reviewing the evidence in diachronic perspective. In D. Bakker & M. Haspelmath (eds.), *Languages across boundaries: Studies in the memory of Anna Siewierska*, 69–93. Berlin & New York: Mouton de Gruyter.

Cristofaro, Sonia. 2014. Competing motivations and diachrony: What evidence for what motivations? In Brian MacWhinney, Andrej Malchukov & Edith A Moravcsik (eds.), *Competing motivations in grammar and usage*, 282–98. Oxford: Oxford University Press.

Croft, William. 2000. *Explaining language change: An evolutionary approach.* Harlow, Essex: Longman.

Croft, William. 2003. *Typology and universals.* 2nd edition. Cambridge: Cambridge University Press.

Cyffer, Norbert. 1998. *A sketch of Kanuri.* Köln: Rüdiger Köppe.

Dixon, R. M. W. 1994. *Ergativity.* Cambridge: Cambridge University Press.

Greenberg, Joseph H. (ed.). 1966. *Universals of language.* Cambridge: MIT Press.

Greenberg, Joseph H. 1978. How does a language acquire gender markers? In Joseph H. Greenberg, Charles H. Ferguson & Edith A. Moravcsick (eds.), *Universals of human language*, vol. 3, 47–82. Stanford: Stanford University Press.

Haspelmath, Martin. 2006. Against markedness (and what to replace it with). *Journal of Linguistics* 42. 25–70.

Haspelmath, Martin. 2008. Creating economical morphosyntactic patterns in language change. In J. Good (ed.), *Linguistic universals and language change*, 185–214. Oxford: Oxford University Press.

Hawkins, John A. 1983. *Word order universals.* New York: Academic Press.

Hawkins, John A. 2004. *Efficiency and complexity in grammars.* Oxford: Oxford University Press.

Heine, Bernd. 1982. African noun class systems. In H. Seiler & C. Lehmann (eds.), *Apprehension: Das sprachliche Erfassen von Gegenständen*, 189–216. Tübingen: Narr.

Heine, Bernd, Ulrike Claudi & Friederike Hünnemeyer. 1991. *Grammaticalization.* Chicago: University of Chicago Press.

Iemmolo, Giorgio. 2010. Topicality and differential object marking: Evidence from Romance and beyond. *Studies in Language* 34(2). 239–72.

Kakati, Banikanta. 1962. *Assamese, its formation and development. 2nd edition.* Gauhati: Lawyer's Book Stall.

Kutsch Lojenga, Constance. 1994. *Ngiti: A central-Sudanic language of Zaire.* Köln: Rüdiger Köppe.

Leslau, Wolf. 1995. *Reference grammar of Amharic.* Wiesbaden: Harassowitz.

McMahon, April M. S. 1994. *Understanding language change.* Cambridge: Cambridge University Press.

Mithun, Marianne. 1999. *The languages of native North America.* Cambridge: Cambridge University Press.

Mossé, Fernand. 1949. *Manuel de l'anglais du moyen âge des origines au XIVme siècle. II. Moyen-Anglais. Tome premier: Grammaire et textes.* Paris: Aubier.

Nichols, Johanna. 1988. On alienable and inalienable possession. In W. Shipley (ed.), *In honor of Mary Haas*, 557–609. Berlin: Mouton de Gruyter.

Nitz, Eike & Sebastian Nordhoff. 2010. Subtractive plural morphology in Sinhala. In J. Wohlgemuth & Michael Cysouw (eds.), *Rara & Rarissima: Collecting and interpreting unusual characteristics of human languages*, 247–66. Berlin & New York: Mouton de Gruyter.

Sapir, Edward. 1930. *The Southern Paiute language.* Boston: American Academy of Arts & Sciences.

Scott-Phillips, Thomas C., Thomas E. Dickins & Stuart A. West. 2011. Evolutionary theory and the ultimate-proximate distinction in the human behavioral sciences. *Perspectives on Psychological Science* 6(1). 38–47.

Seiler, Walter. 1985. Imonda, a Papuan language. *Pacific Linguistics. Series B-* 93. 1–236.

Traugott, Elizabeth C. & Richard B. Dasher. 2005. *Regularity in semantic change.* Cambridge: Cambridge University Press.

Chapter 3

New approaches to Greenbergian word order dependencies

Jennifer Culbertson

School of Philosophy, Psychology and Language Sciences, University of Edinburgh, Edinburgh, UK

1 Cognitive explanations for language typology

1.1 Introduction

Implicational typological universals (e.g., Greenberg 1963) represent a class of dependencies that linguists have been seeking to document, refine and explain for decades. From a functionalist typological viewpoint, the goal of such explorations is to understand how these distributions of patterns arose through a combination of geography, history and cultural evolution. From a generative linguistic viewpoint, the goal is to relate dependencies to features of the human language faculty and thus inform and constrain grammatical theories. While these two perspectives could in principle be mutually informative (Hawkins 2004; Baker & McCloskey 2007), foundational differences have often prevented cross-talk between researchers (Bickel 2007; Haspelmath 2000; Newmeyer 1998). The goal of this chapter is to highlight a strand of behavioral research which can advance the goals of both functionalists and generativists alike. Evidence from controlled laboratory experiments brings to light cognitive biases which might play a causal role in constraining language change, and opens the door to investigating the extent to which they reflect properties of the language faculty narrowly construed, or rather domain-general forces potentially shared across cognitive systems (and even species). This source of evidence therefore adds to our understanding of why language is the way it is–by refining the set of factors likely to have shaped a particular distribution of linguistic patterns–and how we should characterize linguistic competence. I illustrate this with two case studies investigating the connection between two Greenbergian word order universals and asymmetrical learning outcomes in the lab.

1.2 Mental universals and typology

Under a traditional nativist view, typological universals are treated as a source of direct evidence from which to make inferences about the content of genetically encoded *mental* universals. The latter are formalized as grammatical constraints ensuring languages change in particular ways and not others, and relatedly, limiting the space of hypotheses entertained by language learners (e.g., Lightfoot 1989; Baker 2001). For example, Greenberg's Universals 3 and 4 state implicational relationships between word order across phrases: if a language is VSO it will have prepositions, by contrast SOV languages tend to have postpositions (Greenberg 1963). If these relations constrain how languages change, then one might expect that if the basic word order changes from VSO to SOV, the order of adpositions will also change (or at least will be more likely to do so).

Perhaps the most problematic aspect of this view is the idea that typology is the observable result of cognitive constraints. Most obviously, this is because distributions of patterns across the world's languages are undoubtedly affected by cognition-external factors–indeed in some cases they may be completely accounted for by appealing to the influence of historical coincidence, areal factors and/or culturally-driven influence. Teasing apart such factors is at best extremely challenging (Cysouw 2005; Ladd, Roberts & Dediu 2015; Piantadosi & Gibson 2014). Further, even if some cognitive constraint *is* part of the explanation for a particular typological universal, a number of questions necessarily remain: Is the underlying mechanism functionally motivated? Is the constraint innately encoded or learned? Is it domain-specific (either evolved specifically for language, or representationally specific to language) or does it operate across cognitive domains? This is particularly important since most typological "universals" are statistical rather than absolute. Universal 4, for example, describes a strong tendency for SOV languages to have postpositions, but this only holds in 472/486 or 97% of cases in a large sample (Dryer 2013c). If this universal is the reflection of an underlying cognitive constraint, it would not immediately be compatible with the notion of inviolable principle employed to formalize constraints in many generative frameworks.

1.3 Probing cognitive explanations experimentally

A growing body of research has begun to investigate the existence and content of mental universals through behavioral experiments, specifically using artificial language learning (ALL) paradigms. Although ALL has been used most extensively to test phonological pattern learning, studies featuring ALL experiments can now be found across all linguistic domains, including syntax (see Moreton & Pater 2012; Culbertson 2012 for literature reviews). This approach treats typology as a source of hypotheses about possible constraints or BIASES in language learning or use rather than as direct evidence for them. While converging evidence supporting a particular hypothesized bias could potentially come from studies of natural language acquisition, ALL paradigms have important advantages. Most obviously, the characteristics of the input language can be precisely controlled and contributions from multiple factors can be independently tested. In addition, it is relatively straightforward to test learning of rare or unattested patterns which might otherwise be very difficult if not impossible to investigate.

These paradigms also make it possible to test the nature and scope of hypothesized biases, for example by instantiating parallel patterns or structures in non-linguistic stimuli. Both domain-general and linguistically specific biases uncovered using these methods could in principle be formalized as inviolable constraints (hard limits on the space of possible languages) of the sort typically posited by mainstream generative linguistic theories. However, just as typological data are often in the form of statistical trends, behavioral data typically reveal probabilistic biases. This suggests they may be better captured by models which allow for probabilistic constraints (e.g., using Maximum Entropy or Probabilistic Harmonic Grammar formalisms; Goldwater & Johnson 2003; Wilson 2006). For example, Culbertson, Smolensky & Wilson (2013) create a probabilistic model of biases in noun phrase word order which also incorporates a bias for regularization – reducing of unconditioned variation – that is outside the grammar itself. Models like this therefore allow biases of different types to combine with one another to predict learning outcomes, and in principle could further take into account non-cognitive factors to more precisely model typological distributions. While many ALL studies focus on learning in individual participants, recent work has involved creating particular social conditions, adding communicative pressures, and transmitting learning outcomes across sets of participants to model language change (e.g., Fay et al. 2010; Kirby et al. 2015; Kirby, Cornish & Smith 2008). These factors can be straightforwardly incorporated into probabilistic models in order to formalize hypotheses and make further predictions about what shapes typology.

To give the reader a clear picture of how ALL works and the kinds of learning biases one can investigate using it, in what follows I discuss in more detail two case studies. These case studies highlight the use of two distinct ALL paradigms in testing the psychological reality of three biases in the learning of nominal word order predicted from Greenbergian Universals 18 and 20.

2 Greenberg's Universal 18

2.1 Introduction

Greenberg's Universal 18 (U18) is stated in (1) below.

(1) If Adj-N then Num-N.

This implicational universal rules out one of the four logically possible patterns in Table 1, namely the one which combines Adj-N with N-Num. The geographic distribution of these four patterns is shown using data from a much larger sample in Figure 1. This map in fact highlights the difficulty with interpreting raw typological frequency data: they may turn out to be misleading once genetic and areal relationship are taken into account. In this case, the larger sample shows that Adj-N & N-Num languages are in fact attested, however they may be over-represented in the raw numbers since the languages are clearly clustered in three small areas. Similarly, many of the languages classified as N-Adj & N-Num (numerically most frequent) are found clustered in Africa. This strongly suggests the need for additional empirical data in understanding this typological tendency.

Beyond Universal 18, Table 1 reveals a second trend in the raw frequency data: ordering patterns which place both Adj and Num on the same side of the noun are by far the most common in the sample. This type of pattern is sometimes called HARMONIC, while the other two are NON-HARMONIC (for discussion of this terminology see Croft 2003: 59-62). A trend toward harmony across phrases is a well

Table 1: Four possible combinations of {N, Adj} and {N, Num} with corresponding frequencies in the languages of the world based on Dryer (2013a,b).

	Adj-N	N-Adj
Num-N	251 (27%)	168 (17%)
N-Num	37 (4%)	509 (52%)

3 New approaches to Greenbergian word order dependencies

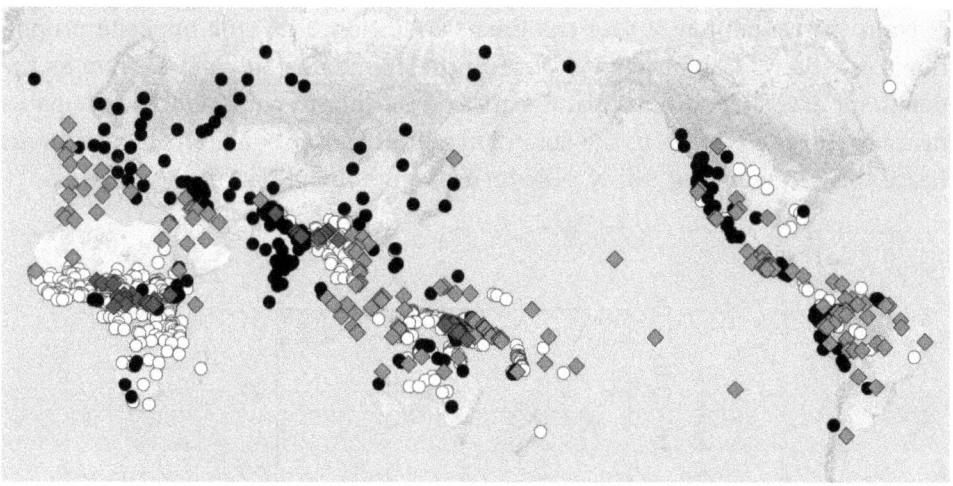

Figure 1: Geographical distribution of ordering patterns based on Dryer (2013a,b). Circles are harmonic (black: Adj-N, Num-N, white: N-Adj, N-Num), diamonds are non-harmonic (green: N-Adj, Num-N, red: Adj-N, N-Num).

known typological universal (many other Greenbergian universals are relevant for this, e.g., 2-6), which has been the subject of much research (e.g., Hawkins 1983; Travis 1984; Chomsky 1988; Dryer 1992; Baker 2001). To summarize then, we can hypothesize two biases based on these typological data: (i) a bias in favor of harmonic patterns, and (ii) a bias against the particular non-harmonic pattern combining pre-nominal adjectives with post-nominal numerals.

2.2 Testing Universal 18

The four patterns in Table 1 are intuitively simple and are all clearly learnable. How, then, might one uncover potentially subtle *differences* in learnability? In Culbertson, Smolensky & Legendre (2012) we did this by introducing variation into the input, essentially allowing us to see which patterns are more easily learnable under noisy conditions. Native-English-speaking adult learners were trained on phrases comprised of a noun and single modifier (adjective or numeral word), the order of which varied between a dominant order–heard in 70% of utterances–and the opposite–heard in 30% of phrases. The dominant order varied randomly across participants in the experiment and instantiated one of the four possible patterns in Table 1. The conditions are represented in Figure 2, with numbers 1–4 indicating the four conditions. For example, in condition 1, learners heard pre-nominal Adj-N and Num-N 70% of the time, and post-nominal N-Adj,

N-Num the remaining 30% of the time. Condition 2 has the opposite proportions, and therefore participants heard post-nominal N-Adj and N-Num as the dominant order. Conditions 3 and 4 are non-harmonic; condition 3 participants heard N-Adj and Num-N as the dominant pattern, while condition 4 participants heard the U18-violating Adj-N, N-Num as the dominant pattern.

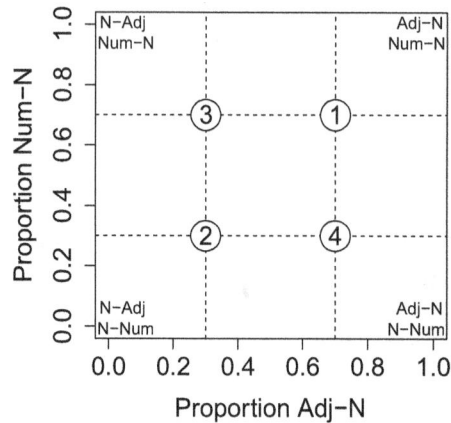

Figure 2: Illustration of experiment conditions. The corners of this space represent deterministic patterns, while inset numbers represent the four variable conditions used in the experiment. Note that condition 1 and 2 are harmonic, while 3, 4 are non-harmonic. Condition 4 is a variable version of the U18-violating pattern.

Independent evidence from natural language and ALL studies (e.g., Singleton & Newport 2004; Hudson Kam & Newport 2009) suggests that learners tend to *regularize* unpredictable (unconditioned) variation of the sort we used in this experiment. We hypothesized that learners would be most likely to regularize variable patterns which conformed to their biases, and would not regularize those they found more difficult to learn. This predicts that participants learning a variable version of one of the two harmonic patterns (1: Adj-N, Num-N, or 2: N-Adj, N-Num) should regularize the majority order, using it more than 70% of the time. By contrast, participants learning the non-harmonic pattern targeted by Universal 18 (4: Adj-N, N-Num) should *not* regularize that pattern.

These predictions were borne out by the results, as shown in Figure 3(a): participants in conditions 1 and 2 regularized the variation in their input–using the majority order substantially more than 70% of the time–while participants in condition 4 did not regularize. Participants in condition 3, who were exposed to

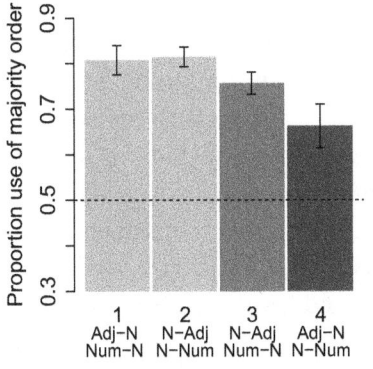
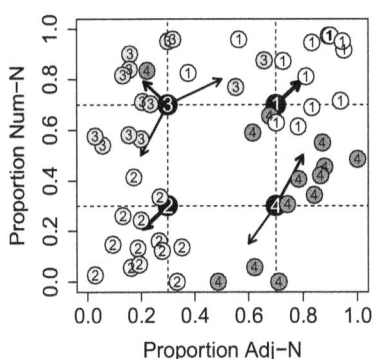

(a) Average use of the majority order in each condition.

(b) Behavioral outcomes for individual participants in each condition relative to their input.

Figure 3: Experiment results.

the non-harmonic pattern not violating U18, show some regularization but not as much as those in the harmonic conditions. Another way to visualize the behavioral outcomes in the experiment is in terms of the space shown in Figure 3(b), which plots individual participants' use of each order relative to their input. This illustrates how learners *shift* or change the language they are exposed to according to their biases. In conditions 1 and 2, learners' tendency to regularize aligns with their bias for harmonic patterns, therefore their output is shifted toward the deterministic corners relative to the input. In non-harmonic condition 3, some learners shift toward a more regular version of their input, but others actively move the language toward one of the two preferred harmonic patterns. In non-harmonic condition 4, this shifting toward a harmonic pattern is much more dramatic and *no* learners have regularized their input pattern. Interestingly, in this experiment native English-speaking participants showed only a small preference for their native-language order: the average regularization was the same across conditions 1 and 2, however more participants in the non-harmonic conditions shifted toward the pre-nominal harmonic pattern (for additional discussion about prior language experience and an alternative explanation of this difference see Culbertson, Smolensky & Legendre 2012; Culbertson & Newport 2015).

To summarize, in Culbertson, Smolensky & Legendre (2012), we started with Universal 18 and generated a set of hypothesized biases. We tested the psychological reality of these biases using an artificial language learning paradigm which exploits learners' tendency to regularize unpredictable variation. We confirmed that regularization of variation is indeed modulated by the particular type of pattern being learned; when the majority pattern in the input conforms to learners' biases, they regularize. When the majority pattern is dispreferred, learners actively change the language to bring it in line with their preferences. With this evidence in hand, researchers interested in constructing explanations for the typological distribution of nominal word order can more confidently add these factors into their models. Moreover, additional research using experimental methods can begin to explore *why* Universal 18 holds in the population tested, and *why* learners might prefer harmonic patterns. This could involve testing structurally similar patterns in non-linguistic domains or investigating the role of language experience in the development of these biases.

3 Greenberg's Universal 20

3.1 Introduction

Greenberg's Universal 20 (U20), as reformulated by Cinque (2005), is stated in (2) below.

(2) In pre-nominal position: Dem-Num-Adj
     In post-nominal position: Dem-Num-Adj or Adj-Num-Dem

The explanation for this implicational universal has received significant attention in the literature, particularly after additional typological work by Cinque (2005) and Dryer (2009). Figure 4 plots the frequency of each of the 24 possible combinations of N, Dem, Num, Adj in descending order. The two post-nominal orders picked out by Greenberg are highlighted in black. To account for this distribution, or key aspects it, a number of distinct proposals have been made (e.g., Cinque 2005; Abels & Neeleman 2012; Dryer 2009; Cysouw 2010; Steddy & Samek-Lodovici 2011). All of these proposals include a notion of the semantic or structural distinctions among the modifiers that can be described in terms of SCOPE, as illustrated in Figure 5. In this case, adjectives can be said to take innermost scope since they modify dimension inherent to noun meaning, while numerals serve to count these larger units. Demonstratives take highest scope because they serve to connect the internal material to the surrounding discourse.

These scope relations do not determine linear order, instead a given language can map these structural relations to linear order in various ways. Importantly, of the 24 possible patterns, eight preserve the underlying scope relations in the

3 New approaches to Greenbergian word order dependencies

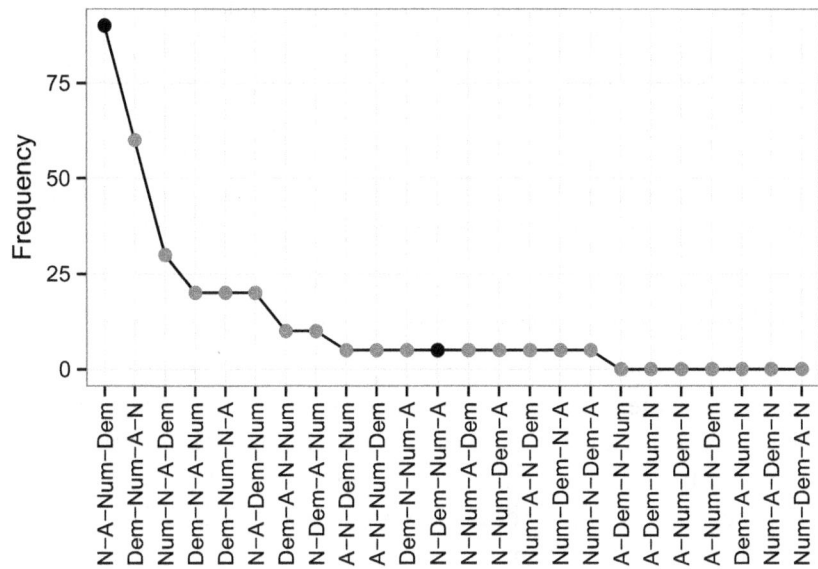

Figure 4: Frequency of 24 possible combinations of N, Dem, Num, Adj as reported in Dryer (2009). Post-nominal orders in Greenberg's Universal 20 are the black points.

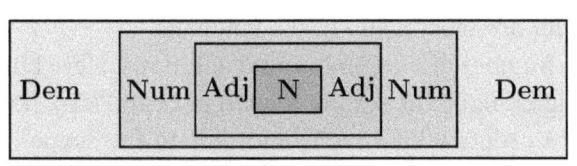

(a) Illustration of nested scope relationship among nominal modifiers.

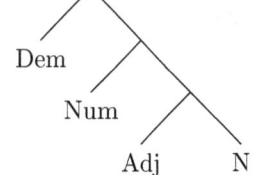

(b) Hierarchical representation of scope. Dem takes widest scope, Adj takes innermost scope.

Figure 5: Scope relationship among nominal modifiers

31

surface linear order. If in addition to preservation of the scope relations, harmony is also a factor which constrains language change, then we can explain why Dem-Num-Adj-N and the mirror order N-Adj-Num-Dem are the most frequent. Indeed, a principle encoding a harmony preference is present in most analyses of Universal 20, and harmonic patterns were shown to be preferred by learners in Culbertson, Smolensky & Legendre (2012). By the same reasoning, the alternative post-nominal pattern cited by Greenberg, N-Dem-Num-Adj, is expected to be less frequent since it is harmonic but does *not* maintain the isomorphism between scope and the linear order.

3.2 Testing U20

The two post-nominal orders in Greenberg's Universal, N-Adj-Num-Dem and N-Dem-Num-Adj differ from one another in two important ways. First, as described above, N-Adj-Num-Dem maintains the underlying scope relations in the linear order, while N-Dem-Num-Adj does not (in fact it perturbs them maximally). Second, N-Dem-Num-Adj has the same linear order of the modifiers as English, while N-Adj-Num-Dem does not (in fact it is the opposite). In Culbertson & Adger (2014), we capitalized on this pattern of differences to test whether English speakers learning a new language will transfer their knowledge of linear order, or their knowledge of scope-to-surface isomorphism. We did this by using the POVERTY-OF-THE-STIMULUS PARADIGM, in which learners are presented with examples from a new language in a way that withholds critical evidence about its structure. At test, learners must generalize to held-out data that will disambiguate the alternative hypotheses. In this experiment, participants heard phrases with a noun and a single post-nominal modifier and then at test were asked about the relative order of modifiers. For example, they might be trained on N-Dem and N-Adj sequences, and then be asked at test whether phrases with N-Adj-Dem or N-Dem-Adj order are most likely in the language.

We trained participants in a number of different input conditions. Here I highlight one set, summarized in Figure 6(a). The results, shown in Figure 6(b), reveal a striking preference at test for orders which are isomorphic to the scope over those with are more surface-similar to English. Interestingly, this preference was most dramatic when the input included Dem and Adj. This suggests that preserving the scope relations among the two most structurally distant modifiers (Dem and Adj) may be more important than the closer ones (either Dem, Num or Num, Adj). This prediction turns out to be typologically accurate; languages which perturb the scope of Adj, Num or Num, Dem are about twice as common as Adj, Dem.

3 New approaches to Greenbergian word order dependencies

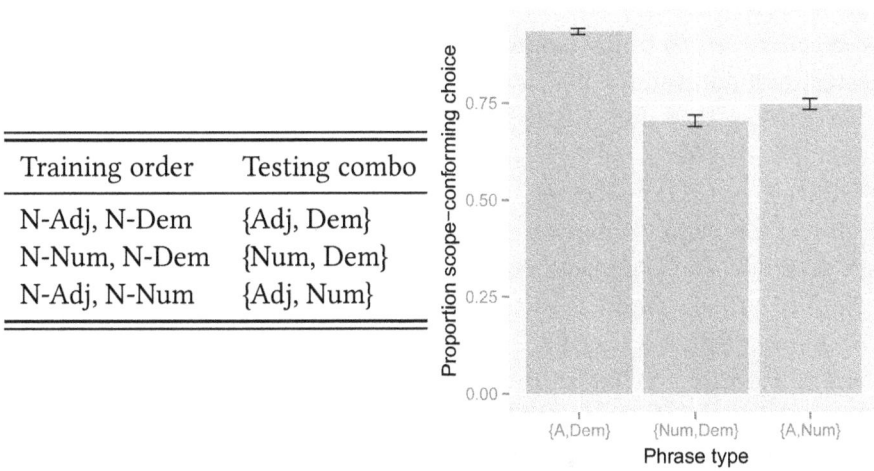

Training order	Testing combo
N-Adj, N-Dem	{Adj, Dem}
N-Num, N-Dem	{Num, Dem}
N-Adj, N-Num	{Adj, Num}

(a) Experimental conditions (b) Results by condition from Experiment 1

Figure 6: Conditions and results as reported in Culbertson & Adger (2014).

To summarize, this result provides the first experimental evidence for a bias favoring linear orders that maintain an isomorphism with the underlying semantic scope. The evidence is preliminary to the extent that participants' bias may come from knowledge of this abstract property of English. To determine whether the bias can be found in learners without direct experience with it, future work will need to target a population whose language *violates* this preference–for example Kikuyu is one of the few languages with N-Dem-Num-Adj. Nevertheless, combined with a preference for harmony, as shown in Culbertson, Smolensky & Legendre (2012), this provides a promising potential explanation for the typological asymmetry among these 24 ordering patterns. As with Universal 18, the scope of this bias remains an open question which can be investigated further using experimental techniques. It could be the case that the mapping between hierarchical structure and linear order in other domains (i.e. motor/action planning) respects similar kinds of constraints.

4 Conclusion

Research in typology is critical for generative linguistics, where the enterprise is to characterize the human language faculty, including any constraints on the systems it can generate. Although there is disagreement as to whether these constraints must be hard-and-fast limits, or soft biases, and whether they are necessarily special features of language, typology is a source of crucial data. I have suggested here that these data should be used in formulating hypotheses about possible biases rather than treated as their observable result. Accordingly, the goal of much research using ALL paradigms is to provide behavioral evidence for hypothesized connections between typological patterns, like Greenberg's word order universals, and properties of the human cognitive system. The two case studies described above present examples of this kind of research; in both cases, biases are hypothesized on the basis of typological data, and predicted effects on learning are tested using ALL. These experiments corroborate the typological evidence, suggesting that (1) learners are biased in favor of harmonic word order patterns and disfavor one non-harmonic pattern especially (Adj-N, N-Num), and (2) learners tend to infer relative orders of nominal modifiers that preserve the underlying semantic relations among them.

To the extent that connections between typological frequency and ease of learning are borne out, I would argue that the results also bear on major questions addressed by work in functionally-oriented typology; distinctions among patterns in terms of learnability (or use-ability) can be integrated into theories constructed to explain pathways of language change and, ultimately, typological distributions. The methods themselves are also increasingly used to further investigate the content and scope of biases, and whether they might be amplified or altered by social or communicative context. The case studies I have highlighted here illustrate, I hope, the kind of work that is informed by and can make progress in addressing important issues for both typology and generative linguistics.

Acknowledgements

I would like to thank Nick Enfield and attendees of the *Dependencies Among Systems of Language* workshop, held June 2014 in Ardennes, Belgium. I also thank Larry Hyman for comments on a previous version of this paper.

References

Abels, Klaus & Ad Neeleman. 2012. Linear asymmetries and the LCA. *Syntax* 15(1). 25–74.
Baker, Mark. 2001. *The atoms of language: The mind's hidden rules of grammar*. New York, NY: Basic Books.

Baker, Mark & James McCloskey. 2007. On the relationship of typology to theoretical syntax. *Linguistic Typology* 11(1). 273–284.
Bickel, Balthasar. 2007. Typology in the 21st century: Major current developments. *Linguistic Typology* 11(1). 239–251.
Chomsky, Noam. 1988. *Language and problems of knowledge: The Managua lectures*. Cambridge, MA: MIT Press.
Cinque, Guglielmo. 2005. Deriving Greenberg's Universal 20 and its exceptions. *Linguistic Inquiry* 36(3). 315–332.
Croft, William. 2003. *Typology and universals*. 2nd edition. New York: Cambridge University Press.
Culbertson, Jennifer. 2012. Typological universals as reflections of biased learning: Evidence from artificial language learning. *Language and Linguistics Compass* 6(5). 310–329.
Culbertson, Jennifer & David Adger. 2014. Language learners privilege structured meaning over surface frequency. *Proceedings of the National Academy of Sciences* 111(16). 5842–5847. DOI:10.1073/pnas.1320525111
Culbertson, Jennifer & Elissa L. Newport. 2015. Harmonic biases in child learners: In support of language universals. *Cognition* 139. 71–82.
Culbertson, Jennifer, Paul Smolensky & Géraldine Legendre. 2012. Learning biases predict a word order universal. *Cognition* 122. 306–329.
Culbertson, Jennifer, Paul Smolensky & Colin Wilson. 2013. Cognitive biases, linguistic universals, and constraint-based grammar learning. *Topics in Cognitive Science* 5(3). 392–424. DOI:10.1111/tops.12027
Cysouw, Michael. 2005. Quantitative methods in typology. In Reinhard Köhler, Gabriel Altmann & Rajmund G. Piotrowski (eds.), *Quantitative linguistics: An international handbook*, 554–578. Berlin: Mouton de Gruyter.
Cysouw, Michael. 2010. Dealing with diversity: Towards an explanation of NP-internal word order frequencies. *Linguistic Typology* 14(2). 253–287.
Dryer, Matthew S. 1992. The Greenbergian word order correlations. *Language* 68(1). 81–183.
Dryer, Matthew S. 2009. On the order of demonstrative, numeral, adjective and noun: An alternative to Cinque. Talk presented at Theoretical approaches to disharmonic word orders, Newcastle University, May-June 2009.
Dryer, Matthew S. 2013a. Order of adjective and noun. In Matthew S. Dryer & Martin Haspelmath (eds.), *The world atlas of language structures online*. Leipzig: Max Planck Institute for Evolutionary Anthropology. http://wals.info/chapter/87.

Dryer, Matthew S. 2013b. Order of numeral and noun. In Matthew S. Dryer & Martin Haspelmath (eds.), *The world atlas of language structures online.* Leipzig: Max Planck Institute for Evolutionary Anthropology. http://wals.info/chapter/89.

Dryer, Matthew S. 2013c. Relationship between the order of object and verb and the order of adposition and noun phrase. In Matthew S. Dryer & Martin Haspelmath (eds.), *The world atlas of language structures online.* Leipzig: Max Planck Institute for Evolutionary Anthropology. http://wals.info/chapter/95.

Fay, Nicolas, Simon Garrod, Leo Roberts & Nik Swoboda. 2010. The interactive evolution of human communication systems. *Cognitive Science* 34(3). 351–386.

Goldwater, Sharon & Mark Johnson. 2003. Learning OT constraint rankings using a maximum entropy model. In *Proceedings of the workshop on variation within optimality theory*, 111–120. Stockholm: Stockholm University.

Greenberg, Joseph H. 1963. Some universals of grammar with particular reference to the order of meaningful elements. In Joseph H. Greenberg (ed.), *Universals of language*, 73–113. Cambridge, MA: MIT Press.

Haspelmath, Martin. 2000. Why can't we talk to each other? *Lingua* 110(4). 235–255.

Hawkins, John A. 1983. *Word order universals.* New York: Academic Press.

Hawkins, John A. 2004. *Complexity and efficiency in grammars.* Oxford: Oxford University Press.

Hudson Kam, Carla & Elissa L. Newport. 2009. Getting it right by getting it wrong: When learners change languages. *Cognitive Psychology* 59(1). 30–66.

Kirby, Simon, Hannah Cornish & Kenny Smith. 2008. Cumulative cultural evolution in the laboratory: An experimental approach to the origins of structure in human language. *Proceedings of the National Academy of Sciences* 105(31). 10681–10686.

Kirby, Simon, Monica Tamariz, Hannah Cornish & Kenny Smith. 2015. Compression and communication in the cultural evolution of linguistic structure. *Cognition* 141. 87–102.

Ladd, D. Robert, Seán G. Roberts & Dan Dediu. 2015. Correlational studies in typological and historical linguistics. *Annual Review of Linguistics* 1. 221–241.

Lightfoot, David. 1989. The child's trigger experience: Degree-0 learnability. *Behavioral and Brain Sciences* 12(02). 321–334.

Moreton, Elliott & Joe Pater. 2012. Structure and substance in artificial-phonology learning, part I: Structure. *Language and Linguistics Compass* 6(11). 686–701.

Newmeyer, Frederick J. 1998. The irrelevance of typology for grammatical theory. *Syntaxis* 1. 161–197.

Piantadosi, Steven T & Edward Gibson. 2014. Quantitative standards for absolute linguistic universals. *Cognitive Science* 38(4). 736–756.

Singleton, Jenny L. & Elissa L. Newport. 2004. When learners surpass their models: The acquisition of American Sign Language from inconsistent input. *Cognitive Psychology* 49(4). 370–407.

Steddy, Sam & Vieri Samek-Lodovici. 2011. On the ungrammaticality of remnant movement in the derivation of Greenberg's Universal 20. *Linguistic Inquiry* 42(3). 445–469.

Travis, Lisa. 1984. *Parameters and effects of word order variation*. MIT Ph.D. dissertation.

Wilson, Colin. 2006. An experimental and computational study of velar palatalization. *Cognitive Science* 30(5). 945–982.

Chapter 4

From biology to language change and diversity

Dan Dediu
Max Planck Institute for Psycholinguistics, Nijmegen, The Netherlands

1 Introduction

Establishing CAUSALITY (or at least, attempting to) must rank as one of the most important aims of science, but despite the widespread impression to the contrary, any cursory look at the vast literature dedicated to it or, for that matter, to the scientific literature where claims to have established, supported or refuted causal stories abound, shows that this is a very complex, multifaceted and slippery concept. Indeed, the philosophical literature abounds with proposals of what causality is and how it can be established, as well as counter-examples and counter-proposals, while there recently has been an explosion in the methodological literature mostly fueled by the seminal work of Judea Pearl (Pearl 2000; see also Blasi & Roberts 2017, in this volume).

Given the complexity of this literature and the brevity of this chapter, I will use here the guide laid down by the "Causality in the Sciences" (CitS) movement[1] (Illari, Russo & Williamson 2011; Illari & Russo 2014) which, very helpfully, distinguishes between SCIENTIFIC and PHILOSOPHICAL questions. The five scientific questions concern INFERENCE (what are the causal relations between X and Y and what is their quantitative form, what are the causes of effects, what are the effects of causes), PREDICTION (how do we know and with what accuracy), EXPLANATION (how to causally explain, how much is explained by statistics, what level of explanation), CONTROL (how and when to control for confounds, the experimental setting, how to interfere with a system), and REASONING (how to think about

---

[1] This is far from being the only proposal (or non-controversial), but I find it the best available framework for the practicing scientist with limited time and resources.

Dan Dediu. 2017. From biology to language change and diversity. In N. J. Enfield (ed.), *Dependencies in language*, 39–53. Berlin: Language Science Press. DOI:10.5281/zenodo.573779

causality, what concepts underlie a causal story, how to "sharpen up" causal reasoning). The five philosophical questions are EPISTEMOLOGICAL (how do we know causal relations), METAPHYSICAL (what is causality, what features must causes have, what sort of entities are causes), METHODOLOGICAL (how to study causality; this is related to INFERENCE), SEMANTIC (what do we mean by causality, what concept of causality is used), and USE (what are we using causal knowledge for). Keeping these problems distinct helps not only by keeping the research questions and methods on the right track, but also avoids muddled discussions and debates where different questions are addressed (knowingly or not) by different parties, arguing at cross purposes. Moreover, there are two very important distinctions that are sometimes glossed over, namely the relation between the POPULATION (or type)-level and INDIVIDUAL (or token)-level causes (e.g., dry climate might reduce the probability of tone but how does that relate to Berber not having tone but Khoekhoe having a complex tone system?), and the difference between DIFFERENCE-MAKING (or probability-altering, e.g., correlations, associations, counterfactuals) and MECHANISTIC (or production, e.g., substantive mechanisms, process, information flow) views of causality.

With these in mind, we must acknowledge first that causal explanations in linguistics (broadly speaking) are hard not only because of historical accidents that meant that important sections of our discipline were quite reluctant to use numbers, viewed variation with suspicion and felt that it must be explained away, and resisted non-linguistic factors as (partial) causes of interesting linguistic patterns, but also because language is intrinsically difficult. It spans multiple levels of organization, spatio-temporal scales and scientific disciplines, and it involves humans and their cultures. This complexity means that, ideally, claims should be supported by multiple strands of evidence possibly from different disciplines and using different methodologies, each reinforcing each other and the overall proposal, but this is unfortunately very hard to achieve in practice. Nevertheless, if we want to have a full, convincing and coherent account of why language is the way it is and how it came to be so, we must embrace these challenges and try to build causal bridges from molecules to linguistic diversity, bridges that will differ in complexity depending on the particular proposals concerned, but that share a common blueprint.

2 From molecules to linguistic diversity

I will briefly review two examples of such attempts at building bridges across levels and disciplines, one focusing on tone and the other on clicks. Even if either (or both) of these accounts should prove false (which in itself will be proof that the scientific methods work as they should even for such complex cases!), I hope the overarching program will be successful in advancing our understanding, methodology and way of thinking about language and its causes.

3 Tone and genes (and climate)

All spoken languages use voice pitch to convey information as intonation (Ladd 2008) but in about half of the world's languages (so-called TONE languages; Maddieson 2013b and the associated map at http://wals.info/feature/13A) it is also used to encode words and grammatical distinctions (Yip 2002). While the distinction between languages that do and do not have tone (and the type and number of tones in the tone languages) is not clear-cut and simple to establish, a typology of tone can be usefully applied. The geographic distribution of tone languages is non-random (Maddieson 2013b) and tone is a dynamic phenomenon in the sense that tone can be gained (TONOGENESIS) and lost, tends to be retained in language families (i.e., it carries a genealogical signal)but can be influenced by contact with other languages too. This pattern thus requires a causal account, and there are several proposals appealing to language-internal factors (such as universal properties of speech production and perception), treating the dynamics of tone as a purely linguistic phenomenon (Yip 2002).

However, this pattern might very well be also influenced by extra-linguistic factors that combine with the linguistic ones to produce a more complex, nuanced and – ultimately – interesting causal account. One such factor was suggested by Bob Ladd and myself almost a decade ago (Dediu & Ladd 2007), based on the idea that *very weak biases* at the individual level (so weak in fact that they cannot be detected without very sensitive experimental techniques) might be amplified by the inter-generational cultural transmission of language, influencing the trajectory of language change and resulting in observable patterns of linguistic diversity (Dediu 2011b; Ladd 2008). This mechanism has been shown to work in computer models (Dediu 2008; Kirby & Hurford 2002; Kirby, Dowman & Griffiths 2007) and iterated learning experiments with human participants (Kirby, Cornish & Smith 2008; Smith & Wonnacott 2010).

Our specific proposal concerned two genes involved in brain growth and development (*ASPM* and *Microcephalin*) for which two so-called DERIVED ALLELES exist whose population frequency correlate very strongly with the probability that a population speaks a tone language or not. Of course, correlations can be spurious and a major concern for correlational studies, especially using large databases, is that such meaningless correlations are bound to pop up, and proper methods to control for them are required (Ladd, Roberts & Dediu 2015). However, even after controlling for the historical relatedness and the geographic distance between the languages in our sample (within the limits of our data and the methods available), and even after comparing the relationship between tone, *ASPM* and *Microcephalin* with the (literally) millions of possible relationships between 26 structural features of languages and 981 genetic loci spread across the genome, we found that tone is predicted by the population frequency of these two genes much better than expected by chance.[2]

We then tried to spell out an as-detailed-as-possible proposal for how these two genes could affect tone: at the individual level, these genes influence (during development and/or afterwards) a weak bias affecting the acquisition, perception, production and/or processing of tone, a bias that differs among individuals carrying different genotypes at these two genes. Therefore, populations with varying frequencies of these different individuals experience different types and level of this bias, an inter-population difference that is amplified by the intergenerational cultural transmission of language (in a feed-back loop) resulting in different trajectories of language change and, finally, a patterned distribution of tone (Dediu 2011b; Dediu & Ladd 2007)[3].

The evidence so far for this causal account is patchy and consists (besides the correlation between population genetics and tone distribution in our original paper) of computer models showing that such biases can work and might result in observable geographic patterns (e.g., Dediu 2008; 2009) and Wong, Chandrasekaran & Zheng's (2012) finding that *ASPM* is associated with lexical tone perception within individuals.[4] However, it is still unclear, at the molecular, cel-

---

[2] A better control for the fact that our hypothesis was prompted by the maps of tone and the two derived alleles would be represented by testing the hypothesis on a new set of populations and languages but, unfortunately, this is still not feasible. However, our testing against the 26 features and 981 markers does support the strength of the hypothesized association within the limits of available data.

[3] Another feed-back loop that we did not discuss is the logical possibility that existing patterns of linguistic diversity (such as for tone) might in turn generate pressure on our genomes resulting in adaptations for particular types of languages through some form of the Baldwin effect. However, even though this proposal has been repeatedly suggested to us, I believe that the time-scales and putative selective pressures (if any) involved make such a scenario quite improbable.

[4] This study, while very interesting and using two different measures of lexical tone, suffers from a small sample size and, apparently problematic for us, while finding an effect where we predicted it should be, the effect is seemingly in the opposite direction (but see the caveats in Wong, Chandrasekaran & Zheng's (2012) and the fact that their measure is probably a measure of intonation and not of lexical tone, making their result match perfectly with our prediction; see Caldwell-Harris et al. 2015).

lular and neuro-cognitive levels, what exactly these derived alleles might do to influence a bias affecting tone, and what precisely this bias looks like (and not for want of testing hypotheses, ranging from the missing fundamental Ladd et al. 2013, artificial tone language learning Asaridou et al. 2016 and syllable segmentation using tone Caldwell-Harris et al. 2015), but, so far, the decisive evidence one way or the other is still lacking (such as a well-designed sufficiently powered inter-individual genetic association study), making this hypothesis still open to empirical testing.

A new exciting twist, making this complex causal story even more interesting, is represented by the suggestion that climate influences the patterning of tone (Everett, Blasi & Roberts 2015) in the sense that air dryness biases against the retention of tone. Moreover, Collins (2017, in this volume) suggests that tone simply reflects past demographic movements as captured by mitochondrial haplotypes, which raises interesting questions about the genealogical stability of tone (Dediu 2011a). Nevertheless, the really intriguing prospect is that all these factors (and many more) play a role in shaping the temporal dynamics and geographic patterning of tone, weaving a complex and fascinating causal story involving multiple different factors (phonetics, genetics, climate, demography) acting at different scales and levels.

4 Why are clicks so rare?

The production of clicks involves the rarefaction of air within an enclosed space in the oral cavity requiring thus no airstream from the lungs. While many languages use clicks *paralinguistically* to convey affective meanings (such as irritation and disappointment), to express negation, or to interact with animals (see Gil 2013), there are very few languages (10 as counted by Maddieson 2013a), geographically restricted to southern and eastern Africa (Maddieson 2013a and associated map at http://wals.info/feature/19A), that incorporate clicks in their phonological inventory. Phonological inventories with clicks are primarily found in the "Khoisan languages", a set of language families (e.g., Khoe-Kwadi, Tu and Kxa[5]) and isolates (e.g, Hadza and Sandawe) but they have also been borrowed in some Bantu languages (such as Zulu and Xhosa) and the Cushitic language Dahalo. The present-day fragmented range of the click languages and the known recent Bantu expansion suggest that click languages might have had a much more extensive range in sub-Saharan Africa.

---

[5] I use here the language families as given by the WALS (Dryer & Haspelmath 2013) given that I also refer to WALS feature descriptions and maps.

This rarity and geographic clustering (notwithstanding the putative earlier extended range), combined with their prevalence as paralinguistic sounds and the fact that they can be borrowed into other languages, raises some intriguing questions. Of course, their restricted distribution can simply be a statistical fluctuation expected to obtain when enough features are considered, even in the case where there is a bias against clicks due to properties related to their acoustics, perception or production that universally disfavor them.

Alternatively (Moisik & Dediu 2015), it has been suggested that their particular geographic range is explained by the relaxation of a bias against their production due to the anatomy of the hard palate in the click-language speakers: more precisely, Traill (1985; see also Traunmüller 2003) observed that of his five !Xóõ (Tu family) speakers, four do not have an alveolar ridge (see tracings in Traill 1985 and Moisik & Dediu 2015 for a comparison with a palate featuring a prominent alveolar ridge); this pattern seems to hold for much larger and comprehensive samples (reviewed in Moisik & Dediu 2015). The suggestion was that somehow, the lack of an alveolar ridge helps in producing lingual clicks, weakening the bias against clicks in the populations with a high incidence of palates without an alveolar ridge.

Scott Moisik (Moisik & Dediu 2015) has refined this proposal by suggesting that the shape of the alveolar ridge impacts clicks production because a smooth hard palate requires less effort for the tongue to form the anterior contact, and also allows a better change in the cavity's volume during click release. He tested these hypotheses by building a realistic bio-mechanical model of (dental) click production with ArtiSynth (www.artisynth.org; Lloyd, Stavness & Fels 2012) in which different shapes of the alveolar ridge were simulated. He found that when there is a large alveolar ridge more muscle effort is required and the volume change was negatively impacted, suggesting that indeed, within the limits of this initial simulation,[6] a hard palate without an alveolar ridge favors the production of (dental) clicks.

Assuming these preliminary results will be supported by later refinements in the simulation, are they sufficient to support the suggested conjecture? What sort of empirical data should we attempt to collect and what type of tests should we conduct? Finally, what really is the causal structure of such claims?

---

[6] Currently, he is exploring ways to improve this simulation and to also include estimates of the acoustic effects of hard palate shape.

4 From biology to language change and diversity

5 The causal anatomy of language

The two examples above are, in fact, special cases of a general framework that attempts to causally link biology[7] and language, a framework that is the foundation of the Genetic Biases in Language and Speech (G[3]bils) project funded by the Netherlands Organisation for Scientific Research (NWO) and hosted at the Max Planck Institute for Psycholinguistics in Nijmegen. The idea is that an individual's genotype (in interaction with its environment), during and after development, produces and maintains a vocal tract[8] whose structure affects the individual's speech and might result in (very weak) biases in speech production, which might be expressed and amplified in populations of such biased individuals through cultural evolution, finally affecting the large-scale observable patterns of language (see Figure 1).

Several important observations are in order. First, development (and maintenance) are extremely complex dynamic processes resulting from tight interaction between the genotype and the environment, involving large and structured networks of genes with surprising evolutionary histories (e.g., Carroll 2011). These processes (Fitch & Giedd 1999) result in individual anatomies of the vocal tract structures (for example, focusing on the hard palate only, its morphogenesis requires a delicate orchestration of gene networks controlling the growth, elevation, adhesion and fusion of the palatal shelf that quite often fail to a certain degree and result in pathologies such as cleft palate; see Bush & Jiang 2012; Dixon et al. 2011 for reviews), and differences between individuals in the genes involved in these processes (or in the relevant environmental factors[9]) result in inter-individual variation in the anatomy of their vocal tracts (a still under-researched topic but see Praveen et al. 2011; Lammert, Proctor & Narayanan 2013; Lammert et al. 2011; You et al. 2008; Liu et al. 2012). Establishing these causal links requires investigations of normal and pathological evolution and development, understanding the genetic bases of clinical phenotypes affecting the vocal tract (e.g., cleft lip and palate), animal and cell-based models of vocal tract development, and the transfer of these findings to the normal range of variation in

---

[7] This framework can be easily adapted for other extra-linguistic factors such as climate (see, for example, Everett, Blasi & Roberts 2015, or Ladd, Roberts & Dediu 2015).

[8] and ears, and a brain, and hands, etc., but here we are focusing on vocal tracts for reasons to do with the tractability of the problem space, the availability of reliable methods of measurement and the relatively well understood principles of bio-mechanics and acoustics.

[9] A fascinating case is represented by type of food consumed, with the varying amount of masticatory effort affecting the anatomy of the lower jaw explaining some of the variation between hunter-gatherer and agricultural populations (Cramon-Taubadel 2011).

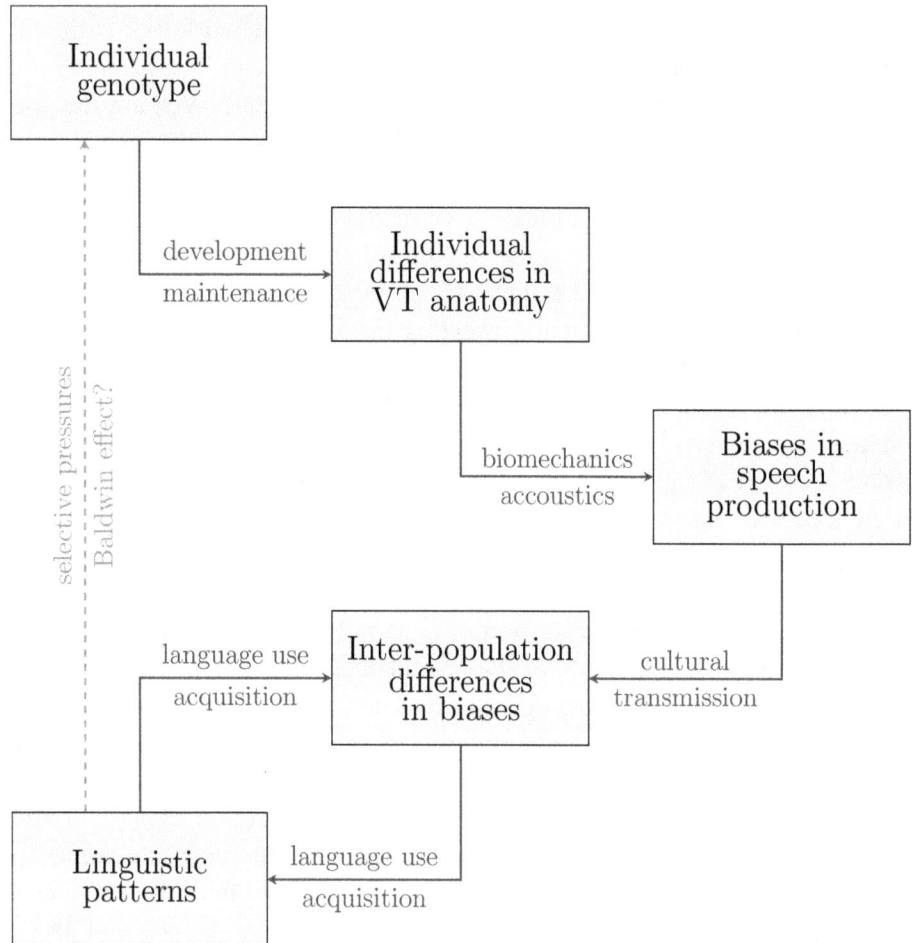

Figure 1: The general causal framework connecting the molecular bases of inter-individual variation in vocal tract anatomy to language change and patterns of linguistic diversity. The boxes and links are discussed in the text (except for the feedback from linguistic patterns to the genome mediated from something like the Baldwin effect; this is a separate issue not covered in this chapter). This framework can easily be extended to also include auditory perception (see Butcher 2006 for an intriguing proposal involving Chronic Otitis Media in Australia) and cognitive processing (as forcefully argued by Christiansen & Chater 2008; see also Christiansen 2017, this volume and Culbertson 2017, this volume).

humans through large-scale genetic association studies. These causal chains are long, complex, and probabilistic, both mechanistic and difference-making, and must bridge from molecular mechanisms to measurable anatomical differences but, on the bright side, they stay largely within the bio-medical sciences which ensures agreed-upon standards of what a good causal story is and how it should be supported or rejected.

Second, these inter-individual differences in vocal tract anatomy might cause differences between individuals in their articulatory behavior and acoustic output (Brunner, Fuchs & Perrier 2005; 2009; Debruyne et al. 2002); these relationships can be empirically measured and quantified using techniques such as MRI, intra-oral scans, X-rays or 3D digitized casts and bone structures. Based on these primary data we can build computer models to investigate the articulatory and acoustic outputs, we can conduct statistical analyses (using classical and geometric morphometrics; Zelditch et al. 2012) and we can correlate them with measured acoustic behavior. These causal chains are relatively short, stay within articulatory phonetics, but are highly probabilistic, involve a high degree of complexity (in the sense of chaos theory) and offer many opportunities for mediation (what phoneticians usually call "compensation"; e.g. Brunner et al. 2006).

Third, these inter-individual biases in speech production are found within populations of speakers; if there are systematic differences between populations in their make-up in what concerns these biases (i.e., the distribution[10] of their types and strength), then it is possible that inter-population differences will emerge, these differences will be amplified and expressed through the cultural evolution that governs language and will result in differences between the languages spoken by those populations (Levinson & Dediu 2013). This feedback loop is an essential causal engine and there are many opportunities for mediation resulting from population heterogeneity and other cultural forces that affect language change (Dediu 2011b). We can investigate this using computer models, experimental manipulations of cultural transmission in the lab, actual historical linguistic processes, and statistical correlations between biases and cross-linguistic variation. A possible complicating factor is that we need to straddle several disciplines including historical linguistics, typology, phonetics, phonology, cognitive neuroscience, and studies of cultural evolution, which might result in different standards for causality and fundamental disagreements; moreover we probably must stay mostly within the realm of difference-making accounts as mechanistic processes are not yet understood well enough.

---

[10] Importantly, we are not talking here only about the frequency of such biases in the population (a first approximation, easy to measure and model) but, crucially, about the biases' relation to the communicative networks present in the population.

6 Conclusions

Establishing convincing causal stories that link language and extra-linguistic factors is inherently difficult and complex, but we can make substantial progress if we agree to take seriously the complexity of the task, the need to talk across disciplines and methods, and to think about what solid causal accounts actually imply. There is no single golden path to causality (despite what some experimentalists might think!) and we can only progress if we take a pluralistic approach that builds upon experiments (when feasible, relevant and valid), natural experiments (when we're lucky enough to find them), advanced statistical analyses of large databases (keeping in mind good practices and the highest standards of skepticism), computer models of many kinds (built on current theories and calibrated on empirical findings), recent advances in methods such as Directed Acyclic Graphs (DAGs) and Structural Equation Modeling (SEM), and any other methods that can offer valid and reliable information concerning the problems at hand.

In the end, having such an overarching causal story connecting multiple levels, scales and disciplines will not only allow us to answer all five scientific questions of causality with increased clarity and detail with respect to language and its evolution, but more importantly, to discover new interesting questions we did not even know were possible to meaningfully ask.

Acknowledgements

I wish to thank Scott Moisik specifically for his work on clicks used here as an example, but also for his and Rick Janssen's more general contributions to the G[3]bils project; Carly Jaques for invaluable help with ArtiVark; Alexandra Dima for illuminating discussions and pointers to the literature concerning causality; Nick Enfield, the participants in the "Dependencies in Language" Workshop in Ardennes, June 2014, and the organizers and participants to the "Causality in the Language Sciences" Workshop in Leipzig, April 2015, for fascinating discussions and suggestions. This work was supported by a VIDI grant from the Netherlands Organisation for Scientific Research (NWO).

References

Asaridou, Salomi, Atsuko Takashima, Dan Dediu, Peter Hagoort & James M. McQueen. 2016. Repetition suppression in the left inferior frontal gyrus predicts tone learning performance. *Cerebral Cortex* 26(6). 2728–2742. DOI:10.1093/cercor/bhv126

Brunner, Jana, Susanne Fuchs & Pascal Perrier. 2005. The influence of the palate shape on articulatory token-to-token variability. *ZAS Papers in Linguistics* 42. 43–67.

Brunner, Jana, Susanne Fuchs & Pascal Perrier. 2009. On the relationship between palate shape and articulatory behavior. *Journal of the Acoustic Society of America* 125(6). 3936–3949. DOI:10.1121/1.3125313

Brunner, Jana, Phil Hoole, Pascale Perrier & Susanne Fuchs. 2006. Temporal development of compensation strategies for perturbed palate shape in German/sch/-production. *Proceedings of the 7th International Seminar on Speech Production* 7. 247–254. http : / / halshs . archives - ouvertes . fr / hal - 00403289/.

Bush, Jeffrey O. & Rulang Jiang. 2012. Palatogenesis: Morphogenetic and molecular mechanisms of secondary palate. *Development* 139(2). 231–243. DOI:10.1242/dev.067082

Butcher, Andy. 2006. Australian Aboriginal languages. In J. Harrington & M. Tabain (eds.), *Speech production: Models, phonetic processes, and techniques (pp,* 187–210. New York: Pyschology Press.

Caldwell-Harris, Catharine L., A. Lancaster, D. Robert Ladd, Dan Dediu & Morten H. Christiansen. 2015. Factors influencing sensitivity to lexical tone in an artificial language. *Studies in Second Language Acquisition* 37(2). 335–357. DOI:10.1017/S0272263114000849

Carroll, Sean B. 2011. *Endless forms most beautiful: The new science of evo devo and the making of the animal kingdom.* London: Quercus Publishing.

Christiansen, Morten H. & Nick Chater. 2008. Language as shaped by the brain. *Behavioral and Brain Sciences* 31. 489–558.

Cramon-Taubadel, N. von. 2011. Global human mandibular variation reflects differences in agricultural and hunter-gatherer subsistence strategies. *Proceedings of the National Academy of Sciences* 108(49). 19546–19551. DOI:10.1073/pnas.1113050108

Debruyne, Frans, Wivine Decoster, Annemie Van Gijsel & Julie Vercammen. 2002. Speaking fundamental frequency in monozygotic and dizygotic twins. *Journal of Voice* 16(4). 466–471.

Dediu, Dan. 2008. The role of genetic biases in shaping language-genes correlations. *Journal of Theoretical Biology* 254. 400–407. DOI:10.1016/j.jtbi.2008.05.028

Dediu, Dan. 2009. Genetic biasing through cultural transmission: Do simple Bayesian models of language evolution generalize? *Journal of Theoretical Biology* 259(3). 552–561. DOI:10.1016/j.jtbi.2009.04.004

Dediu, Dan. 2011a. A Bayesian phylogenetic approach to estimating the stability of linguistic features and the genetic biasing of tone. *Proc R Soc B* 278. 474–479. DOI:10.1098/rspb.2010.1595

Dediu, Dan. 2011b. Are languages really independent from genes? If not, what would a genetic bias affecting language diversity look like? *Human Biology* 83(2). 279–296. DOI:10.3378/027.083.0208

Dediu, Dan & D. Robert Ladd. 2007. Linguistic tone is related to the population frequency of the adaptive haplogroups of two brain size genes, ASPM and microcephalin. *Proceedings of the National Academy of Sciences* 104(26). 10944–9.

Dixon, Michael J., Mary L. Marazita, Terri H. Beaty & Jeffrey C. Murray. 2011. Cleft lip and palate: Synthesizing genetic and environmental influences. Nature reviews. *Genetics* 12(3). 167–178. DOI:10.1038/nrg2933

Dryer, Matthew S. & Martin Haspelmath (eds.). 2013. *WALS online*. Leipzig: Max Planck Institute for Evolutionary Anthropology. http://wals.info/.

Everett, Caleb, Damián E. Blasi & Seán G. Roberts. 2015. Climate, vocal folds, and tonal languages: Connecting the physiological and geographic dots. *Proceedings of the National Academy of Sciences* 112(5). 1322–1327.

Fitch, W. Tecumseh & Jay Giedd. 1999. Morphology and development of the human vocal tract: A study using magnetic resonance imaging. *The Journal of the Acoustical Society of America* 106(3). 1511–1522.

Gil, David. 2013. Para-linguistic usages of clicks. In Matthew S. Dryer & M. Haspelmath (eds.), *The world atlas of language structures online*. Leipzig: Max Planck Institute for Evolutionary Anthropology. http://wals.info/chapter/142.

Illari, Phyllis McKay & Federica Russo. 2014. *Causality: Philosophical theory meets scientific practice*. Oxford: Oxford University Press.

Illari, Phyllis McKay, Federica Russo & Jon Williamson. 2011. *Causality in the sciences*. Oxford: Oxford University Press.

Kirby, Simon, Hannah Cornish & Kenny Smith. 2008. Cumulative cultural evolution in the laboratory: An experimental approach to the origins of structure in human language. *Proceedings of the National Academy of Sciences* 105(31). 10681–10686.

Kirby, Simon, Mike Dowman & Thomas L. Griffiths. 2007. Innateness and culture in the evolution of language. *Proceedings of the National Academy of Science USA* 104(12). 5241–5.

Kirby, Simon & James Hurford. 2002. The emergence of linguistic structure: An overview of the iterated learning model. In A. Cangelosi & D. Parisi (eds.), *Simulating the evolution of language (pp,* 121–148. London: Springer Verlag.

Ladd, D. Robert. 2008. *Intonational phonology.* 2nd edn. Cambridge: Cambridge University Press.

Ladd, D. Robert, Seán G. Roberts & Dan Dediu. 2015. Correlational studies in typological and historical linguistics. *Annual Review of Linguistics* 1(1). 221–241. DOI:10.1146/annurev-linguist-030514-124819

Ladd, D. Robert, R. Ainscough, C. Assmann, C. Caldwell-Harris, L. Y. Ganushchak, K. Swoboda & Dan Dediu. 2013. Patterns of individual differences in the perception of missing-fundamental tones. *Journal of Experimental Psychology: Human Perception and Performance* 39 (5). 1386–97.

Lammert, Adam, Michael Proctor & Shrikanth Narayanan. 2013. Morphological variation in the adult hard palate and posterior pharyngeal wall. *Journal of Speech, Language and Hearing Research* 56(2). 521–530.

Lammert, Adam, Michael Proctor, Athanasios Katsamanis & Shrikanth Narayanan. 2011. Morphological variation in the adult vocal tract: A modeling study of its potential acoustic impact. In *Twelfth annual conference of the international speech communication association.* http://www.mproctor.net/docs/lammert11_IS2011_morphology.pdf.

Levinson, Steven C. & Dan Dediu. 2013. The interplay of genetic and cultural factors in ongoing language evolution. In P. J. Richerson & Morten H. Christiansen (eds.), *Cultural evolution: Society, technology, language, and religion (vol. 12, pp,* 219–232. Cambridge, Mass: MIT Press.

Liu, Fan, Fedde van der Lijn, Claudia Schurmann, Gu Zhu, M. Mallar Chakravarty, Pirro G. Hysi, Andreas Wollstein, Oscar Lao, Marleen de Bruijne, M. Arfan Ikram, Aad van der Lugt, Fernando Rivadeneira, André G. Uitterlinden, Albert Hofman, Wiro J. Niessen, Georg Homuth, Greig de Zubicaray, Katie L. McMahon, Paul M. Thompson, Amro Daboul, Ralf Puls, Katrin Hegenscheid, Liisa Bevan, Zdenka Pausova, Sarah E. Medland, Grant W. Montgomery, Margaret J. Wright, Carol Wicking, Stefan Boehringer, Timothy D. Spector, Tomáš Paus, Nicholas G. Martin, Reiner Biffar & Manfred Kayser. 2012. A genome-wide association study identifies five loci influencing facial morphology in Europeans. *PLOS Genetics* 8(9). 1–13. DOI:10.1371/journal.pgen.1002932

Lloyd, John E., Ian Stavness & Sidney Fels. 2012. Artisynth: A fast interactive biomechanical modeling toolkit combining multibody and finite element simulation. In *Soft tissue biomechanical modeling for computer assisted surgery*, 355–394. New York: Springer. http://link.springer.com/chapter/10.1007/8415_2012_126.

Maddieson, Ian. 2013a. Presence of uncommon consonants. In Matthew S. Dryer & Martin Haspelmath (eds.), *The world atlas of language structures online*. Leipzig: Max Planck Institute for Evolutionary Anthropology. http://wals.info/chapter/19.

Maddieson, Ian. 2013b. Tone. In Matthew S. Dryer & M. Haspelmath (eds.), *The world atlas of language structures online*. Leipzig: Max Planck Institute for Evolutionary Anthropology. http://wals.info/chapter/13.

Moisik, Scott R. & Dan Dediu. 2015. Anatomical biasing and clicks: Preliminary biomechanical modelling. In L. Hannah (ed.), *The evolution of phonetic capabilities: Causal constraints, consequences*. 18th International Congress of Phonetic Sciences, 8–13. Brussels: Vrije Universiteit Brussel Artificial Intelligence Lab.

Pearl, Judea. 2000. *Causality: Models, reasoning, and inference*. New York: Cambridge University Press.

Praveen, B. N., Sunita Amrutesh, Sumona Pal, A. R. Shubhasini & Syed Vaseemuddin. 2011. Various shapes of soft palate: A lateral cephalometric study. *World Journal of Dentistry* 2. 207–210.

Smith, Kenny & Elizabeth Wonnacott. 2010. Eliminating unpredictable variation through iterated learning. *Cognition* 116(3). 444–449. DOI:10.1016/j.cognition.2010.06.004

Traill, Anthony. 1985. *Phonetic and phonological studies of !Xóõ Bushman*. Hamburg: Helmut Buske Verlag.

Traunmüller, Hartmut. 2003. Clicks and the idea of a human protolanguage. *PHONUM* 9. 1–4.

Wong, Patrick C. M., Bharath Chandrasekaran & Jing Zheng. 2012. The derived allele of ASPM is associated with lexical tone perception. *PLoS ONE* 7(4). e34243. DOI:10.1371/journal.pone.0034243

Yip, Moira. 2002. *Tone*. Cambridge: Cambridge University Press.

You, M., X. Li, H. Wang, J. Zhang, H. Wu, Liu Y. & Z. Zhu. 2008. Morphological variety of the soft palate in normal individuals: A digital cephalometric study. *Dento Maxillo Facial Radiology* 37(6). 344–349. DOI:10.1259/dmfr/55898096

Zelditch, Miriam Leah, Donald L. Swiderski, H. David Sheets & William L. Fink. 2012. *Geometric morphometrics for biologists: A primer*. New York: Elsevier Academic Press.

Chapter 5

Language intertwined across multiple timescales: Processing, acquisition and evolution

Morten H. Christiansen
Department of Psychology, Cornell University, Ithaca, NY, USA
Centre for Interacting Minds, Aarhus University, Denmark

Theories of language invoke different types of causal dependencies to explain a variety of linguistic phenomena, ranging from typological patterns (e.g., "verb-final languages tend to have postpositions," Greenberg 1966) to psycholinguistic regularities (e.g., "hearing a passive construction increases the likelihood of producing one," Bock 1986). Several chapters in this volume provide important insights into such dependencies across a variety of domains (see, for example, chapters by Cristofaro, Culbertson, Dediu, Hyman, and Rice). This chapter, however, concerns itself with a different kind of dependency: the fundamental theoretical interdependencies between different timescales of language, from processing to acquisition to evolution.

In the mainstream generative grammar tradition, possible interdependencies between language processing, acquisition and evolution are rarely ever explored (but see Pinker 1994; Jackendoff 2002). This is likely a consequence of Chomsky's methodological dictums that the study of language proper should be separated from how it is used and processed (Chomsky 1965), acquired over development (Chomsky 1975), and how it evolved (Chomsky 2005). Christiansen & Chater (2016a) refer to the theoretical impact of these methodological dictums as "Chomsky's hidden legacy", and note that its influence has gone well beyond generative approaches. For example, typological and usage-based approaches to language processing typically downplay issues related to the acquisition and evolution of language (e.g., Clark 1996; Hawkins 1994). Similarly, work on language acquisition tends not to consider questions pertaining to the processing and evolution of language (e.g., Cowie 1999; Hirsh-Pasek & Golinkoff 1996; O'Grady 1997), and studies of language evolution usually pay little attention to research on language acquisition and processing (e.g., Botha 2003; Burling 2005; Corballis 2002; Dunbar 1998; Lieberman 2000). In contrast, Christiansen & Chater (2016a) argue that there are strong theoretical constraints between the processing, acquisition and evolution of language–allowing each to shed light on the others–and that key questions within each area can only be fully addressed through an integrated approach. As an example, I briefly discuss how the immediacy of language processing has implications for both language acquisition and evolution.

1 The Now-or-Never bottleneck

Language happens in the here-and-now. Our memory for acoustic information is incredibly short-lived, disappearing within less than 100 msec (Remez et al. 2010). At the same time spoken language comes at us at a very rapid rate, at about 10-15 phonemes per second (Studdert-Kennedy 1986), with the further complication that our auditory system is only able to keep track of about 10 separate (non-speech) sounds per second (Miller & Taylor 1948). To make matters worse, our ability to keep track of sound sequences is also very limited: we are able to recall less than four non-speech sounds (Warren et al. 1969) and only four to seven unrelated linguistic items (Cowan 2001; Miller 1956). Thus, during a normal conversation, we are faced with an immense challenge by the combined effects of poor acoustic memory, fast input, and severely limited sequence memory.[1] As a consequence of this NOW-OR-NEVER BOTTLENECK (Christiansen & Chater 2016b), new material will constantly overwrite and interfere with previous material unless it is processed immediately.

The Now-or-Never bottleneck has direct implications for language processing. To deal with the immediacy of language, Christiansen & Chater (2016b) suggest that the language system must engage in CHUNK-AND-PASS processing: compress and recode language input as rapidly as possible into increasingly more abstract levels of linguistic representation, from sound-based units to words (or word combinations) to discourse-level representations. This passing up of chunks allows for increasingly longer retention of linguistic information at higher levels of linguistic abstraction, consistent with recent neuroimaging data (e.g., Ding et al. 2016; Stephens, Honey & Hasson 2013).

---

[1] Communication using sign language involves a similar problem (see Christiansen & Chater 2016b for discussion)

The time-sensitive nature of Chunk-and-Pass processing leads to a strong pressure toward incremental processing because chunking will primarily happen across neighboring units, resulting in a bias toward local dependencies (in line with evidence for garden path effects in language comprehension; e.g., Bever 1970). The multiple levels of linguistic structure that result from the Chunk-and-Pass process provides a possible processing-based explanation for why linguistic theories tend to be couched in terms of multiple levels of representation, from phonology and morphology to syntax and discourse.[2] Importantly, though, in the proposed framework, higher levels of representations will contain less of the original detail of the input as it becomes more compressed through repeated Chunk-and-Pass processing.

Because the Now-or-Never bottleneck prevents any significant backtracking, the language system employs prediction to use as much available information as possible to be right the first time. In doing so, the processing system will build the most abstract and complete representation that is justified, given the linguistic input–a "good-enough" representation (Ferreira, Bailey & Ferraro 2002; Ferreira & Patson 2007). Through prediction, top-down information from discourse expectations, world knowledge, and so on, is used to guide the incremental interpretation of linguistic input. Language production follows the same principles but in the opposite direction, from discourse representations of the intended message and intonational phrases to words and articulatory motor commands (see Chater & Christiansen 2016; Chater, McCauley & Christiansen 2016 for discussion).

The effects of the Now-and-Never bottleneck go beyond the timescale of processing to the timescale of acquisition. In order to become a competent language user, the child must learn how to create and integrate the right chunks as rapidly as possible, before the input is gone. From this perspective, language acquisition does *not* consist in identifying the right grammar but rather, *language acquisition is learning to process*, to become more efficient at Chunk-and-Pass processing. That is, the child is not a "mini-linguist" but a developing language user, acquiring the necessary skills to comprehend and produce language. To deal with the Now-or-Never bottleneck, the child must learn in the "here-and-now," relying only on currently available information, instead of abstracting over large

---

[2] Although this perspective is consistent with standard levels of linguistic abstraction, from phonology through syntax to pragmatics, a complete model might incorporate more fine-grained levels that, for example, would distinguish between multiple levels of discourse representation (e.g., as in Enfield 2013).

swaths of data[3]. Learning is therefore local and piecemeal, constrained by limited memory, in line with item-based approaches to language acquisition (e.g., Tomasello 2003). Children gradually learn to apply top-down knowledge to facilitate Chunk-and-Pass processing via prediction. Thus, predictive abilities emerge over time as children develop their chunking skills and learn to rapidly apply the multiple constraints that are crucial to adult incremental processing (Borovsky, Elman & Fernald 2012).

The theoretical impact of the Now-or-Never bottleneck not only affects the timescales of processing and acquisition, but also extends to the longer timescales of language evolution and change. Given the hypothesis that language evolution may be explained primarily by the cultural evolution of linguistic structure rather than biological adaptations for language (e.g., Christiansen & Chater 2008; Hurford 1999; Smith & Kirby 2008; for a review, see Dediu et al. 2013), we might expect that linguistic patterns that can be processed through the bottleneck will tend to proliferate. That is, language is a product of piecemeal tinkering, with the long-term evolution of language resulting from the compounding of a myriad local short-term processes of language change. This means that *language change is item-based* in nature, with specific changes arising from constraints on Chunk-and-Pass processing–both within and across individuals–providing a possible cognitive foundation for grammaticalization.

The Now-or-Never bottleneck provides a constant pressure towards reduction and erosion across different levels of linguistic representation, from discourse syntacticization and semantic bleaching to morphological reduction and phonetic erosion (see Christiansen & Chater 2016b for further discussion). Language change, more broadly, will be local at the level of individual chunks, consistent with theories of lexical diffusion suggesting that sound change originates in a small set of words and then spreads throughout the vocabulary (e.g., Wang 1977). Similarly, morpho-syntactic change is also predicted to be local in nature, resulting in what Christiansen & Chater (2016b) term "constructional diffusion."

Importantly, the process of piecemeal tinkering that drives item-based language change is subject to constraints deriving not only from Chunk-and-Pass

---

[3] The Now-or-Never bottleneck thus has important implications for computational models of language, many of which use so-called batch-learning either over large corpora (e.g., Perfors, Tenenbaum & Wonnacott 2010) or large memory windows (e.g., Kolodny, Lotem & Edelman 2015) incompatible with psychological constraints on memory. In contrast, the Chunk-Based Learner (McCauley & Christiansen 2014; 2016) was developed with the Now-and-Never bottleneck in mind, providing a computational account of aspects of early language acquisition, including the interconnected nature of comprehension and production (Chater, McCauley & Christiansen 2016).

processing but also from the specific trajectory of cultural evolution that a language follows. More generally, in this perspective, there is no sharp distinction between language evolution and language change: language evolution is simply the result of language change writ large (see also Heine & Kuteva 2007), constrained by processing and acquisition (see Christiansen & Chater 2016a for more details).

2 Language intertwined across multiple timescales

In this chapter, I have discussed how the Now-or-Never bottleneck not only provides constraints on the processing of language but also on the nature of language acquisition and evolution (with further implications for the structure of language itself, as discussed in Christiansen & Chater 2016a,b). Figure 1 provides an illustration of how the Now-or-Never bottleneck affects language across these different timescales.

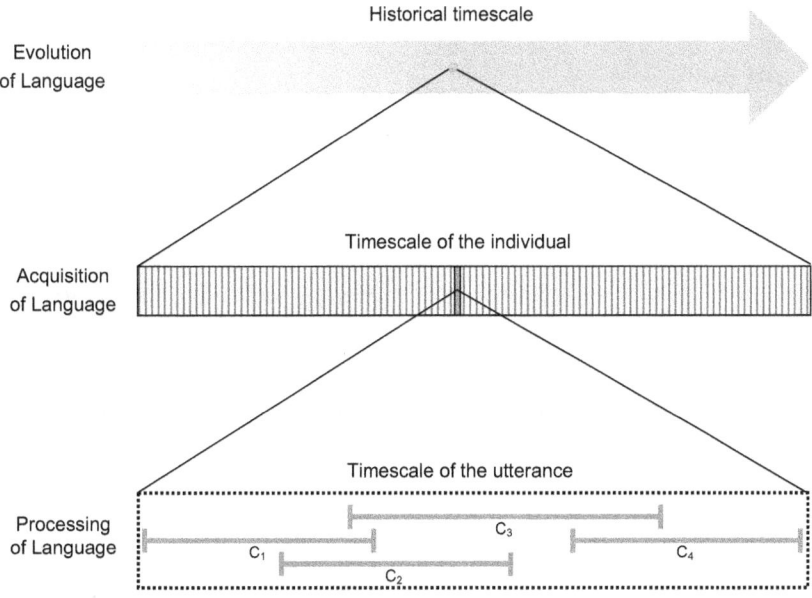

Figure 1: Illustration of how Chunk-and-Pass processing at the utterance level (with the C_{1-4} referring to different chunks) constrains the acquisition of language by the individual, which, in turn, influences how language evolves through learning and use by groups of individuals on a historical timescale. Adapted from Christiansen & Chater (2016a).

At the timescale of the utterance (seconds), Chunk-and-Pass processing carves the input–or output–into chunks at various levels of linguistic abstraction. At the timescale of the individual (tens of years), these chunks provide the comprehension and production events from which children learn (and adults update) their ability to process language. And, on a historical timescale (hundreds or thousands of years), each learner is part of a community of language users that together change language, based on patterns that are easy to acquire and process. Of course, the Now-or-Never bottleneck works together with other constraints deriving from the brain and body to shape the cultural evolution of language (Christiansen & Chater 2008; 2016a), where the brain and body are embedded in a social network of interactions. Thus, to reach a complete understanding of how language works, we need to study it as intertwined across the multiple timescales of processing, acquisition and evolution.

Acknowledgments

Thanks to Erin Isbilen for comments on a previous version of this chapter.

References

Bever, Thomas G. 1970. The cognitive basis for linguistic structures. In J. R. Hayes (ed.), *Cognition and the development of language*, 279–362. New York: Wiley & Sons.

Bock, J. Kathryn. 1986. Meaning, sound, and syntax: Lexical priming in sentence production. *Journal of Experimental Psychology: Learning, Memory, and Cognition* 12. 575–586.

Borovsky, Arielle, Jeffrey L. Elman & Anne Fernald. 2012. Knowing a lot for one's age: Vocabulary skill and not age is associated with anticipatory incremental sentence interpretation in children and adults. *Journal of Experimental Child Psychology* 112. 417–436.

Botha, Rudolf P. 2003. *Unravelling the evolution of language*. Amsterdam: Elsevier.

Burling, Robbins. 2005. *The talking ape: How language evolved*. Oxford: Oxford University Press.

Chater, Nick & Morten H. Christiansen. 2016. Squeezing through the now-or-never bottleneck: Reconnecting language processing, acquisition, change and structure. *Behavioral and Brain Sciences* 39 e62.

Chater, Nick, Stewart M. McCauley & Morten H. Christiansen. 2016. Language as skill: Inter-twining comprehension and production. *Journal of Memory and Language* 89. 244–254.

Chomsky, Noam. 1965. *Aspects of the theory of syntax.* Cambridge, MA: MIT Press.

Chomsky, Noam. 1975. *Reflections on language.* New York: Pantheon Books.

Chomsky, Noam. 2005. Three factors in language design. *Linguistic Inquiry* 36. 1–22.

Christiansen, Morten H. & Nick Chater. 2008. Language as shaped by the brain. *Behavioral and Brain Sciences* 31. 489–558.

Christiansen, Morten H. & Nick Chater. 2016a. *Creating language: Integrating evolution, acquisition, and processing.* Cambridge, MA: MIT Press.

Christiansen, Morten H. & Nick Chater. 2016b. The now-or-never bottleneck: A fundamental constraint on language. *Behavioral and Brain Sciences* 39 e62.

Clark, Herbert H. 1996. *Using language.* Cambridge: Cambridge University Press.

Corballis, Michael C. 2002. *From hand to mouth: The origins of language.* Princeton: Princeton University Press.

Cowan, Nelson. 2001. The magical number 4 in short-term memory: A reconsideration of mental storage capacity. *Behavioral and Brain Sciences* 24. 87–114.

Cowie, Fiona. 1999. *What's within? Nativism reconsidered.* New York: Oxford University Press.

Dediu, Dan, Michael Cysouw, Steven C. Levinson, Andrea Baronchelli, Morten H. Christiansen, William. Croft, Nicholas D. Evans, Simon Garrod, Russel D. Gray, Anne Kandler & Elena Lieven. 2013. Cultural evolution of language. In P. J. Richerson & M. H. Christiansen (eds.), *Cultural evolution: Society, technology, language and religion,* 303–332. Cambridge, MA: MIT Press.

Ding, Nai, Lucia Melloni, Hang Zhang, Xing Tian & David Poeppel. 2016. Cortical tracking of hierarchical linguistic structures in connected speech. *Nature Neuroscience* 19. 158–164.

Dunbar, Robin I. M. 1998. *Grooming, gossip, and the evolution of language.* Cambridge, MA: Harvard University Press.

Enfield, N. J. 2013. *Relationship thinking: Agency, enchrony, and human sociality.* New York: Oxford university Press.

Ferreira, Fernanda, Karl G. Bailey & Vittoria Ferraro. 2002. Good-enough representations in language comprehension. *Current Directions in Psychological Science* 11. 11–15.

Ferreira, Fernanda & Nikole D. Patson. 2007. The "good enough" approach to language comprehension. *Language and Linguistics Compass* 1. 71–83.

Greenberg, Joseph H. 1966. Some universals of grammar with particular reference to the order of meaningful elements. In Joseph H. Greenberg (ed.), *Universals of language (second edition)*, 73–113. Cambridge, MA: MIT Press.

Hawkins, John A. 1994. *A performance theory of order and constituency*. Cambridge: Cambridge University Press.

Heine, Bernd & Tania Kuteva. 2007. *The genesis of grammar: A reconstruction*. Oxford: Oxford University Press.

Hirsh-Pasek, Kathy & Roberta Golinkoff (eds.). 1996. *Action meets word: How children learn verbs*. New York: Oxford University Press.

Hurford, James. 1999. The evolution of language and languages. In R. Dunbar, C. Knight & C. Power (eds.), *The evolution of culture*, 173–193. Edinburgh, UK: Edinburgh University Press.

Jackendoff, Ray. 2002. *Foundations of language: Brain, meaning, grammar, evolution*. New York: Oxford University Press.

Kolodny, Oren, Arnon Lotem & Shimon Edelman. 2015. Learning a generative probabilistic grammar of experience: A process-level model of language acquisition. *Cognitive Science* 39. 227–267.

Lieberman, Phillip. 2000. *Human language and our reptilian brain*. Cambridge, MA: Harvard University Press.

McCauley, Stewart M. & Morten H. Christiansen. 2014. Acquiring formulaic language: A computational model. *Mental Lexicon* 9. 419–436.

McCauley, Stewart M. & Morten H. Christiansen. 2016. Language learning as language use: A cross-linguistic model of child language development. Manuscript in preparation.

Miller, George Armitage. 1956. The magical number seven, plus or minus two: Some limits on our capacity for processing information. *Psychological Review* 63. 81–97.

Miller, George Armitage & Walter G. Taylor. 1948. The perception of repeated bursts of noise. *Journal of the Acoustical Society of America* 20. 171–182.

O'Grady, William. 1997. *Syntactic development*. Chicago, IL: University of Chicago Press.

Perfors, Amy, Joshua B. Tenenbaum & Elizabeth Wonnacott. 2010. Variability, negative evidence, and the acquisition of verb argument constructions. *Journal of Child Language* 37. 607–642.

Pinker, Steven. 1994. *The language instinct: How the mind creates language*. New York, NY: William Morrow & Company.

Remez, Robert E., Daria F. Ferro, Kathryn R. Dubowski, Judith Meer, Robin S. Broder & Morgana L. Davids. 2010. Is desynchrony tolerance adaptable in the perceptual organization of speech? *Attention, Perception & Psychophysics* 72. 2054–2058.

Smith, Kenny & Simon Kirby. 2008. Cultural evolution: Implications for understanding the human language faculty and its evolution. *Philosophical Transactions of the Royal Society B* 363. 3591–3603.

Stephens, Greg J., Christopher J. Honey & Uri Hasson. 2013. A place for time: The spatiotemporal structure of neural dynamics during natural audition. *Journal of Neurophysiology* 110. 2019–2026.

Studdert-Kennedy, Michael. 1986. Some developments in research on language behavior. In N. J. Smelser & D. R. Gerstein (eds.), *Behavioral and social science: Fifty years of discovery: In commemoration of the fiftieth anniversary of the "Ogburn Report: Recent social trends in the United States"*, 208–248. Washington, DC: National Academy Press.

Tomasello, Michael. 2003. *Constructing a language: A usage-based theory of language acquisition*. Cambridge, MA: Harvard University Press.

Wang, William S. (ed.). 1977. *The lexicon in phonological change*. The Hague: Mouton.

Warren, Richard M., Charles J. Obusek, Richard M. Farmer & Roslyn P. Warren. 1969. Auditory sequence: Confusion of patterns other than speech or music. *Science* 164. 586–587.

Chapter 6

What comes first in language emergence?

Wendy Sandler
University of Haifa

There has been much speculation about what came first in the evolution of human language – repetitive syllables that took on meaning (MacNeilage 1998) or that provided a structural basis for syntax (Carstairs-McCarthy 1999); words (Bickerton 1990; Jackendoff 1999); undecomposable holophrases (e.g., Arbib 2012); or musical protolanguage (Darwin 1871; Fitch 2010; see Newmeyer 2002 and Fitch 2005 for informative overviews).[1] Others have argued that the defining property at the evolutionary core of the human language faculty is syntactic recursion (Hauser, Chomsky & Fitch 2002), more recently described as a computational operation combining and recombining linguistic units (Bolhuis et al. 2014), or "discrete infinity" (Hauser et al. 2014). Whatever one takes to have been fundamental, it is reasonable to assume that language must have evolved in stages, and that, in some cases, the emergence of one property must have depended on another that preceded it, in the sense that it could not have evolved without it.

It is difficult to support, refute, or flesh out hypotheses about these stages of evolution with evidence from spoken languages alone, because they are all thousands of years old, or descended from old languages, with their full linguistic structure intact. However, sign languages can arise anew at any time, and linguists look to them for clues to the course of language emergence.

The fact that the emergence of sign languages can be observed in real time does not guarantee that they will provide clues to the course of evolution of the human language capacity. If these young sign languages were to make their appearance replete with complex linguistic structures, they would be of little

---

[1] Some theorists have proposed that spoken language emerged from gesture (Corballis 2002; Armstrong, Stokoe & Wilcox 1995; Arbib 2012). I do not deal with that issue here, but see also e.g., MacNeilage (1998); and Sandler (2013); Emmorey (2013); and other papers in Kemmerer (2013) for discussion.

Wendy Sandler. 2017. What comes first in language emergence? In N. J. Enfield (ed.), *Dependencies in language*, 63–84. Berlin: Language Science Press.
DOI:10.5281/zenodo.573788

help in determining how such structure emerged in evolution. It is only if they develop gradually, and if the stages in this process can be identified, that they might offer concrete contemporary evidence of the path of language emergence.

Here I will identify such evidence in a new sign language that arose in relative isolation, to show that modest linguistic machinery – holistic words and prosodic organization of semantically related words – are the first things to emerge, and that they are enough to support fully functional language. Other, more computational, aspects of linguistic form, such as phonological, morphological,[2] and syntactic structuring, are later arrivals, apparently requiring the prior scaffolding provided by simplex words and by prosodic constituents that temporally organize semantically related units and characterize them with intonation.[3]

Of course, it cannot be assumed that the emergence of new sign languages in biologically modern humans faithfully replicates the evolution of language in our species. But the modernity of these languages does not nullify their significance in the context of evolution, and it would be a mistake to dismiss them. Emerging sign languages offer an exciting opportunity to identify two central facets of language emergence that no other naturally occurring system can provide. One is the nature of the communicative elements that are required minimally in order for a system to function as language. The other facet, relevant for the theme of this volume, is the path along which one kind of structure follows, or is dependent on, another over time before arriving at the kind of rule governed complexity in language that we often take for granted. In this sense, new sign languages can offer a uniquely empirical and plausible reference point for models of language evolution.

New sign languages have a heuristic advantage over spoken languages in another way as well. The nature of the physical system, in which movements of different parts of the body (the two hands, the head, the face, the torso) visually manifest different linguistic functions, makes it possible for linguists to match form to function more directly than they can for spoken languages, and literally to see it unfold (Sandler 2012a). I refer to this correspondence between the recruitment of articulators for linguistic purposes and language form as the Grammar of the Body.

---

[2] Sign languages in general have certain types of modality-typical complex morphology (e.g., Aronoff, Meir & Sandler 2005). We were surprised not to have found this complexity at the morphological level in Al Sayyid Bedouin Sign Language, although the beginnings of a system can be discerned in compounds. See Meir et al. (2010) and Padden et al. (2010) for treatments of the emergence of morphology in ABSL.

[3] I am assuming here that prosody includes intonation as well as rhythm (timing) and stress.

6 What comes first in language emergence?

Investigation of Al-Sayyid Bedouin Sign Language (ABSL), a young sign language that arose in relative isolation, has shown that a language does not spring forth fully formed, but rather evolves gradually across generations (see Aronoff et al. 2008; Sandler et al. 2014 for overviews).[4] Studying this language in different age groups, and tracing the step-by-step recruitment of different articulators to create a linguistic system (Sandler 2012a), allows us to observe the gradual emergence of linguistic form over time.

Our data suggest that language develops very efficiently, first, by creating holistic units to signify concepts – words with no phonology. This is followed by combining words into short propositions and later into larger discourse units, and organizing them prosodically into a fully functional linguistic system. Word order comes in early as well (Sandler et al. 2005), although we now have reason to believe that it is determined by the fundamental opposition between human and inanimate referents, and not by syntax (Meir et al. 2017).

I will extrapolate from our findings on Al-Sayyid Bedouin Sign Language to propose that certain basic elements of language must be present before other components commonly thought of as fundamental can arise. First, the crystallization of phonology depends on conventionalization of lexical items, which in turn depends on repeated social interactions with the same social group. These factors lead to automaticity, which results in a split between form and meaning. This split paves the way for duality of patterning (Hockett 1960) – meaningful and meaningless (phonological) levels of structure. The second two related properties are prosody and syntax. In ABSL, prosodic structure organizes semantic relations in the absence of concrete evidence for any syntactic means of marking the same relations. With little evidence for syntax in ABSL, I conclude that syntactic structure is not a prerequisite for the emergence of prosodic organization.

The pattern of emergence we see suggests that central properties of language that are considered universal – phonology and autonomous syntax – do not come ready-made in the human brain, and that a good deal of language can be present without clear evidence for them. I begin with a snapshot of the Grammar of the

---

[4] As Keren Rice pointed out to me, no criteria are offered for measuring whether language emergence is gradual or abrupt, and indeed, the characterization depends a lot on one's expectations. Coming from the generative tradition that attributes a fair amount of linguistic structure to innate propensities, our group was surprised by the lack of much linguistic structure in the early stages of ABSL, and by the seemingly arduous path to its accrual and conventionalization, leading us us to characterize emergence of linguistic form as gradual. For an overview of our ABSL findings, see Sandler et al. 2014.

Body in established sign languages to show how linguistic structure manifests itself in these visual languages[5], and then go on to emergence.

1 The Grammar of the Body

Sign languages are sometimes described as manual languages because the hands convey words, the most essential linguistic units. But sign languages also systematically exploit the whole upper body to convey language: movements of the head, facial articulators, and the torso, and independent use of the nondominant hand. Different movements of the extra-manual bodily articulators individually and in combination convey important elements of structure, including subordination, adjectival- or adverbial-type modification, contrast, intonation, and more, as shown in Figure 3 below.[6] The two levels to be traced here are the word and prosody/intonation.

In established sign languages, words have phonological structure: different configurations of the fingers, orientations of the palm, and movements of the hand on or near different body locations are combined to create signs and to distinguish them from one another, and they are altered in phonological processes such as assimilation (Stokoe 1960; Sandler 1989; Liddell & Johnson 1989; Brentari 1998). Figure 1 shows a minimal pair in Israeli Sign Language (ISL) distinguished by differences in major place of articulation alone.

A sign in sign language roughly corresponds to a word in spoken language: it bears a conventionalized form-meaning relation and is constrained in form both phonotactically (Battison 1978; Mandel 1981) and prosodically (Sandler 1999). Signs are typically monosyllabic, characterized by a single movement of the hands from one location to another. Even morphologically complex signs are usually monosyllabic, since grammatical morphemes are nonconcatenatively (simultaneously) overlaid on the base sign, by changes in locations, types of movement, and/or rhythm, and with particular conventionalized facial expressions (Sandler 1999).

At the level of phrasal prosody, manual timing establishes rhythm, and facial expression and head movement function systematically as intonation (Nespor & Sandler 1998; Dachkovsky, Healy & Sandler 2013). To prepare for the discussion

---

[5] For comprehensive treatments of sign language linguistic structure at all levels, see Sandler & Lillo-Martin (2006) and Pfau, Steinbach & Woll (2012).

[6] There is a large literature on nonmanual linguistic use of the body in sign languages. See Pfau & Quer (2010), Sandler (2012b), and a special issue of *Sign Language and Linguistics* (2011), Hermann and Steinbach (Eds.).

6 What comes first in language emergence?

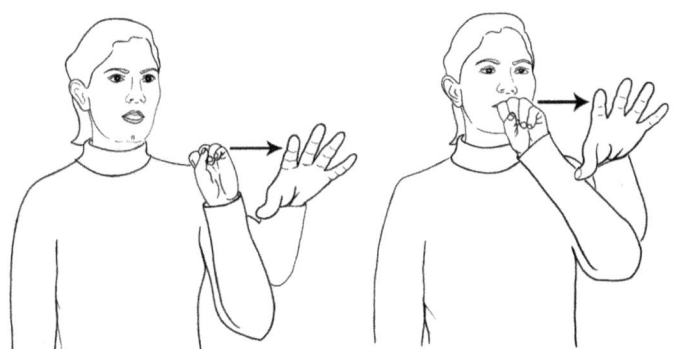

Figure 1: Minimal pair in Israeli Sign Language distinguished by place of articulation: (a) SEND (torso) and (b) TATTLE (head)

of prosody as an early feature of ABSL, a brief discussion of the way the body expresses prosody in sign languages is in order.

In an established sign language, the end of an intonational phrase is signaled by phrase final lengthening on the hands, coordinated with a change in facial expression and head position.[7] Figure 2 shows the boundary between the two intonational phrases in the Israeli Sign Language sentence glossed roughly [[DOG SMALL THAT] [WEEK-AGO I FIND IT]] // [[ESCAPE]] meaning 'The little dog that I found last week // ran away.'[8] Figure 2 shows that there is an across the board change in facial expression and head position between the end of the first constituent (...FIND IT) and the second (ESCAPE).[9]

In this sentence of ISL, the dependency between the two constituents is indicated by raised brows and head forward and down at the end of the first major constituent, the sentence topic, and by an across the board change of face and head configurations for the second, the comment. Squinted eyes indicate shared information – the little dog that the signer and addressee know about – a reliable signal for relative clauses (Nespor & Sandler 1998; Dachkovsky & Sandler 2009). The nondominant hand retains its shape and position from 'small dog' throughout the first constituent (through 'find it'), signaling topic continuity. This means that the anaphoric pronoun 'it' and the topic antecedent 'small dog' overlap tem-

---

[7] These intonational phrase markers are documented for two unrelated sign languages: Israeli and American (Dachkovsky, Healy & Sandler 2013).
[8] The first intonational phrase in the sentence is comprised of two lower level phonological phrases.
[9] In the context of language typology featured in this volume, it is worth mentioning that well studied established sign languages seem to have similar articulator-to-linguistic function correspondence to that shown in Figure 3, and thus constitute a language type.

Wendy Sandler

Figure 2: Complete change in facial expression and head position at intonational phrase boundary between (a) [[...IT]] and (b) [[ESCAPE]] i.e., between the topic, 'The little dog that I found a week ago,' and the comment, 'ran away'.

porally in the signal, as do the intonational and rhythmic markings of prosodic structure. In Figure 3a, a close-up of Figure 2a, the articulators are labeled for the specific functions they convey at the end of the first constituent. Figure 3b lists some of the linguistic functions conveyed by movements of articulators in the language generally. This complex simultaneous layering of bodily signals systematically organizes information in sign language sentences (Wilbur 2000). We can now turn to the order of emergence of the two pairs of structures of interest here: words and phonology, and prosody and syntax.

In the case of words, it is commonly believed that it would not be possible to amass a large vocabulary with holistic signals, and that a lower level of recombinable meaningless units (i.e., phonology) must have been a prerequisite for a large lexicon (Hockett 1960; Pinker & Jackendoff 2005). As for prosody, two competing predictions can be put forward, either prosody and then syntax or syntax and then prosody. Specifically, it has been hypothesized that, in a young language, such as a pidgin, prosody might precede syntactic marking to indicate different sentence types and subordination (Givón 1979). On the other hand, synchronic linguistic theory typically points in the opposite direction, holding that prosodic constituents are projected from syntactic constituents (Selkirk 1984; Nespor & Vogel 1986).

6 What comes first in language emergence?

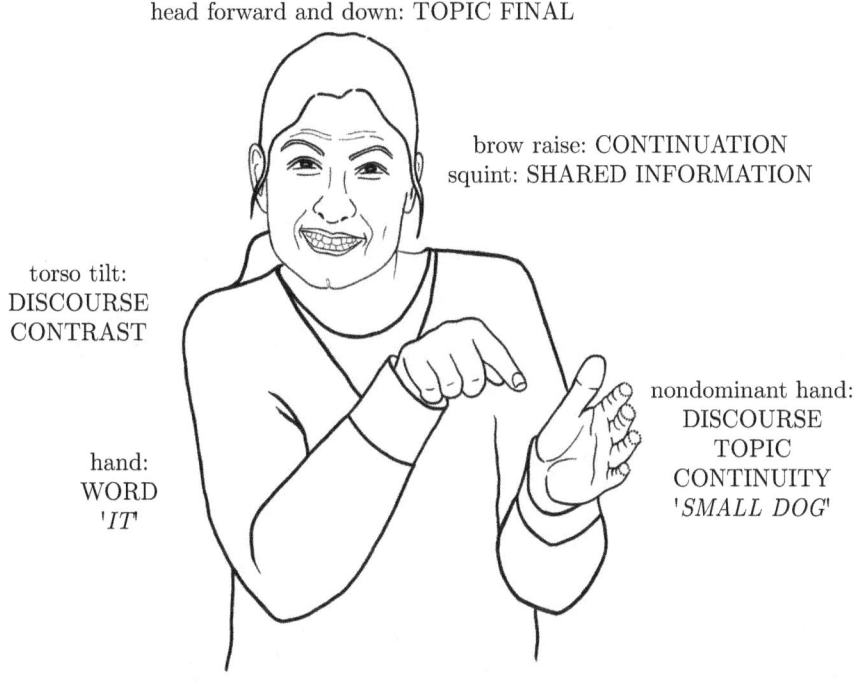

- **Eyeballs**: gaze (pointing; questioning; referential shift)
- **Head**: topic marking; question marking; prominence; continuation/dependency; referential shift; constituent boundary marking
- **Upper Face (brows, lids, cheeks)**: utterance type and information status (questions; old information; focus, etc.); constituent boundary marking (with blink); character perspective
- **Lower Face (tongue lips, cheeks)**: adj., adv. modification; mouthing of spoken words
- **Torso**: referential shift; discourse contrast
- **Hand(s)**: words (phonology; morphology); rhythm; prominence; boundary strength
- **Nondominant Hand**: phonological element in words; independent classifier morpheme; discourse topic continuity

Figure 3: (a) Functions signalled by movement of articulators at the end of the topic constituent. (b) list of functions signaled by various articulators in the language generally.

It is striking that neither in the case of words/phonology nor of prosody/syntax, do these paired elements appear at the same time in ABSL. Instead, one precedes the other: the language accrues a relatively large lexicon before phonological structure crystallizes, and prosodic markers of relations such as coordination and dependency between propositions appear in the absence of identifiable syntactic marking of these relations. While there is already evidence for the beginnings of phonology, there is in fact very little in the way of overt syntax even in third generation ABSL signers.

2 Words first, phonology later

We have followed the emergence of ABSL by recording and analyzing the language of people of different ages in the village. This investigation reveals that the word is the first linguistic unit to appear, and that this symbolic pairing of form and meaning is at the heart of human language (Sandler 2013). Zooming in to the structure of words in an emerging language shows a considerable amount of variation as well as the beginnings of structure.

2.1 Lexical form

Our earliest data consist of a videotaped story told by an elderly man who was one of the first four deaf children born into one family in the village. His utterances consist mainly of a series of one or two word-like manual signs, e.g., RIFLE, or HORSE RUN, occasionally interspersed with pantomimic movement of the whole body, e.g., 'strike-with-sword'.[10,11]

Restriction of linguistic form to the hands is in stark contrast with the linguistic uses of the body schematized in Figure 3. Given the availability of the whole body, and the complex and systematic use of different parts of the body in established sign languages, it is striking that only the hands are used for linguistic function at the beginning of language (Sandler 2012a), to symbolize word-level concepts.

In fact, the language used by this first generation signer is as simple and vague as the content of his story is detailed and complex, suggesting that a high level of cognitive complexity is possible without a concomitant degree of linguistic

---

[10] Pantomimic use of the body means that the body represents a human body performing some action: the hands are hands; the head is a head; the torso is a torso.

[11] Some utterances in the narrative have more words in a constituent, including what might be analyzed as a complex sentence or two. However, the majority of utterances are minimal, and often vague, as exemplified here.

complexity. The story comes from the history of Al-Sayyid, and was translated for us by the man's hearing son, who filled in a good deal of information shared by members of the community which was necessary for understanding the story but was not overtly conveyed.

Studying vocabulary in ABSL generally, we were surprised to find quite a lot of variation in lexical items across this small community, with more convergence within families, prompting us to coin the term, "familylect". Certain patterns can be identified at the level of the word, such as iconically motivated regularities in lexeme formation (Padden et al. 2013; Lepic et al. 2016). The only evidence we have found of complexity at the word level is in the formation of compounds, which show considerable variation in structure, with the exception of a language-particular subset involving classifier morphemes that typically follow a noun (Meir et al. 2010; Sandler et al. 2011b).

2.2 Articulatory variation: no crystallized phonological system

In our investigation of sign production across the community, we also found a surprising amount of articulatory variation in the production of the same lexical item (Israel & Sandler 2011). In this way, the words of ABSL are unlike the words of more established sign languages because they function as iconic wholes, and we concluded that a phonological system has not yet crystallized across the community (Sandler et al. 2011b).

Our team created a dictionary with 300 entries, presumably only a fraction of the lexicon in the language, since the signs had mostly been elicited through picture naming and the majority are thus concrete nouns. Yet, despite a relatively large vocabulary, we could not detect evidence of a discrete, systematic, meaningless level of structure. Even broad phonological specifications in established sign languages, such as major place of articulation categories, on a par with LABIAL or DORSAL in spoken languages, varied across signers for the same sign, as exemplified in Figure 4 for the sign DOG. The two places of articulation shown here, head and torso, are major place categories and contrastive in more established sign languages (cf., SEND and TATTLE in ISL, Figure 1).

We did discover kernels of phonology. For example, we encountered signs among younger signers whose form had been consistently altered to accommodate ease of articulation, resulting in signs that are counter-iconic. This suggests that smaller units of meaningless form are taking precedence over iconic, holistic signals. Within what we dubbed a "familylect", we also found consistent form-based handshape assimilation in a frequently used compound rendering it, too, non-iconic, and suggesting the beginning of a phonological level (Sandler et al.

Figure 4: The ABSL sign DOG signed by different signers at two different places of articulation, the head (a) and torso (b). The same two places of articulation are contrastive in established sign languages (see Figure 1).

2011b; Sandler 2014). We deduce from these studies that the emergence of phonology, at least in a contemporary sign language, depends first on the conventionalization of words and then on frequency of use and automaticity. The answer to the empirical question of how many meaningful holistic signals humans can produce and perceive in the vocal/auditory modality is not known, and it is possible that sign languages can tolerate a larger number than spoken languages can, due to the iconicity of form and the nature of visual perception. But even if there is some difference between modalities in this regard, ABSL shows surprisingly that it is possible for a functioning human language to have a relatively large vocabulary without a crystallized phonological system, making phonology dependent, in the sense intended here, on a stable, conventionalized, and frequently shared lexicon.

3 Prosodic organization first, syntax later

How are these words combined into meaningful utterances? In established languages, prosodic signals – rhythm, intonation, and phrasal stress – are typically coextensive with syntactic constituents such as the phrase or the clause. It has been argued that phrasal stress is determined by the order of heads and complements in a language (Nespor & Vogel 1986), and that children, sensitive to prosody of their native language since infancy (e.g., Mehler & Dupoux 1994; Jusczyk 1997), use the prominence patterns of prosody to bootstrap the syntactic structure (e.g., Nespor, Guasti & Christophe 1996).

6 What comes first in language emergence?

Because of this syntax-prosody correspondence, linguists propose that the prosody is read off the syntax, and is in this sense dependent on it (Selkirk 1984; Nespor & Vogel 1986). Given these observations, one might expect syntactic structure to be a prerequisite for prosodic structure in a new language. This prediction runs contrary to that of Givón (1979) and others who reason that prosody is likely to precede syntax in young languages.

The difference between these two views may depend to some extent on what one calls syntax. Our approach throughout has been to refrain from attributing autonomous syntactic form to an expression in ABSL without explicit evidence for it.[12] We find word groupings by meaning and even consistencies in word order (Sandler et al. 2005), but no evidence so far that favors autonomous syntactic structure over a much more basic driving force. In a recent and detailed study, Meir et al. (2017) show that word order in new sign languages and in gesture (without speech) is governed by the salience of human referents and not by syntactic rules.[13] In ABSL, the groupings of words into constituents and the relations between them are marked by prosody, which emerges gradually over time in the community (Sandler et al. 2011a).

On the whole, evidence from a small sample of narratives in four ABSL age groups suggests that prosody – consisting of timing and intonation – is the earliest organizing force, and that it emerges gradually. This overall picture is tempered by the fact that certain indications of syntactic relations *within* clauses begin to appear together with intonational marking of dependency *across* them. The findings are summarized in Tables 1 and 2. We are currently investigating these preliminary results further, across three young sign languages.

Age group 1. As I pointed out in the introduction, the story told by the oldest signer (age group 1), is characterized largely (though not exclusively) by one or two-word propositions, separated by pauses. Only the *hands* are recruited for linguistic components.

---

[12] Apart from overt markers, syntactic tests can identify syntactic structure. For example, early research on American Sign Language distinguished coordinate from subordinate clauses by the coreference properties of a process called final subject pronoun copy (Padden 1988). In ABSL we have not found syntactic processes of this kind, nor do we see evidence of morphosyntax, such as verb agreement (Padden et al. 2010), although it is common in established sign languages (Aronoff, Meir & Sandler 2005), or case marking. While one cannot rule out the covert presence of syntactic structure driving the prosodic structure we see, neither can we identify evidence for its existence. The more parsimonious account, therefore, is one that takes prosody as the prior mechanism for organizing and relating essentially semantic constituents.

[13] Based on word orders of ABSL and other new sign languages, and on experimental work with gesture, Meir et al. (2017) found that human arguments occur before inanimate arguments, irrespective of their syntactic or semantic roles.

Table 1: Recruitment of additional articulators for grammatical functions according to age group, from oldest (group 1, the earliest stage of the language) to youngest (group 4, the later stage)

Age group	Hands	Head	Face	Body	Nondominant hand
1	×				
2	×	×			
3	×	×	×		
4	×	×	×	×	×

Table 2: Complexity added through recruitment of additional articulators for linguistic functions (adapted from Sandler et al. 2011a; Sandler 2012a)

Age group	Words	Complex sentences	Discourse/reference cohesion
1	Signs		
2	Signs	Unsystematic clause linking (coordination); 1 NP per 2.5 predicates (vague one-word constitutents); 1st person subject pronouns only	
3	Signs	Many dependent constituents (conditionals, temporal expressions, reported speech); 1-2 NPs per predicate; 3rd person pronouns	Parentheticals, reported speech
4	Signs	Addition of modifiers, quantifiers, embedding inside reported speech (double embedding)	Addition of topic continuity marker and torso shift for different discourse referents

6 What comes first in language emergence?

Age group 2. In the second age group (short stretches of narratives of two people in the study reported in Sandler et al. 2011a), movement of the *head* was added to the hands to separate constituents. Some separated constituents were lists, and some (e.g., temporal expressions such as DAYS THREE meaning 'for three days') were related semantically to adjacent propositions, but no special syntactic or prosodic marking distinguished these from coordinated units. Many propositions in this age group did not associate nominal arguments with verbs in the same constituent, and no pronouns were used except occasionally first person (pointing to the chest).

Age group 3. In the third age group (short stretches of narratives of two younger people), *facial expression* was added to show continuation/dependency between constituents such as conditionals, and, together with head position, to signal parentheticals in a discourse. Although utterances clearly involve subordination semantically (e.g., in conditionals), this subordination is not marked syntactically – no complementizers, time adverbials, or conditional expressions like 'if'. Instead it is marked with prosodic signals of timing of the hands and intonation of the face and head.

Together with prosodic signaling of dependency between clauses, we see somewhat richer structure within clauses: verbs are more likely to occur with nominal arguments, and third person pronouns – abstract syntactic elements – are common. Relations between clauses are signaled prosodically by timing and intonation, and not syntactically, but a tendency that might be considered syntactic is emerging: an increase in overt arguments associated with verbs, some of them pronominal forms. We see no implicational relation between these syntactic elements within clauses and the prosody connecting them, however.

While we cannot rule out the covert presence of syntactic structure driving the prosodic structure we see, neither can we identify evidence for its existence. The more parsimonious account, therefore, is one that takes prosody as the prior mechanism for organizing and relating essentially semantic constituents. We conclude that the mechanism for connecting clauses and indicating dependency relations between them is prosodic, and that syntactic mechanisms serving this function have not (yet) arisen. For further discussion of what you can say without syntax, see Jackendoff & Wittenberg's (2014) paper with that title.

Age group 4. We are just beginning to analyze the language of age group 4. The narrative of a single signer in the fourth age group was chosen for analysis for two reasons: he is the oldest of five deaf siblings in one household and his deaf mother and hearing father know only ABSL and no ISL,[14] so that the young man is able to distinguish the two languages and provide a good example of "pure", fluent ABSL in his age group.

In his signing we found refinement and coordination of the nonmanual signals for subordination/dependency (cf. ISL example in Figure 3). Even double embedding of constituents occurs. An example is an utterance translated (with the help of prosody) as, "Father (said to) me about marriage, 'If you marry a deaf girl, all of your children will be deaf. No way.'" The boldface constituent in the gloss has conditional prosody: FATHER ME MARRIAGE, **DEAF TWO DEAF BOTH MARRY**, OFFSPRING DEAF ALL – REJECT. As with age group 3 signers, this embedding of one proposition within another is signaled by prosody only and not by overt morpho-syntactic elements such as a conditional word like 'if'.

In his narrative, the signer added the *nondominant hand* for topic continuity (essentially, discourse level coreference) and shifts in *body posture* to identify referents in a discourse. All of these phenomena are structural advances over the narratives of the earlier stages of the language of the older people studied. Table 3 is a gloss and translation to English of an excerpt in which he describes the vocations (professions) he had to choose from at vocational school. A parenthetical segment is set off in the gloss by square brackets. The large curly bracket along the side indicates the stretch of signing during which the nondominant hand is held in the signal to mark continuity of the topic – 'the third vocation' (welding) – dropping to his side at the end of the discourse segment relating to the topic. Figure 5 illustrates the physical manifestation of linguistic properties of the utterance. The signer's budding Grammar of the Body may not yet be as systematic and complex as that of more established sign languages, but it has the scaffolding in place.

---

[14] The young people of the Al-Sayyid village have had a good deal of exposure to signs from Israeli Sign Language in school settings, while exposure to ISL grammatical structure as it is signed by deaf people is limited. In school, the teachers speak Arabic, accompanied by ISL signs. This is not ISL, since the grammar of the sign language is very different from that of the spoken language, and, as with other sign-supported speech systems, when both channels are used at the same time, one or the other (usually the sign language) is seriously disrupted. Some of the young deaf men in Al-Sayyid (including the Group 4 example discussed here) did have extended exposure to ISL in their late teens when they attended a mixed vocational high school (Jewish and Arab pupils with ISL signing deaf teachers), now closed down. The bottom line is that people under the age of 30 have had considerable exposure to ISL vocabulary and sporadic, uneven exposure to its grammatical structure. A general description of the spoken and signed linguistic mosaic in Israel is offered in Sandler (2014).

6 What comes first in language emergence?

Table 3: Excerpt from 4th age group signer's narrative (from Sandler 2012a)

Gloss	Translation
ONE COOKING TWO MECHANICS THREE WELDING	[[One, cooking, two, mechanics, three, welding.
[I LONG-AGO I SMALL FATHER ME HE WELD REMEMBER WELL NOT, REJECT]	[Long ago, when I was small, my father was a welder. I remembered it well and didn't want that, not welding.]
FOUR, COMPUTERS ALL PROFESSIONS	Four computers, all the professions.]]
ME MECHANICS.	I wanted mechanics.

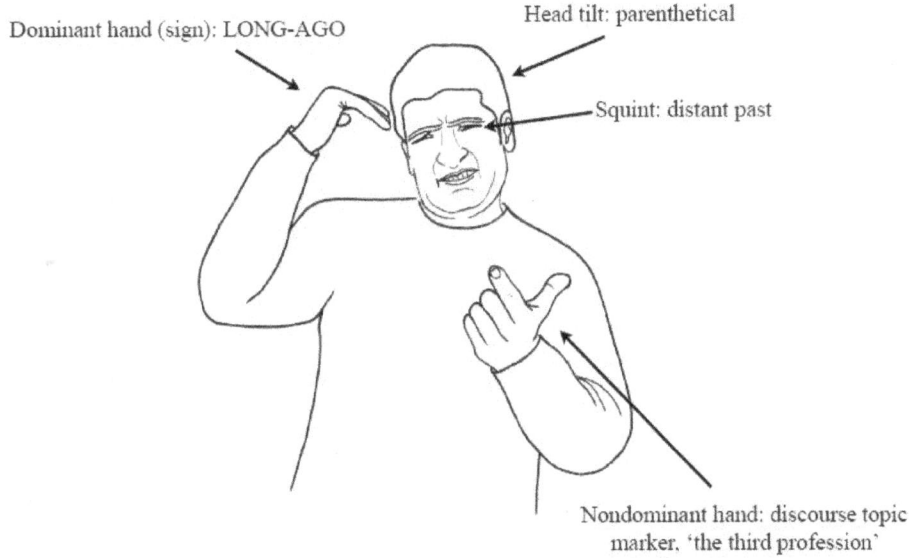

Figure 5: Use of the body for grammatical functions (from Sandler 2012a).

77

4 Conclusion

From a grammatical point of view, ABSL across the community is relatively simple. Nevertheless, the semantic/cognitive conceptualization and relations it reflects are far from simple. With these conceptualizations and relations, and minimal linguistic machinery, ABSL functions as a full language. Its users talk about life histories, folk remedies no longer in use, dreams, fertility, deafness, national insurance, wedding preparations, suspicions, personal relations – all fluently, without hesitation or pantomimic "acting out", and without noticeable communication failures. While further grammatical structures may develop over time, it seems that fully functional language is possible with relatively simple linguistic structure (see Klein & Perdue 1997; Gil 2005; Jackendoff & Wittenberg 2014 for more support for this claim).

ABSL and other new languages provide novel evidence for theories about the relation between community structure and language structure (Meir et al. 2012). For example, the language of age groups 1 and 2 corresponds to Bernstein's (1971) notion of a restricted code used in circumstances where the speakers share knowledge and assumptions. A restricted code is economical in that it can convey a good deal of meaning with a few words, as speakers can rely on the shared knowledge of their interlocutors to interpret what they say.

We have reported elsewhere that tolerance of irregularity, in the form of lexical variation and variation in the order of constituents in compounds in the Al-Sayyid village, reported in Meir et al. (2010), is compatible with Wray & Grace's (2007) conception of an esoteric code. Acquired in childhood and used within a homogeneous group with shared culture and environment, esoteric codes are characterized by irregularities of form that are less typical of more regular exoteric codes, used with outsiders.[15]

The overview presented here suggests that the emergence of a crystallized phonological system follows – in other words, depends on – the prior existence of a sizable, conventionalized lexicon. As for the emergence of prosody and syntax, our findings suggest that an autonomous syntax is not a prerequisite for prosody, or, in other words, that prosody does not depend on syntax. Prosody is a critical factor in organizing semantic relations relatively early in a language, while overt indications of syntax have yet to emerge. Language needs this basic scaffolding of words and prosody, which emerges gradually over a few generations, and it

---

[15] As a very young language, ABSL has not had a chance to develop characteristics attributed to esoteric codes such as morphophonemic alternations and irregular morphological paradigms.

seems that it is all the linguistic machinery you need for a perfectly good human language. Simple maybe, compared to millennia-old languages. But no other species even comes close.

Acknowledgements

The research on ISL is supported by grant 580/09 from the Israel Science Foundation to Irit Meir and the author. The ABSL research is supported by a grant from the U.S. Israel Binational Science Foundation and by NIH grant R01 DC006473. The Grammar of the Body project is supported by a grant to the author by the European Research Council, project 340140. Many thanks to Nick Enfield and other participants for useful and stimulating discussions at the meeting on Dependencies among Systems of Language, Ardennes, June 2014. I am grateful to Mark Aronoff, Ray Jackendoff, and Keren Rice for their insightful comments and suggestions on this paper.

References

Arbib, Michael. 2012. *How the brain got language: The mirror system hypothesis.* Oxford: Oxford University Press.
Armstrong, David F., William C. Stokoe & Sherman E. Wilcox. 1995. *Gesture and the nature of language.* Cambridge: Cambridge University Press.
Aronoff, Mark, Irit Meir & Wendy Sandler. 2005. The paradox of sign language morphology. *Language* 81. 301–344.
Aronoff, Mark, Irit Meir, Carol Padden & Wendy Sandler. 2008. The roots of linguistic organization in a new language. In Derek Bickerton & Michael Arbib (eds.), *Holophrasis, compositionality and protolanguage (special issue of Interaction Studies),* 133–149. Amsterdam: John Benjamins Publishing Company.
Battison, Robbin. 1978. *Lexical borrowing in American Sign Language.* Silver Spring, MD: Linstok Press.
Bernstein, Basil. 1971. *Class, codes and control, volume 1.* London: Routledge & Kegan Paul.
Bickerton, Derek. 1990. *Language and species.* Chicago: Chicago University Press.
Bolhuis, Johan, Ian Tattersal, Noam Chomsky & Robert Berwick. 2014. How could language have evolved? *PLOS Biology* 12(8). 1–7.
Brentari, Diane. 1998. *A prosodic model of sign language phonology.* Cambridge, MA: MIT Press.

Carstairs-McCarthy, Andrew. 1999. *The origins of complex language.* Oxford: Oxford University Press.

Corballis, Michael C. 2002. *From hand to mouth: The origins of language.* Princeton: Princeton University Press.

Dachkovsky, Svetlana, Christina Healy & Wendy Sandler. 2013. Visual intonation in two sign languages. *Phonology* 30(2). 211–252.

Dachkovsky, Svetlana & Wendy Sandler. 2009. Visual intonation in the prosody of a sign. *Language and Speech* 52(2-3). 287–314.

Darwin, Charles. 1871. *The descent of man and selection in relation to sex.* London: John Murray.

Emmorey, Karen. 2013. The neurobiology of sign language and the mirror system hypothesis. In David Kemmerer (ed.), *Language and cognition 5/2-3*, 205–210. Berlin: De Gruyter.

Fitch, W. Tecumseh. 2005. The evolution of language: A comparative view. *Biology and Philosophy* 20. 193–230.

Fitch, W. Tecumseh. 2010. *The evolution of language.* Cambridge: Cambridge University Press.

Gil, David. 2005. Word order without syntactic categories: How Riau Indonesian does it. In H. Harley A. Carnie & S.A. Dooley (eds.), *Verb first: On the syntax of verb-initial languages*, 243–262. Amsterdam: John Benjamins.

Givón, Talmy. 1979. From discourse to syntax: Grammar as a processing strategy. In Talmy Givón (ed.), *Discourse and syntax* (Syntax and Semantics, vol. 12), 81–111. New York: Academic Press.

Hauser, Marc, Noam Chomsky & W. Tecumseh Fitch. 2002. The faculty of language: What is it, who has it, and how did it evolve? *Science* 298. 1569–1579.

Hauser, Marc, Charles Yang, Robert Berwick, Ian Tattersall, Michael Ryan, Jeffrey Watumull, Noam Chomsky & Richard Lewontin. 2014. The mystery of language evolution: Frontiers in psychology. *Language Sciences* 401(5). 1–12.

Hockett, Charles F. 1960. The origin of speech. *Scientific American* 203. 89–96.

Israel, Assaf & Wendy Sandler. 2011. Phonological category resultion: A a study of handshapes in younger and older sign languages. In Rachel Channon & Harry van der Hulst (eds.), *Formational units in sign language*, vol. 3, 177–202. Berlin: Mouton de Gruyter.

Jackendoff, Ray. 1999. Possible stages in the evolution of the language capacity. *Trends in Cognitive Science* 3. 272–279.

Jackendoff, Ray & Eva Wittenberg. 2014. What you can say without syntax: A hierarchy of grammatical complexity. In Frederick Newmeyer & Lauren Preston (eds.), *Measuring grammatical complexity*, 65–83. Oxford: Oxford University Press.

Jusczyk, Peter. 1997. *The discovery of spoken language*. Cambridge MA: MIT Press.

Kemmerer, David (ed.). 2013. Language and cognition. 5(2-3): *Special issue in response to arbib (2012)*.

Klein, Wolfgang & Clive Perdue. 1997. The basic variety (or: Couldn't natural languages be much simpler?) *Second Language Research* 13. 301–347.

Lepic, Ryan, Carl Börstell, Gal Belsitzman & Wendy Sandler. 2016. Taking meaning in hand: Iconic motivation in two-handed signs. *Sign Language and Linguistics* 19(1). 37–81.

Liddell, Scott K. & Robert E. Johnson. 1989. American Sign Language: The phonological base. *Sign Language Studies* 64. 195–277.

MacNeilage, Peter F. 1998. The frame/content theory of evolution of speech production. *Behavior and Brain Science* 21. 499 – 546.

Mandel, Mark. 1981. *Phonotactics and morphophonology in ASL*. University of California, Berkeley PhD thesis.

Mehler, Jacques & Emmanuel Dupoux. 1994. *What infants know*. Cambridge, MA: Blackwell.

Meir, Irit, Mark Aronoff, Wendy Sandler & Carol Padden. 2010. Sign languages and compounding. In Sergio Scalise & Irene Vogel (eds.), *Compounding*, 301–322. Amsterdam: John Benjamins Publishing Company.

Meir, Irit, Assaf Israel, Wendy Sandler, Carol Padden & Mark Aronoff. 2012. The influence of community on language structure: Evidence from two young sign languages. *Linguistic Variation* 12(2). 247–291.

Meir, Irit, Mark Aronoff, Carl Börstell, So-One Hwang, Deniz Ikbasaran, Itamar Kastner, Ryan Lepic, Adi Lifshitz Ben Basat, Carol Padden & Wendy Sandler. 2017. The effect of being human and the basis of grammatical word order: Insights from novel communication systems and young sign languages. *Cognition* 158. 189–207.

Nespor, Marina, Maria-Theresa Guasti & Anne Christophe. 1996. Selecting word order: The rhythmic activation principle. In Ursula Kleinhenz (ed.), *Interfaces in phonology*, 1–26. Berlin: Akademie Verlag.

Nespor, Marina & Wendy Sandler. 1998. Prosodic phonology in Israeli Sign Language. *Language and Speech* 52(2-3). 143–176.

Nespor, Marina & Irene Vogel. 1986. *Prosodic phonology*. Dordrecht: Foris.

Newmeyer, Frederick J. 2002. Uniformitarian assumptions and language evolution research. In Alison Wray (ed.), *The transition to language*, 359–375. Oxford: Oxford University Press.

Padden, Carol. 1988. *Interaction of morphology and syntax in American Sign Languages* (Outstanding Dissertations in Linguistics). New York: Garland.

Padden, Carol, Irit Meir, Mark Aronoff & Wendy Sandler. 2010. The grammar of space in two new sign languages. In Diane Brentari (ed.), *Sign languages*, 573–595. New York: Cambridge University Press.

Padden, Carol, Irit Meir, So-One Hwang, Ryan Lepic & Sharon Seegers. 2013. Where do nouns come from? *Gesture* 13(3). 287–308.

Pfau, Roland & Josep Quer. 2010. Nonmanuals: Their grammatical and prosodic roles. In Diane Brentari (ed.), *Sign languages*. 381–402. New York: Cambridge University Press.

Pfau, Roland, Markus Steinbach & Bencie Woll (eds.). 2012. *Sign language: An international handbook*. Berlin: De Gruyter Mouton.

Pinker, Steven & Ray Jackendoff. 2005. The faculty of language: What's special about it? *Cognition* 95. 201–236.

Sandler, Wendy. 1989. *Phonological representation of the sign: Linearity and non-linearity in American Sign Language*. Dordrecht: Foris.

Sandler, Wendy. 1999. Cliticization and prosodic words in sign language. In Tracy Hall & Ursula Kleinhenz (eds.), *Studies on the phonological word*, 223–255. Amsterdam: John Benjamins Publishing Company.

Sandler, Wendy. 2012a. Dedicated gestures and the emergence of sign language. *Gesture* 12(3). 265–307.

Sandler, Wendy. 2012b. Visual prosody. In Roland Pfau, Markus Steinbach & Bencie Woll (eds.), *Sign language: An international handbook*, 55–76. Berlin: De Gruyter Mouton.

Sandler, Wendy. 2013. Vive la différence: Sign language and spoken language in language evolution. *Language and Cognition* 5(2-3). 189–203.

Sandler, Wendy. 2014. The emergence of phonetic and phonological features in sign language. *Nordlyd* 41(1). 183–212.

Sandler, Wendy & Diane Lillo-Martin. 2006. *Sign language and linguistic universals*. Cambridge UK: Cambridge University Press.

Sandler, Wendy, Irit Meir, Carol Padden & Mark Aronoff. 2005. The emergence of grammar in a new sign language. *Proceedings of the National Academy of Sciences* 102(7). 2661–2665.

Sandler, Wendy, Irit Meir, Svetlana Dachkovsky, Carol Padden & Mark Aronoff. 2011a. The emergence of complexity in prosody and syntax. *Lingua* 121. 2014–2033.

Sandler, Wendy, Mark Aronoff, Irit Meir & Carol Padden. 2011b. The gradual emergence of phonological form in a new language. *Natural Language and Linguistic Theory* 29. 503–543.

Sandler, Wendy, Mark Aronoff, Carol Padden & Irit Meir. 2014. Language emergence Al-Sayyid Bedouin Sign Language. In Jack Sidnell, Paul Kockelman & N. J. Enfield (eds.), *The Cambridge handbook of linguistic anthropology*, 246–278. Cambridge UK: Cambridge University Press.

Selkirk, Elizabeth. 1984. *Phonology and syntax: The relation between sound and structure.* Cambridge, MA: MIT Press.

Stokoe, William C. 1960. *Sign language structure: An outline of the visual communications systems of the American deaf* (Studies in Linguistics: Occasional Papers 8). Buffalo: University of Buffalo.

Wilbur, Ronnie B. 2000. Phonological and prosodic layering of nonmanuals in American Sign Language. In Karen Emmorey & Harlan Lane (eds.), *The signs of language revisited: An anthology to honor Ursula Bellugi and Ed Klima*, 190–214. Mahwah, NJ: Lawrence Erlbaum Associates.

Wray, Alison & George W. Grace. 2007. The consequences of talking to strangers: Evolutionary corollaries of socio-cultural influences on linguistic form. *Lingua* 117. 543–578.

Chapter 7

Is language development dependent on early communicative development?

Elena Lieven

ESRC International Centre for Language and Communicative Development (LuCiD)
Division of Human Communication, Development and Hearing
University of Manchester

1 Introduction

Children diagnosed with Autism Spectrum Disorder (ASD) show impairments in communication, social interaction and a restricted behavioural repertoire. One influential hypothesis in the literature is that the understanding of other minds (i.e. that one's interactants are communicating intentionally) is *the* (or *a*) necessary precondition to learning language. Since, on the one hand, most children subsequently diagnosed with autism show disruption in measures of early intention reading and, on the other, some children diagnosed with autism learn to talk – in some cases with real proficiency – this seemingly challenges the above hypothesis (but see Carpenter & Tomasello 2000).

Studies of later language development in autism have come to highly variable conclusions, some finding considerable differences with matched typically developing (TD) controls, others finding almost no differences in vocabulary or syntax though pragmatic skills may be impaired. A recently published survey of language and communicative development in autism (Arcuili & Brock 2014) which covers many aspects from prelinguistic communication through to literacy, narrative, and conversational development shows this lack of agreement in the field for almost every aspect studied. In this chapter, I will first outline the claim that shared intentionality is a necessary foundation for language development before covering studies that have examined this in children who develop autism. I will then look at the evidence for language impairments in autistic children.

Elena Lieven

2 Shared intentionality as the precondition for language development

There is pretty unanimous agreement that typically developing children show a qualitative change in interactive behaviour starting sometime around the last trimester of the first year. Of course, this is preceded by other important developmental milestones: for instance, the onset of social smiling and the development of attachment-related behaviours. Although termed the "9-month revolution" by Tomasello and others, this overstates the abruptness of the shift in interactional behaviours, which show continuous development over this period. The underlying theoretical construct is that of "shared intentionality" – a new world of shared intersubjectivity in which infants start to realise that others have intentions and that these can be related to their own intentions, i.e., that others are intentional agents like themselves. The behavioural manifestations of this change in the understanding of other minds are "triadic" interactions: interactions in which children involve their interactive partners in their own interests and actions and understand that the communicative behaviours of others are intentional. The following behaviours are taken as evidence for this shift to "intention reading": sharing joint attention to objects and knowing that you are doing so; showing objects to the other; using pointing to draw attention to events or objects; understanding what is new for the other; giving information to the other. Tomasello characterises this as part of the human biological inheritance which allows for the cultural inheritance that we acquire through the specifically human behaviours of imitation, learning and teaching. In turn, these form the basis for the "cultural ratchet": the rapid rate of social and technological innovation and change in modern humans (Tomasello 1999: 6).

There does seem to be good evidence for a relatively universal developmental timetable for these early skills of shared intentionality (Brown 2011; Callaghan et al. 2011; Liszkowski et al. 2012; Lieven & Stoll 2013), though as these studies also report, there are some differences resulting from the different cultural contexts (most importantly while Callaghan et al. report language comprehension as starting at around 9-10 months in all the studied cultures, production is, on average, 3 months later in the non-technologically complex cultures). There also seems to be considerable consistency within a culture. A study by Carpenter, Nagell & Tomasello (1998) investigated the emergence of joint attentional skills in a group of 24 children in the USA aged between 9-15 months, as measured by 9 different tasks. They found that infants first shared attention, then started to follow the attention of the mother and finally started to direct attention. There were also strong correlations between the emergence of each pair of skills and their sub-components: they emerged in close developmental synchrony and with a consistent ordering pattern.

Why should the development of shared intentionality be the necessary basis for language development? The argument depends on understanding the importance of "common ground" in all intentional communication. The meaning of a communicative act can only be understood in a shared context. For instance *The door is open* will be interpreted quite differently if someone is complaining about being cold rather than about being bored. Therefore, the argument goes, infants will only be able to start to acquire language once they "realise" that utterances addressed to them carry meaning based on shared common understandings. Symbolic representations do not, therefore, exist cut off from their context but are always intersubjective (socially shared) and perspectival (they pick out a particular way of viewing a phenomenon, Tomasello 1999, Levinson 2006, Enfield 2013). This potentially deals with the Quinian problem of how an infant can interpret the reference of an utterance, given the multitude of possibilities when the caretaker points and/or uses a word/sentence. To support this position, Carpenter & Tomasello ask why word learning takes off at 12-14 months and not much earlier given the enormous number of words that most infants hear during the first year of life. Their answer is that the development of shared intentionality is crucial to providing the context in which word meaning can be interpreted, and therefore learned, and there is plenty of evidence that preverbal infants do, in fact, understand a good deal about what is given and new for another and can interpret other's communication on this basis (Tomasello & Haberl 2003; Moll et al. 2008). This is supported by the many studies of typically developing children showing strong correlations between early joint attentional skills and vocabulary size (e.g. Carpenter, Nagell & Tomasello 1998).

3 Studies of language development in autistic and ASD children

A third to half of the children diagnosed with ASD never develop a functional language. The rest do learn but with very varying degrees of sophistication (Wetherby & Prizant 1992; Noens et al. 2006). The biggest problem in trying to understand these children's language development is that different studies conflict in critically important ways. There are a number of reasons for this. The first is methodological: studies use different diagnostic criteria, different types of control groups and different methods of assessing children's language and communicative development. In the latter case, this is almost always done using standardised tests which do not give much insight into the underlying processes involved in developing language. In addition, with the exception of the "prodromal" studies mentioned below, since an autism diagnosis is rare before 3 years of age, the crucial early stages of breaking into language have not been available for study. However there are some general conclusions that one can draw from this literature. Children diagnosed with ASD usually show difficulties in communicative reciprocity and discourse management (Anderson et al. 2009) and jargon echolalia is often present (Roberts 2014). On standardised language tests, children diagnosed with ASD are almost always behind compared to age-matched, TD controls. However, if they are matched for mental age or vocabulary size, a number of studies find no difference in syntax or morphology. For instance, Brock & Caruana (2014) found that reading for words and sentences is largely predicted by degree of language impairment and level of oral language and Norbury (2005) concludes that the oral comprehension of the children diagnosed with ASD in her study was predicted by their language skills and not the severity of their autism. But how do these general findings for children aged 3;0 and above relate to the early development of shared intentionality?

4 Prelinguistic communication in children who develop ASD

There is a complex literature on the possible social interactional antecedents to language development in autism. Different studies have focussed on particular aspects of early social interaction with Mutual Shared Attention, Joint Engagement, Response to Joint Attention and Initiation of Joint Attention held out as critical in different models with variable levels of evidence to support the claims. Sigman & Ruskin (1999) followed 51 children with an autism diagnosis aged between 3-5 years of age when they were first recruited, into the mid-school years. They found that joint attention behaviours by the children were strongly concurrently related to language skills. Another study shows clear evidence of the involvement of child joint attention in predicting later communicative and language skills (Siller & Sigman 2002). As well, they also found that parental behaviours that were synchronised with their child's focus of attention and ongoing activity were associated with higher levels of joint attention in their children a year later and with better language outcomes 10 and 16 years later and this was independent of the child's initial language age, IQ and joint attention skills. In a separate study of a group of children who entered with a mean age of 16

7 Is language development dependent on early communicative development?

months (and a standard deviation of 7 months), the same authors (Siller & Sigman 2008) found that, on the one hand, child characteristics on entry (Non-verbal IQ, language age as well as joint attention) were correlated and predicted language outcomes. But, on the other hand, *rate* of language growth was independently predicted by (a) children's responsiveness to others' bids for joint attention and (b) parents' responsiveness to their children's attention and activity during play and neither of these relations could be explained by initial variation in mental age or initial language abilities. Thus there seems to be clear evidence that aspects of joint attention in children with ASD are implicated in subsequent language development and that parental success in achieving synchronous joint attention with their children is independently associated with more successful language outcomes. However the fact remains that impaired joint attention is almost universally found in children with ASD and yet many do achieve competence in language at least to the level of using phrasal speech and sometimes to much more sophisticated language.

A major development in the attempt to explore the developmental antecedents to autism comes from prodromal studies with the younger siblings of children already diagnosed with an autism spectrum disorder in which the probability of a sibling also developing the disorder is 20% (Ozonoff et al. 2011). This has led to a number of studies in which "prodromal" children's early communicative interaction is compared with that of low-risk children and then related to the subsequent outcome in terms of an ASD diagnosis (Jones et al. 2014; Wan et al. 2013; Green et al. 2013)

The Wan et al. (2013) study which compared a prodromal high-risk group and a low risk group, used a global measure of the quality of mother-infant interaction at 8 and 14 months. The study showed that when compared to low-risk infants, at risk infants show significantly lower scores at 8 months than non at risk infants on global measures of the quality of parent-child interaction (PCI), differences that at 14 months are increased and are associated with an autism outcome at 3 years of age. It should be emphasised that the authors consider that the lower measures of PCI quality are due to aspects of the infants' behaviour (e.g. lack of eye contact) which arise from the infant's condition, which then, in turn, disrupts the interaction between parent and child and thus the child's functional social experience. A targeted intervention study between 9-14 months succeeded in improving the quality of these interactions as well as suggesting a reduction of autism pre-symptoms at 14 month endpoint (Green et al. 2013). These improvements were sustained at 24 month follow up (Green et al. 2015). At 14 months the non-significant trend in the data was for there to be, if anything, a slowing in language acquisition – however by 24 months the treatment group showed a trend towards improved function, especially in receptive language development. There was however no equivalent effect on "structural" language development, suggesting a possible relative dissociation in this context between the quality of PCI and attention on the one hand and syntax growth on the other. This suggests that while being able to respond to joint attention initiatives and caregivers' ability to synchronise communication with the child are facilitatory in learning language, they may well not be essential, potentially contra to a strong version of the Tomasello hypothesis.

5 Implications

There are, of course, many interpretations of what it means to learn language. Minimally, I mean the ability to produce and understand what is said in some relation to actions and events, at least one's own, and to be able to adapt one's utterances to different situations with at least some ability to go beyond reproducing utterances learned by rote.

The suggestion that the development of language within autism progresses in rather a different way to that of typical language development has often been raised but the evidence currently is not sufficient to decide whether this is the case nor to understand the mechanisms which might underpin any such differences. Karmiloff-Smith, in her studies of children with Williams syndrome (2006), has suggested that these children's facility with language (relative to very low levels of cognitive ability) might represent a different learning route. Can we suggest the same thing for those children with ASD who learn language? How might children who are more or less impaired on early intention reading skills learn language? Clearly there is an innate basis to the learning of language but this leaves open a very wide range of possibilities. First, language learning might actually be independent of the communicative basis with which language is used. The best known version of this position argues for an innate set of specifically linguistic modules, one of which is Universal Grammar (others that have been proposed are for phonology and semantics). In this approach, communication may be largely what language is used for but this has nothing to do with how phonology, semantics and syntax develop. This has been argued very strongly within the Generativist tradition but has recently met strong challenges from a constructivist, usage-based approach (see Ambridge & Lieven 2011, Ambridge, Pine & Lieven 2014). In terms of autism, the immense range of language outcomes seems to challenge the idea of an encapsulated syntactic module, in that children with ASD do not show an "all-or-nothing" profile for syntax or, for that matter, any other aspect of language.

7 Is language development dependent on early communicative development?

An alternative possibility is that since language learning is underpinned by a range of cognitive skills, if some or all of these are relatively intact, structural language can be learned though its use may be pragmatically impaired. For instance, there are word learning studies that suggest that attentional mechanisms and physical context information are sufficient for at least some word learning (Samuelson & Smith 1998). Once children can isolate some words (e.g. own name) this appears to facilitate learning (segmentation) of other words (Fernald & Hurtado 2006; DePaolis, Vihman & Keren-Portnoy 2014). Both are potential non-social routes into language that have some empirical support.

Minimally, infants need to be able to select relevant information, maintain focus/vigilance and move on or unstick from the current focus. Other skills would involve strong statistical learning abilities, an intact working memory and rapid temporal order processing. We know that many autistic children are echolalic, which suggests a good ability to retain short-term phonological information. This is clearly not enough because many echolalic children never develop an innovative ability with language. It is also important to note that there is a variety of definitions of imitation, some of which are much more dependent on the imitator's ability to "mind-read" the goals of the imitated action (e.g. Over & Carpenter 2013). However if the ability to learn from the statistical distribution of the words and inflections that infants hear in the language around them is also present, an enhanced imitative skill might provide a partial route into the learning of language structure. A second pre-requisite might be the ability to "parse" events and objects in the world. This requires, first, the primate-wide abilities to cognitively represent spaces, objects and conspecifics and relational categories as well as the arguably more human cognitive capacities of categorisation, analogy and abstraction. But all of this would require intact attentional skills. The suggestion that some ASD children show abnormal attentional behaviour in infancy (faster to disengage from faces but also difficulties in disengaging from other stimuli (Gliga et al. 2014) might be a factor in inhibiting this ability to relate what they hear to what they see. For instance Ibbotson, Lieven & Tomasello (2014) showed that when mothers use the English progressive this is significantly more likely to overlap with an ongoing event than is the case when the same verb is used with other temporal/aspectual marking. If a child has a problem with rapidly shifting attention, they might well fail to pick up this form-meaning correlation with "upstream" consequences for learning.

These are just a few brief indications about how we might go about addressing this important issue. By putting together findings of particular early impairments from the autism literature with a detailed analysis of how these might impact on the learning of language we could start to explore the possibility of different routes into more or less successful language learning. This would also contribute to understanding the many other factors involved in the learning of language by neuro-typical children and allow us to develop more nuanced theories which attempt to integrate these factors with an understanding of how early social cognition does and does not contribute to different aspects of language development.

A longitudinal prodromal study of the naturalistic communicative and linguistic behaviour of children at risk of an autism diagnosis which relates in depth assessment of language and pragmatic skills to antecedent variables will represent a significant contribution to our understanding of language development within the context of autism. We hope to undertake a study of this kind in the near future.

References

Ambridge, Ben & Elena Lieven. 2011. *Child language acquisition: Contrasting theoretical approaches.* Cambridge: Cambridge University Press.

Ambridge, Ben, Julian Pine & Elena Lieven. 2014. Child language acquisition: Why universal grammar doesn't help. *Language* 90(3). 53–90.

Anderson, Debora K., Rosalind S. Oti, Catherine Lord & Kathleen Welch. 2009. Patterns of growth in adaptive social abilities among children with autism spectrum disorders. *Journal of Abnormal Child Psychology* 37(7). 1019–1034.

Arcuili, Joanne & Jon Brock (eds.). 2014. *Communication in autism.* Amsterdam: John Benjamins Publishing Company.

Brock, Jon & Nathan Caruana. 2014. Reading for sound and reading for meaning in autism. In Joanne Arcuili & Jon Brock (eds.), *Communication in autism,* 125–145. Amsterdam: John Benjamins Publishing Company.

Brown, Penelope. 2011. The cultural organization of attention. In Alessandro Duranti, Elinor Ochs & Bambi B. Schieffelin (eds.), *The handbook of language socialization,* 29–55. Malden: Wiley-Blackwell.

Callaghan, Tara C., Henrike Moll, Hannes Rakoczy, Felix Warneken, Ulf Liszkowski, Tanya Behne & Michael Tomasello. 2011. Early social cognition in three cultural contexts. *Monographs of the Society for Research in Child Development* 76(2). 1–142.

Carpenter, Malinda, Katherine Nagell & Michael Tomasello. 1998. Social cognition, joint attention, and communicative competence from 9 to 15 months of age. *Monographs of the Society for Research in Child Development* 63(4). 1–175.

7 Is language development dependent on early communicative development?

Carpenter, Malinda & Michael Tomasello. 2000. Joint attention, cultural learning, and language acquisition: Implications for children with autism. In Amy Wetherby & Barry M. Prizant (eds.), *Communication and language issues in autism and pervasive developmental disorder: A transactional developmental perspective*, 31–54. Baltimore, MD: Brookes.

DePaolis, Rory A., Marilyn M. Vihman & Temar Keren-Portnoy. 2014. When do infants begin recognizing familiar words in sentences? *Journal of Child Language* 41(1). 226–239.

Enfield, N. J. 2013. *Relationship thinking: Agency, enchrony, and human sociality.* New York: Oxford University Press.

Fernald, Anne & Nereyda Hurtado. 2006. Names in frames: Infants interpret words in sentence frames faster than words in isolation. *Developmental Science* 9(3). 33–40.

Gliga, Teodora, Emily J.H. Jones, Rachael Bedford, Tony Charman & Mark H. Johnson. 2014. From early markers to neuro-developmental mechanisms of autism. *Developmental Review* 34(3). 189–207.

Green, Jonathan, Ming Wai Wan, Jeanne Guiraud, Samina Holsgrove, Janet McNally, Vicky Slonims, Mayada Elsabbagh, Tony Charman, Andrew Pickles, Mark Johnson & BASIS Team. 2013. Intervention for infants at risk of developing autism: A case series. *Journal of Autism and Developmental Disorders* 43(11). 2502–2514.

Green, Jonathan, Tony Charman, Andrew Pickles, Ming W. Wan, Mayada Elsabbagh, Vicky Slonims, Carol Taylor, Janet McNally, Rhonda Booth, Teodora Gliga, Emily J. H. Jones, Clare Harrop, Rachael Bedford, Mark H. Johnson & the BASIS team. 2015. Parent-mediated intervention versus no intervention for infants at high risk of autism: A parallel, single-blind, randomised trial. *The Lancet Psychiatry* 2(2). 133–140.

Ibbotson, Paul, Elena Lieven & Michael Tomasello. 2014. The communicative contexts of grammatical aspect use in English. *Journal of Child Language* 41(3). 705–723. DOI:10.1017/S0305000913000135

Jones, Emily J.H., Teodora Gliga, Rachael Bedford, Tony Charman & Mark H. Johnson. 2014. Developmental pathways to autism: A review of prospective studies of infants at risk. *Neuroscience & Biobehavioral Reviews* 39. 1–33.

Karmiloff-Smith, Annette. 2006. Modules, genes and evolution: What have we learned from atypical development? Processes of change in brain and cognitive development. *Attention and Performance* 21. 563–83.

Levinson, Steven C. 2006. On the human 'interaction engine'. In N. J. Enfield & Stephen C. Levinson (eds.), *Roots of sociality: Culture, cognition, and interaction*, 39–69. Oxford: Berg.

Lieven, Elena & Sabine Stoll. 2013. Early communicative development in two cultures. *Human Development* 56(3). 178–206. DOI:10.1159/000351073

Liszkowski, Ulf, Penny Brown, Tara Callaghan, Akira Takada & Conny de Vos. 2012. A prelinguistic gestural universal of human communication. *Cognitive Science* 36(4). 698–713. DOI:10.1111/j.1551-6709.2011.01228.x

Moll, Henrick, Nadja Richter, Malinda Carpenter & Michael Tomasello. 2008. 14-month-olds know what "we" have shared in a special way. *Infancy* 13(1). 90–101.

Noens, Ilse, Ina van Berckelaer-Onnes, Roger Verpoorten & G. van Duijn. 2006. The ComFor: An instrument for the indication of augmentative communication in people with autism and intellectual disability. *Journal of Intellectual Disability Research* 50(9). 621–632. DOI:10.1111/j.1365-2788.2006.00807.x. PMID 16901289

Norbury, Courtenay. 2005. Barking up the wrong tree? Lexical ambiguity resolution in children with language acquisition impairments and autism spectrum disorders. *Journal of Experimental Child Psychology* 90(2). 142–171.

Over, Harriet & Malinda Carpenter. 2013. The social side of imitation. *Child Development Perspectives* 7(1). 6–11.

Ozonoff, Sally, Gregory S. Young, Alice Carter, Daniel Messinger & Nurit Yirmiya. 2011. Recurrence risk for autism spectrum disorders: A baby siblings research consortium study. *Pediatrics* 128(3). 488–495.

Roberts, Jacqueline. 2014. Echolalia and language development in children with autism. In Joanne Arcuili & Jon Brock (eds.), *Communication in autism*, 55–73. Amsterdam: John Benjamins Publishing Company.

Sigman, Marian & Ellen Ruskin. 1999. Continuity and change in the social competence of children with autism, Down syndrome, and developmental delays. *Monographs of the Society for Research in Child Development* 64(1). 1–142.

Siller, Michael & Marian Sigman. 2002. The behaviors of parents of children with autism predict the subsequent development of their children's communication. *Journal of Autism and Developmental Disorders* 32(2). 77–89.

Siller, Michael & Marian Sigman. 2008. Modeling longitudinal change in the language abilities of children with autism: Parent behaviors and child characteristics as predictors of change. *Developmental Psychology* 44. 1691–1704.

Tomasello, Michael. 1999. *The cultural origins of human cognition*. Cambridge MA: Harvard University Press.

7 Is language development dependent on early communicative development?

Tomasello, Michael & Katharina Haberl. 2003. Understanding attention: 12- and 18-month-olds know what's new for other persons. *Developmental Psychology* 39(5). 906–912.

Wan, Ming Wai, Jonathan Green, Mayada Elsabbagh, Mark H. Johnson, Tony Charman, Faye Plummer & the BASIS Team. 2013. Quality of interaction between at-risk infants and caregiver at 12–15 months is associated with 3-year autism outcome. *Journal of Child Psychology and Psychiatry* 54(7). 763–771.

Wetherby, Amy & Barry M. Prizant. 1992. Facilitating language and communication development in autism: Assessment and intervention guidelines. In Dianne Berkell (ed.), *Autism: Identification, education and treatment*, 107–134. Hillsdale JJ: Lawrence Erlbaum.

Chapter 8

Dependency and relative determination in language acquisition: The case of Ku Waru

Alan Rumsey

Australian National University

In this chapter I discuss what I take to be examples of dependency in children's learning of Ku Waru, a Papuan language spoken in the Western Highlands Province of Papua New Guinea.[1] The first example is a phonological one and has to do with the order of children's acquisition of the four Ku Waru lateral consonant phonemes. The other example is syntactic and has to do with the order of acquisition of simple verbs and two kinds of phrasal verb construction: adjunct+verb constructions and serial verb constructions. I argue that both of these examples show dependencies based on two kinds of constraining factors: 1) intrinsic simplicity *vs* complexity along dimensions which are common to all languages; 2) relational, language specific forms of simplicity *vs* complexity which have to with degrees of "pattern congruity" or "structural congruence" within phonological and syntactic systems respectively.

1 Ku Waru laterals and their acquisition

Ku Waru belongs to the Trans-New Guinea family of Papuan Languages (Pawley 2009). The Ku Waru phonemic inventory is shown in Tables 1 and 2. The characters shown in parentheses are the ones in the practical orthography that is used in §2.

The phonemes in Table 1 that I focus on in this chapter are the laterals. All four of them can occur word initially, medially and finally. Below are some examples,

---

[1] For further details concerning the Ku Waru language and its social setting see Merlan & Rumsey (1991).

Table 1: Ku Waru phonemic inventory: Consonants

	Labial	Apico-Alveolar	Palatal	Velar
Plain stop	p	t		k
Fricative		s		
Prenasalized stop	mb (b)	nd (d)	ɲdʒ (j)	ŋg (g)
Nasal	m	n	ɲ (ny, yn)	ŋ (ng)
Continuant	w	r	j (y)	

	Retroflex flap	Alveolar continuant	Palatal continuant	Prestopped velar
Lateral	ɭ (rlt)	l (l)	ʎ (ly, yl)	ᵍL (l)

Table 2: Ku Waru phonemic inventory: Vowels

	Front	Back
High	i	u
Mid	e	o
Low	a	

which include a minimal quadruplet in medial position (koɭa / koʎa / koᵍLa / kola) and near-minimal contrasting forms in other positions.

Retrofex lateral flap /ɭ/.

(1) a. /ɭim/ → [ɭim] a woman's name
    b. /(kera) koɭa/ → [(kɛrʌ) koɭʌ] '(bird) chicken'
    c. /(kum) piniɭ/ → [(kum)pinIɭ] '(ear) eardrum'

Palatal lateral continuent /ʎ/. In word-initial and word-medial position this consonant is voiced and in word-final position it is voiceless. Examples are:

(2) a. /ʎapi/ → [ʎapi] 'fog'
    b. /koʎa/ → [koʎʌ] 'place'
    c. /paʎ/ → [paʎ̥] 'all'
    d. /kunduʎ/ → [kunduʎ̥] 'red'

Prestopped velar lateral /ᶢʟ/. This is a complex phoneme which in effect combines a velar stop and a velar lateral approximant. When producing it the back of the tongue is first bunched and placed against the velum as for the onset of a velar stop, but instead air is then released to both sides over the bunched tongue. In initial and medial position this phoneme is voiced, and in final position it is voiceless. Examples are:

(3)   a. /ᶢʟapa/ → [ᶢʟapʌ] 'father'
      b. /koᶢʟa/ → [koᶢʟʌ] 'cry'
      c. /paᶢʟa/ → [paᶢʟʌ] 'fence post'
      d. /waᶢʟ/ → [waᵏʟ̥] 'string bag'
      e. /puᶢʟ/ → [puᵏʟ̥] 'base'

Although phonetically complex, this phoneme is by no means a marginal one in Ku Waru. It is in fact the most frequently occurring lateral in the language. Given that it involves both velar occlusion and lateral approximation it is not inevitable that this phoneme should be classed as a lateral rather than a stop. I agree with François (2010) that the choice in such cases is best made on language-internal, distributional grounds rather than purely phonetic ones, and will present evidence of that kind below.

Apico-alveolar /l/. This sound has come into the phonemic inventory of Ku Waru only since the arrival into the region of the mainly English-based lingua franca Tok Pisin, which happened in the 1930s. This is evident from the fact it occurs only in loan words from that language.
    Examples are:

(4)   a. *lo* ([lo]), 'law', from Tok Pisin *lo* 'law',
      b. *kela* ([kɛla]), from Tok Pisin *kela* 'bald head'
      c. *kola* ([kolʌ] from Tok Pisin *kola* 'cola, soft drink'
      d. *gol* ([gol]), from Tok Pisin *gol* 'gold'

The adoption into Ku Waru of /l/ as a phoneme (albeit still a marginal one) was probably facilitated by two preexisting patterns.

The first is that, although /l/ had not been present as a phoneme, [ʟ] and [l] had already been present, as allophones of /ᶢʟ/ before stop consonants. Examples are:

Alan Rumsey

(5) /moꟅ-ku-r/ → [moLkur].
be/stay-PPR-1SG
'I am (staying)'

(6) /sumbuꟅ(u) tuλ/ → [sumbultuʎ̥]
darkness hit:PPL
'night'

(7) /ꟅLku/ → [Lku]
'house'

The appearance of lateral continuants as allophones of /Ʂ/ when it occurs in consonant clusters provides evidence for grouping /Ʂ/ with the laterals rather than stops with respect to its manner of articulation. That interpretation is further supported by the fact that the velar positions in the two stop series are already filled by /k/ and /g/, which are invariably pronounced as stops, whereas /Ʂ/ loses its stop quality in this environment but retains its lateral quality as it does in all other environments.

The second pre-existing pattern that may have facilitated the adoption of /l/ from Tok Pisin into Ku Waru as a phoneme is that [l] has long been present as a pronunciation of /Ʂ/ in the baby talk register of Ku Waru. It is used not only by children, between the ages of approximately 20 months and three years, but also by adults and older children when speaking to them. Examples are shown in Table 3.

Table 3: Some Ku Waru baby talk forms

Adult form	Baby talk form	Meaning
oꟅa	ola	up
maɲa moꟅa	mana mola	Sit down!
moꟅ (>[moᵏꞱ̥])	mol	no

Most children do not learn to produce adult-like versions of the Ʂ/ᵏꞱ̥ sound until they are 5-6 years old. In the meantime, as alternative pronunciations of it they use not only [l] as shown above, but also [k], [g], and later [ɣ] and [x]. Interestingly, adults and older children when speaking to children never use those sounds as baby talk realizations of /Ʂ/, only [l].

The facts that I have reviewed above regarding Ku Waru laterals can, I believe, be at least partially accounted for in terms of relative determination, that is of tendencies that are widely attested in the world's languages and affect how children learn them. The first thing to note in this respect is that from a comparative-typological perspective the Ku Waru inventory of laterals as described above is very unusual. In a survey of 567 of the world's languages, Maddieson (2013) found that by far the most common lateral was /l/, which was found in 76.7% of the languages (cf. Ladefoged 2001: 153–154; Ladefoged, Cochran & Disner 1977; Ladefoged & Maddieson 1996). Only 9.5% of the languages in Maddieson's (2013) sample had lateral obstruents. The inventory of Ku Waru laterals before the adoption of /l/ from Tok Pisin was even more unusual: only 8 or 1.4% of the languages had lateral obstruents but not /l/ (ibid). Of those 8 languages only 5 had two or more obstruent laterals (Maddieson, personal communication March 2016), which places Ku Waru in a class that includes only 0.9% of the sample.

But here I would argue that the exception proves the rule – the rule of what I have called "relative determination". This is true at two different levels – that of distributional patterns within the language and that of speakers' metalinguistic awareness of degrees of complexity *vs* simplicity. With respect to the first level, as I have shown above, even before the adoption of /l/ into Ku Waru from Tok Pisin, [l] and [L] were already present in Ku Waru within a particular environment, namely, when preceding a stop. I would take this to be an instance of the ubiquitous tendency that de Lacy (2006) demonstrates in detail and describes in the following terms: "if there is synchronic non-assimilative, non-dissimilative neutralization $\beta \rightarrow \alpha$ in some prosodic environment, there is a markedness hierarchy in which a feature value of β is more marked than a related feature value of α" (73)[2]. Here, where the β term is /ᶢL/ and the α term is [L], the relevant feature is pre-occlusion, which disappears, leaving only the lateral continuant with which it is otherwise co-articulated. De Lacy's generalization – which is consistent with the results of decades of work on markedness – definitely holds up in this case and is further supported by it, since consonants that involve coarticulation have ever since the foundational work of Trubetzkoy (1931, 1969[1939];

---

[2] Three aspects of this formulation call for comment in the present context. First, while the loss of the velar-stop component of /ᶢL/ before k might be thought of as a dissimilation from the following velar stop, this is counter-indicated by the fact that the same thing happens before t. Second, de Lacy's use of the term 'neutralization' might be thought to render his generalization inapplicable in this case because the process in question does not involve a loss of phonemic contrast between /ᶢL/ and any other phoneme. But de Lacy's use of the term neutralization does not entail loss of contrast (de Lacy 2006: 110). Third, lest De Lacy's formulation appear tautological one must bear in mind that the markedness hierarchies he refers to are not ad hoc ones inferred from single cases but are intended to be universal and are constantly being tested against data from the world's languages and refined on that basis.

cf. Baltaxe 1978: 42) been regarded as more highly marked in their manner of articulation than those that do not.

At the other level, that of metalinguistic awareness, it is surely no accident that the variant of /ʟ̄/ that adults have settled upon as its baby talk equivalent is precisely the one that Maddieson has shown to be by far the most common one around the world: [l]. No doubt that has been determined in part by the fact that [l] is the first lateral sound that Ku Waru children are able to produce. But it also seems to have been determined in part by the language-specific phonological status of /ʟ̄/ within Ku Waru as a lateral rather than as a stop.[3]

2 The acquisition of Ku Waru verbs, verb complexes and copular clauses

2.1 Verbs, verb complexes and copular clauses in Ku Waru adult speech

Ku Waru is typical of Trans-New Guinea languages in having strictly verb-final syntax and three different kinds of finite verbs / verbal constructions as follows:

1. SIMPLE VERBS, consisting of a root and suffixes specifying person/number and tense/aspect/mode. Examples are:

   (8) a. *kang-ayl **pu-ku-m***
            boy-DEF go-PPR-3SG
            'The boy is going.'

        b. *kang-ayl-n   tauwu-ti   **nu-ru-m***
            boy-DEF-ERG banana-IDF eat-RP-3SG
            'The boy ate a banana (before yesterday).'

---

[3] In his very valuable comparative discussion of languages with velar laterals, François (2010) convincingly demonstrates that ʟ̄ sounds are fundamentally ambiguous with respect their manner-of-articulation status as between (laterally released) stop and (pre-stopped) lateral. Based on his work on Hiw, the only Austronesian language known to have a ʟ̄ sound (which he analyses convincingly as a lateral phoneme) and with a speaker of the Papuan language Ekari, François was able to confirm that Ekari has 'exactly the same sound', which is however, best regarded phonologically as a stop, for distributional and phonotactic reasons presented in Doble (1987). François reports that the same is true of Laghuu, a Tibeto-Burman language as described by Edmondson & Ziwo (1999).

2. ADJUNCT+VERB CONSTRUCTIONS (AVC) consisting of an inflecting verb root immediately preceded by another word which functions as a "verbal adjunct".[4] Examples are:

(9) a. kang-ayl **nok** to-ku-m
     boy-DEF cough hit-PPR-3SG
     'The boy is coughing.'

  b. na-n no   **odi le-bu**
     I-ERG water pour put.in.place-FUT:1SG
     'I will pour water.'

All of the inflecting verbs that are used in these constructions can also be used without an adjunct, in which case their meanings are lexically more specific than when used with them. This can be seen in (9a) and (9b), where the verbs have been glossed with the meanings that they have when used without adjuncts.

3. SERIAL VERB CONSTRUCTIONS (SVC), comprising a sequence of two or more verbs, the final one inflected like a simple verb as in (8) and the preceding one(s) inflected with a "non-final" suffix showing person and number but not tense, aspect or mode. Examples are:

(10) a. na langi mare **me-b**   o-ku-r.
      I food some carry-NF:1 come-PPR-1SG
      'I am bringing some food.'

   b. kewa-n koi-d   teman-ti **kodu-pa** nyi-m
      kewa-ERG koy-DAT story-IDF pull-NF:3SG say-PRF:3SG
      'Kewa told a story to Koy.'

In addition to the types of verbal constructions exemplified above, in order to attribute qualities, or to express identity or equivalence between two terms, instead of using a copular verb such as 'be', as in many other languages, Ku Waru speakers do so with verbless clauses in which the two terms are simply juxtaposed. In such clauses, the theme or subject of the

---

[4] For an introductory comparative discussion of these constructions in Papuan languages see Foley (1986: 117–123). For further discussion of the AVC in Ku Waru see Merlan & Rumsey (2018).

clause always comes first and the rheme or predicate always comes last. Examples are:

(11) a. *na Kopia   yi-yl*
    1SG (tribe name) man-DEF
    'I am a Kopia man.'

  b. *wilyi   lku   na-nga*
    up.there house 1SG-GEN
    'The house up there is mine.'

2.2 Verbs and predication in Ku Waru children's speech

Our data on this topic come from audio recordings and transcripts of two Ku Waru speaking children, Enita Don and Jesi Pawa Onga, at ages 1;08,2 (1 year, 8 months, 2 weeks) - 3;01 and 1;09 - 3;01 respectively. When working on the translations, the assistants have often offered what they take to be equivalent adult Ku Waru versions of the children's utterances, based both on their general understanding of how Ku Waru children talk and on their contextual knowledge of what was happening in the interactions that were being recorded. These adult Ku Waru glosses are shown in the following examples in a separate line beneath the forms produced by the children.

Simple verbs are present in the earliest samples for both children. Examples are:

(12) a. ***pa***
    go:IMP
    'Go!' (Enita at 1;08,2)

  b. *no*   ***no-bu***
    liquid consume-FUT:1SG
    'I want to drink. ' (Enita at 1;11,3)

  c. *toti ila   **pum***
    soti ilyi-nga pu-m
    Soti this-GEN go-PRF:3SG
    'Soti went this way.' (Jesi 1;09, responding to: 'Where did Soti go')

8 Dependency and relative determination in children's language acquisition

AVCs first appear from Jesi at 1;09 and from Enita at 1;11,3. Examples are:

(13) a. *ape*   *uta pem*
      wapi   uru pe-ki-m
      (woman's name) sleep be/lie-PPR-3SG

      'Wapi is sleeping.' (Jesi, 1;09)

  b. *papa ku*   *tu*
      papa kur   to-ku-m
      daddy spirit/sickness hit-PPR-3SG

      'Daddy is sick.' (Enita, 1;11,3)

SVCs first appear from Jesi at 1;10,2 and from Enita at 1;11,3. Examples are:

(14) a. *mekal bi kal oba noba*
      mel-ayl bi kalyayl o-ba no-ba
      thing-DEF write that come-NF:3SG eat-FUT:3SG

      'That pen will come and bite you.' (Jesi, 1;10,2)

  b. *das no mom*
      gras no-ba molu-r-um
      grass eat-NF:3SG be/stay-RP-3SG

      'It (the cow) was eating grass.' (Enita, 1;11,3)

As between AVCs and SVCs, based on the data gathered, it seems to be the AVCs that the children acquire earlier; SVCs occur much less frequently in the speech of children in the age range exemplified above. This is illustrated by Tables 4 and 5, which show the results of a search that I have done through the transcripts of speech by the two children and their interlocutors at various ages between 1;08 and 3;01. In addition to the incidence of AVC and SVC the tables also show that of simple verbs, which are much more common than either of the former throughout all the samples.

The developmental trajectories of SVCs and AVCs that are evident from Tables 4 and 5 are shown in graphic form in Figures 1–4.

Table 4: Incidence of verbs and verb constructions in six samples from Enita Don

age of child	sample length	simple verbs tokens	simple verbs types	AVC tokens	AVC types	SVC tokens	SVC types	Ratio AVC/SVC tokens	Ratio AVC/SVC types
1;08,2	45 min	17	7	0	0	0	0	–	–
1;11,3	45 min	91	8	9	3	2	2	82/18	60/40
2;01	45 min	58	12	14	7	20[a]	3	41/59	70/30
2;04	25 min	72	11	8	3	8	3	64/36	50/50
2;09	38 min	77	15	11	5	16	14	41/59	26/74
3;01	38 min	112	19	10	6	19	18	34/66	25/75

[a] Eighteen of these tokens are of one type.

Table 5: Incidence of verbs and verb constructions in five samples from Jesi Pawa Onga

age of child	sample length	simple verbs tokens	simple verbs types	AVC tokens	AVC types	SVC tokens	SVC types	Ratio AVC/SVC tokens	Ratio AVC/SVC types
1;09	45 min	43	6	20	5	0	0	100/0	100/0
1;10,2	38 min	45	12	4	3	1	1	80/20	75/25
2;00	45 min	95	15	31	11	23[a]	6	57/43	65/35
2;05	45 min	205	17	21	15	24	19	47/53	44/66
3;01	45 min	256	27	6	6	38	32	14/86	16/84

[a] Fifteen of these tokens are of one type.

8 *Dependency and relative determination in children's language acquisition*

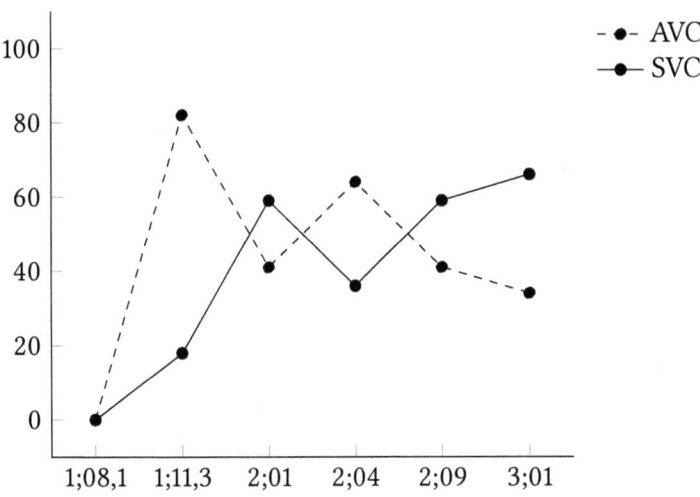

Figure 1: Relative incidence of AVC vs SVC tokens in the samples from Enita (in %)

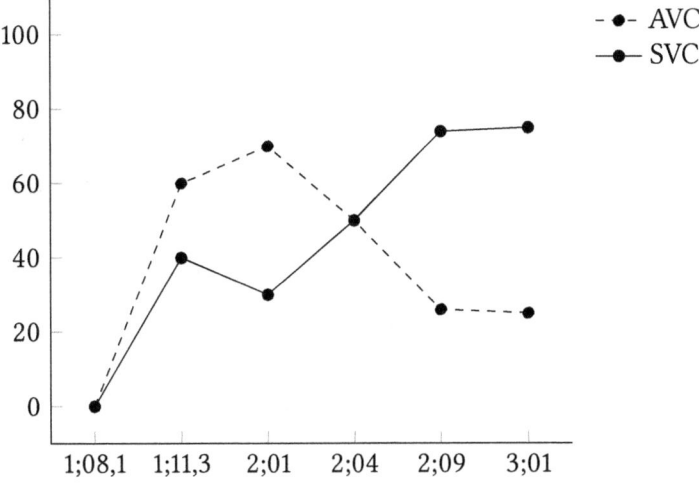

Figure 2: Relative incidence of AVC vs SVC types in the samples from Enita (in %)

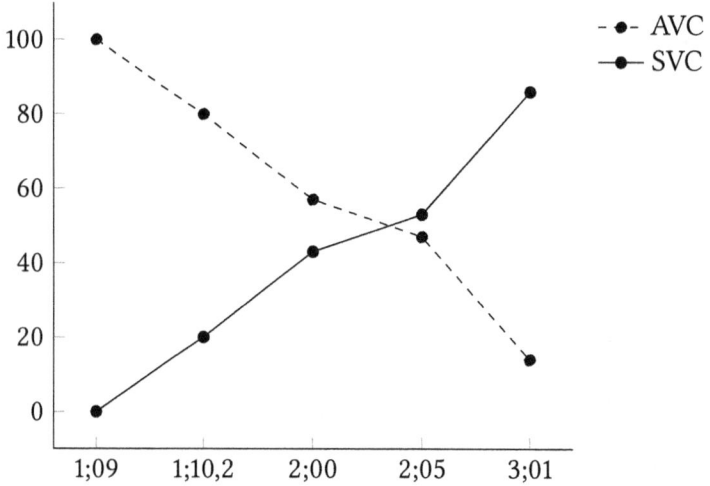

Figure 3: Relative incidence of AVC vs SVC tokens in the samples from Jesi (in %)

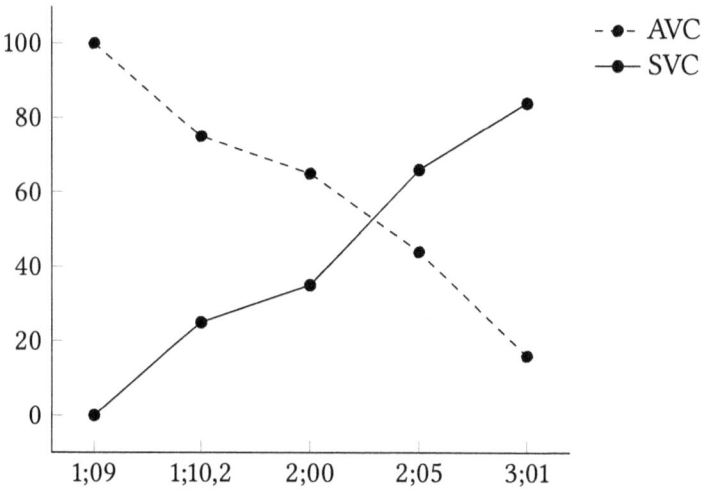

Figure 4: Relative incidence of AVC vs SVC types in the samples from Jesi (in %)

8　*Dependency and relative determination in children's language acquisition*

Besides verb constructions both children make regular use of verbless copular clauses of the kind exemplified from adult speech in (11), always with the subject NP in initial position and the predicate NP in final position, as in adult speech. An example is (15).

(15) i　　na　　popa
　　　i　　na-nga　pepa
　　　This 1SG-GEN paper
　　　This is my paper. (Jesi, 2;00).

Perhaps drawing on the model provided both by these verbless clauses and by AVCs such as (13a-b), children in the 20-25 month age range sometimes (albeit rarely) use adjuncts without accompanying verbs as full predications. An example is (16).

(16) e　　popa　　bi
　　　ekepu pepa-yl　bi　　ta-b
　　　now　paper-DEF write hit:OPT-1SG
　　　'Now I'll write on the paper.' (Jesi, 2:00)

2.3 Discussion

Comparing the above data from Ku Waru children's speech with adults' we can see that in both, predicates always come last in the clause, and arguments come before them. In adult speech this means that the final element in the clause is almost always either a verb or, more rarely, a predicate nominal in a copular clause. The adjuncts in AVCs form part of the predicate, and always precede the inflected verb. In two-year olds' speech there is wider latitude, in that adjuncts are occasionally used in final position as full predicates (as in 16). But in both adult speech and our samples from the two children, if there are one or more verbs in a clause, the final position is always occupied by one of them. Likewise, in both child language and adult speech, if the clause contains both an adjunct and an inflected verb, the verb always occurs after the adjunct and the two of them after any argument NP(s) that may occur in the clause.

A striking *difference* between adults' speech and the earliest samples from Enita and Jesi is in the relative frequency of SVCs *vs* AVCs. In our samples of speech among adults SVCs are roughly three times as frequent as AVCs. By contrast, as can be seen from Figures 1-4, in the children's speech, AVCs greatly outnumber SVCs at first, then begin to be outnumbered by them at about 2;03, until

109

something close to the adult ratio is reached by 3;01. Both this dissimilarity and the commonalities I pointed to above may be understood in terms of the two fundamental patterns that I have described in §2.1, namely: 1) a strict mapping of the functions predicate and argument onto the clause positions final and non-final respectively, and 2) an overall right-to-left mapping of the word classes Verb, Adjunct,[5] and Noun onto the positions final, penultimate and antepenultimate respectively.

These two templates account for the similarities between child speech and adult speech because they are consistently found in both, suggesting that they are one of the most fundamental aspects of Ku Waru grammar. They also account for the differences between child and adult speech in that a sequence of (NP)-Adjunct-Verb comprises a more straightforward realization of both templates than does the sequence (NP)-Verb-Verb, in at least two respects. First, it fills the verb slot in the Noun-Adjunct-Verb template with a single verb, from among the same set of words that the children have begun to learn first as simple verbs, and fills the adjunct slot with a word of a different class, which is never used by adults in final position, and almost never by children. Second, it fills the predicate slot in the argument(s)-predicate template with a single element, an adjunct+verb collocation that is easier to process as a single constituent of the clause than is any serial verb construction, since the words that occur in the adjunct slot are invariant in form and more regularly combined with a single, specific verb root (or small number of alternative ones) than are any of the verbs that enter into SVCs. Underlying the latter consideration is a kind of fractal congruence between the Ku Waru clause and AVC as verb-final constructions.

---

[5] My treatment of 'adjunct' in this chapter as both a word class and a structural position within the AVC is somewhat of an oversimplification in that there are actually two classes of words that can occur in that position. One of them – to which most such words belong – consists of words that can *only* occur only in that position. These we call Adjuncts, distinguishing the word class from the structural position by the use of upper case for it. The other such words can occur either in that position or as a nouns with related senses, e.g. *el* 'arrow'/'fight', *numan* 'mind'/ 'to like'. These we call 'flexibles', after Luuk (2010). In line with Luuk's use of that term, we treat words of this class, and also Adjuncts, as having an intermediate status between nouns and verbs. This is consistent with my claim that the Ku Waru clause shows an overall mapping of the word classes verb, Adjunct, and noun onto the positions final, penultimate and antepenultimate respectively, and renders that mapping more iconic, since the word classes that fill the intermediate position in it have a paradigmatically intermediate status between the preceding and following ones. For a fuller treatment of these issues and discussion of them in relation to much of the same data that is treated in this paper see Merlan & Rumsey (2018).

2.4 The role of adult input

In §2.3 I made some use of data from a sample of adults' speech to other adults, in which the ratio of SVC to AVC tokens was roughly 3 to 1. As discussed there, I compared that ratio with the SVC-AVC ratios in the samples of children's speech treated in this study, and found that those are much lower than that adult ratio at first. But as seen from Tables 4 and 5 and figures 1-4, the SVC-AVC ratios greatly increase by 3;01, at which point they exceed the adult ratio in one of the children's speech and approach it in the other's. As another comparator it is important to consider not only speech by adults to other adults, but also the speech that was used by the adults and older children in their interaction with the children under study at each session that is being considered.[6] For that comparison I have done a count of the relevant tokens and types in the adults' speech to Enita at each of the sessions represented in table 4. Space restrictions preclude my presenting those findings in full (for which see Merlan & Rumsey 2018). Here I will simply note that:

- the frequency of both AVC and SVC in the children's speech is lower – at first much lower – than in that of the adults' speech to the children;

- in the speech of adults and older children when interacting with the children there is a far higher ratio of AVC to SVC than in the sample of speech by adults to other adults.

The second of these two patterns is surely an important factor in accounting for why children begin to use AVCs before SVCs and why they continue to use them at higher rates than in adult-to-adult speech well into their third year at least. For as a large body of research has shown, other things being equal, children's acquisition of given language structures is strongly affected by the relative frequency with which they occur in the speech of adults who speak to them (Lieven 2010; Ambridge & Lieven 2011). But what accounts for pattern 2 itself? I suggest that an important factor there is the adults' intuitive feel for the structural templates I have described in §2.3, and the entailed difference between AVCs and SVCs, whereby a sequence of (NP)-adjunct-verb comprises a more straightforward realization of both templates than does the sequence (NP)-verb-verb. In other words, when speaking to young children the adults orient

---

[6] In all of the samples considered here, the amount of speech by adults to the children under study is far greater than the amount by other children, and in some there is none of the latter at all.

towards to the use of maximally perspicuous structures that will be easier for children to acquire.

3 Conclusions

As is richly exemplified by many of the chapters in this volume and the publications cited in them, there has been much debate among linguists about the nature and viability of cross-linguistic typological comparison, and in particular about the use in it of concepts of markedness. In the heat of that debate I think we are sometimes in danger of throwing the baby out with the bathwater, in that, quite understandably, it tends to highlight theoretical differences among the protagonists rather the common ground among them. With that in mind, in this chapter I have focused on concrete examples that I think demonstrate the validity of basic tenets that inform markedness theory in all its variants, but are generally also accepted by its critics. One is the common-sense notion that some linguistic phenomena are simpler than others, and partly for that reason easier for children to learn, and are therefore learned at a younger age. This is exemplified in §1 by Ku Waru children's much earlier production of the apico-alveolar lateral /l/ than the pre-stopped velar lateral /ᴸL/, and in §2 by their earlier production of simple verbs than of complex verb constructions. I take it that nearly all linguists, regardless of their differences in other respects, would agree with my judgments as to relative simplicity *vs* complexity in these two cases, and with my claim that those differences can be related to the differences in order of acquisition. The relation between those two kinds of difference is one of what I would call "relative determination", in that the greater simplicity of /l/ and of 'simple verbs" at least in part determines the order of their acquisition.

The kinds of simplicity involved in the above examples are, I would claim, universal, or intrinsic to the phenomena themselves. That is, [l] is inherently simpler in its manner of articulation than [ᴸL] and a single verb is inherently simpler than a construction that includes it. In addition to these examples of intrinsic simplicity, I have also discussed kinds of simplicity *vs* complexity that are relational and language-specific. On the phonological side, these included the placement of [ᴸL] as a (pre-stopped) lateral rather than a (laterally released) stop, which I argued is a determining factor in its baby-talk pronunciation as [l]. On the syntactic side, I argued that Ku Waru children's earlier acquisition of AVCs than SVCs was determined in part by the greater structural congruence between AVCs with basic aspects of the structure of the Ku Waru clause. Note that in both of these cases, while the phenomena in question are language specific, my accounts of them appeal to what are widely agreed to be universal tendencies in language: a tendency towards pattern congruity in phonology and a tendency in syntax toward structural congruence, or what Greenberg (1966) called "harmony" among construction types within a given language. While my arguments about these particular Ku Waru phenomena may be disputed, the universal tendencies on which they are based seem to me by now very well established,[7] as does the determining role they play in children's language acquisition. As can be seen from both examples treated here, the influence of such patterning is shown not only in the way children simplify the language when speaking it, but also in the way that adults simplify it when speaking to them, in effect manifesting what I have called an "intuitive feel" for the operation of markedness hierarchies within their language.

Acknowledgements

For their helpful comments on earlier versions of this chapter I thank Katherine Demuth, Francesca Merlan, Hannah Sarvasy, and Tony Woodbury. For their advice concerning aspects of the discussion in §1 thanks to Alex François and Ian Maddieson. For funding the research on which the chapter is based I gratefully acknowledge the Australian Research Council and the Australian National University.

Abbreviations not included in the Leipzig Glossing Rules

| IDF | indefinite | PPR | present progressive |
| NF | non-final | RP | remote past |

References

Ambridge, Ben & Elena Lieven. 2011. *Child language acquisition: Contrasting theoretical approaches.* Cambridge: Cambridge University Press.

Baltaxe, Christiane A. M. 1978. *Foundations of distinctive feature theory.* Baltimore: University Park Press.

---

[7] For phonological examples see Hyman, this volume, Rice, this volume, and references therein. For rich comparative data supporting many of Greenberg's generalizations regarding word order see Dryer (1992); Hawkins (2014).

de Lacy, Paul. 2006. *Markedness: Reduction and preservation in phonology.* Cambridge: Cambridge University Press.

Doble, Marion. 1987. A description of some features of Ekari language structure. *Oceanic Linguistics* 26. 55–113.

Dryer, Matthew S. 1992. The Greenbergian word order correlations. *Language* 68. 81–138.

Edmondson, Jerold A. & Lama Ziwo. 1999. Laghuu or Xá Phó , a new language of the Yi group. *Linguistics of the Tibeto-Burman Area* 22. 1–10.

Foley, William A. 1986. *The Papuan languages of New Guinea.* New York: Cambridge University Press.

François, Alexandre. 2010. Phonotactics and the prestopped velar lateral of Hiw: Resolving the ambiguity of a complex segment. *Phonology* 27. 393 – 434.

Greenberg, Joseph H. (ed.). 1966. *Universals of language.* Cambridge: MIT Press.

Hawkins, John. 2014. *Cross-linguistic variation and efficiency.* Oxford: Oxford University Press.

Ladefoged, Peter. 2001. *Vowels and consonants: An introduction to the sounds of languages.* Malden MA: Blackwell.

Ladefoged, Peter, Anne Cochran & Sandra Disner. 1977. Laterals and trills. *Journal of the International Phonetic Association* 7. 46–54.

Ladefoged, Peter & Ian Maddieson. 1996. *The sounds of the world's languages.* Oxford & Malden: Blackwell.

Lieven, Elena. 2010. Input and first language acquisition: Evaluating the role of frequency. *Lingua* 120. 2546–2556.

Luuk, Erkki. 2010. Nouns, verbs and flexibles: Implications for typologies of word classes. *Language Sciences* 32. 349–365.

Maddieson, Ian. 2013. Lateral consonants. In Matthew S. Dryer & Martin Haspelmath (eds.), *The world atlas of language structures online.* Leipzig: Max Planck Institute for Evolutionary Anthropology. http://wals.info/chapter/8, accessed 2016-03-26.

Merlan, Francesca & Alan Rumsey. 1991. *Ku Waru: Language and segmentary politics in the Western Nebilyer Valley, Papua New Guinea.* Cambridge: Cambridge University Press.

Merlan, Francesca & Alan Rumsey. 2018. Flexibles and polyvalence in Ku Waru: A developmental perspective. In V. Vapnarsky & E. Veneziano (eds.), *Lexical polycategoriality: Cross-linguistic, cross-theoretical and language acquisition approaches.* Amsterdam: John Benjamins Publishing Company, to appear.

Pawley, Andrew. 2009. Trans New Guinea languages. In K. Brown & S. Ogilvie (eds.), *Concise encyclopedia of languages of the world*, 1085–1090. Oxford: Elsevier.

Trubetzkoy, N. S. 1931. Die phonologischen Systeme. *Travaux du Cercle Linguistique de Prague* 4. 96–116.

Trubetzkoy, N. S. 1969. *[1939]. Principles of phonology (translated by C. Baltaxe)*. Berkeley & Los Angeles: University of California Press.

Chapter 9

Beyond binary dependencies in language structure

Damián E. Blasi
University of Zürich,
Max Planck Institute for the Science of Human History

Seán G. Roberts
Max Planck Institute for Psycholinguistics

The study of the regularities in the structures present across languages has always been a quest in close contact with the analysis of data. Traditionally, causal dependencies between pairs of typological variables (like word order patterns or the composition of segment inventories) have been argued for on the basis of language counts, namely how many languages out of a sample exhibit certain patterns in contrast to others. Regularities of this kind have been used in virtually all theoretical camps, and researchers made them part of their discussion on functional pressures on language, cognitive schemes and the architecture of a putative common computational core underlying language, among other things. This popularity resides, without doubt, in the strength and simplicity of the idea: if a set of languages with no recent genealogical history nor traces of areal contact tend to share the same pair of properties again and again, then there seems to be something about the properties of probable languages in general.

While venerable and potentially useful, this procedure is complicated by many factors. First, the nature of a proposed dependency can affect how the pattern of observations translates into support for the dependency. In the first section, we show how different notions of causality and causal strength are appropriate for different types of dependencies involving two variables. Secondly, these dependencies can be distorted not only by historical relations between languages (as usually acknowledged in the literature) but also due to complex causal dependencies involving multiple variables. Addressing these concerns requires appropriate formalisms and statistical techniques. These exist and are widely used for addressing the problem of historical relations (which we cover in the second section), but methods for dealing with relationships between more than two variables are underdeveloped in linguistics. In the final section, we discuss some new approaches to detecting causal dependencies between more than two variables.

1 Probability and causation

There exist several possible formalizations of the concept of causality inspired in concepts from mathematics, logic, computation and philosophy (see Fitelson & Hitchcock 2011). For the kind of regularities and laws governing the language sciences causation appears more naturally described in terms of probabilities.

For the sake of simplicity, we will be dealing in these examples with a hypothesized cause (C) and an effect (E). These will be expressed in terms of total probabilities of the cause or the effect to occur ($P(C)$ and $P(E)$ respectively) and the related conditional probabilities (such as the probability of the effect occurring given that the cause is present $P(E|C)$, or the probability of the effect occurring given that the cause is absent $P(E|\sim C)$). In this context, we can think about causation as probability raising: the probability of the effect taking place is larger when the cause is present than when the cause is absent, $P(E|C) > P(E|\sim C)$.

It is critical to remark that these probabilities and the measures of strength are used as a way of thinking about causal relations instead of definitions suitable for statistical analysis. Identifying probabilities with type frequencies and determining causal dependencies by attesting patterns in language counts can be problematic, and as such the structure of the models we use to think about the data and the data themselves (and their statistical properties) should be always clearly distinguished.

Typically, probabilities are equated to frequencies of occurrence when the statistical assessment takes place. $P(E)$ is approximated to the proportion of times the cause is observed to occur compared to not occurring, and $P(E|\sim C)$ to the proportion of times the effect is observed when the cause is absent. For instance, given the contingency table in 1,

(1)

	C	~C
E	10	5
~E	5	25

9 Beyond binary dependencies in language structure

we could readily estimate $P(C)=15/45=1/3$ and $P(E|\sim C)=5/30=1/5$. This is the usual practice in the field, but it hides a number of assumptions about what is tested and the nature of the sampling process.

First of all, the strategy of counting languages has been used sometimes to say something about probable languages in general and not about the particular relations that hold in the necessarily contingent set of surveyed languages. This is as fundamental as it is uncontroversial and pervades scientific practice, and in particular the language sciences – we infer general properties of cognition from a limited sample of experimental participants and we determine the usage properties of words from samples of text that are diminishingly small in comparison to what is regularly produced by speakers.

In consequence, we assume that the frequency measured in a given set of typological data matches, in some way, the likelihood of picking at random any likely human language and finding that it has a certain property. This becomes explicit in the linguistic typology literature: in the absence of mechanisms or constraints shaping the structure of the grammar, we "would expect each type to have roughly an equal number of representatives" (Comrie 1989). The issue stems from the fact that what "roughly" means here is left unspecified and to a large extent at the discretion of the researcher. In fact, any reasonable sampling model will generate observable differences in the proportions even when no effect is present (Cysouw 2010). Specific distributions of typological variables have been motivated observationally (Nichols 1992), based on concrete models inspired by principles of language change (Cysouw 2010) or borrowed directly from the toolkit of machine learning, the Dirichlet process being a particularly popular choice that is plastic enough as to reflect our lack of certainty (Daumé III 2009; Piantadosi & Gibson 2014).

Assuming for a moment now that we do have access to the true probabilities of causes and effects and their relation (perhaps via a careful consideration of the observed frequencies), let us consider now the two simplest cases of causal relations between C and E (illustrated in Figure 1). Greenberg's seminal work on implicational typological universals already presented a binary classification of dependencies into which we will tap due to its popularity (Greenberg 1966, see Culbertson, this volume Cristofaro, this volume).

Some of Greenberg's universals are bidirectional implications, such as the order of adposition and noun implying the order of genitive and noun, and vice versa. Bidirectional implications contrast with unidirectional implications, which allow the possibility of the effect being present without the cause, but the cause makes the effect more probable. For instance, Greenberg suggested that lan-

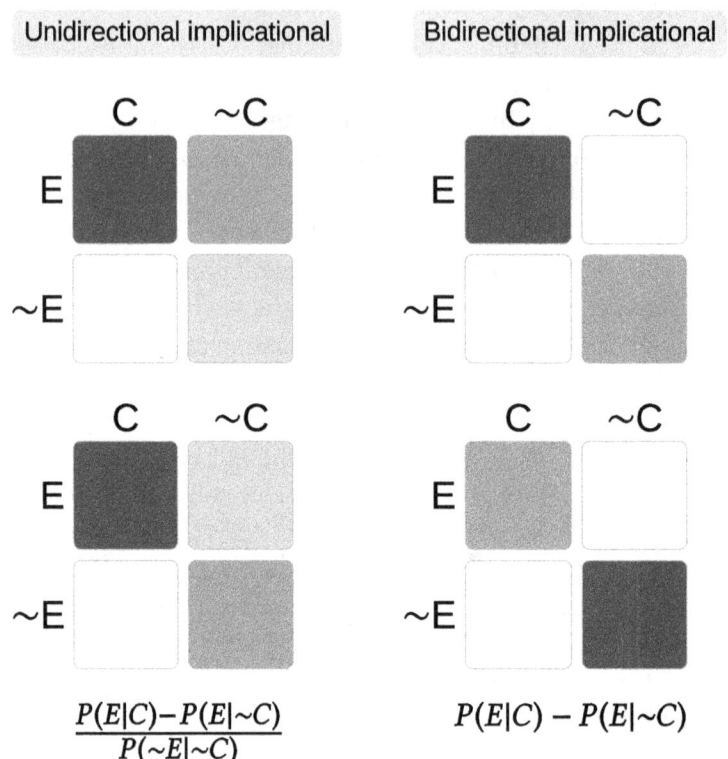

Figure 1: Contingency tables that maximise different measures of causal strength when language type frequencies are equated to type probabilities. On the left are two tables which maximize unidirectional implications and on the right are two tables which maximize bidirectional implication. More intense colour stands for more cases attested with those properties; cells in white represent no counts. The formulas for different notions of causal strength appear at the bottom.

guages with VSO canonical order tend to be prepositional, though this does not claim that all prepositional languages will be VSO: prepositions occur with virtually all other word order combinations, prominently SVO.

While these ideas are intuitive, the formalization of causal strength by means of probabilities sheds light on the kinds of evidence that are needed in order to put forward any claim about causal influence. For the sake of convenience, causal measures are often defined in such a way that 1 stands for the strongest causal relation and 0 for the absence of any evidence of a causal effect, with intermediate values reflecting strengths between these extremes. To start with, Eells (1991)'s view of causal strength captures adequately the causal strength underlying a bidirectional implication, which is defined as:

(2) $CS_e = P(E|C) - P(E|\sim C)$

That is, the change in the probability of the effect when the cause is present and when the cause is absent. The largest difference (CS_e=1) will be achieved when the cause deterministically triggers the effect ($P(E|C)$=1) and where the absence of the cause also implies the absence of the effect ($P(E|\sim C)$=0) – as represented in Figure 1. On the other hand, when the cause does not change the probability of the effect occurring ($P(E|C)=P(E|\sim C)$), Eells' measure of causal strength is minimised (CS_e=0). Notice that the strength of the assertion of a bidirectional implicational universal does not rely on the relative frequencies of each type, i.e. $P(C)$ and $P(E)$ and their complements.

On the other hand, unidirectional implications do not make any predictions with respect to the case in which the cause is absent. $P(E|\sim C)$ could be close to either 1 or 0 without affecting our confidence on the efficacy of the cause – e.g. that smoking leads convincingly to cancer is independent of the fact that cancer might arise due to other factors as well. However, rather than using the plain conditional probability as a measure of the causal strength of a unidirectional implication ($P(E|C)$) the probability $P(E|\sim C)$ plays the role of a baseline to compare against. Thus, a good normalized measure of causal strength for unidirectional implications would be one that (1) becomes 0 when the cause does not make the effect more or less probable than its absence and (2) is 1 only when the cause yields the effect determinstically ($P(E|C)$=1). This leads to none other than Cheng (1997)'s notion of causal strength:

(3) $CS_c = [P(E|C) - P(E|\sim C)] / P(\sim E|\sim C)$

That is, the causal power increases as we observe the effect with the cause and decreases as we observe the effect with the cause, but only to the extent that we also observe no effect without the cause.

In contrast to the idea that causality constitutes a monolithic phenomenon, there are many other approaches to the notion of causal strength (see Fitelson & Hitchcock 2011), each one being suitable for the study of different dependencies. The notion of causal measure will also impact the strategy of inference of the involved probabilities. For example, a unidirectional implication could be assessed by collecting data only on languages which are known to exhibit the cause, while a bidirectional implication requires knowing about languages both with and without the cause.

Damián E. Blasi & Seán G. Roberts

2 Moving towards statistical support

The formalisms above rely on knowing the real probabilities of each cell in the contingency table. The question of practical interest, then, is how to make a statistically valid case for a dependency based on language counts. These counts might differ considerably from the true probabilities since simple co-occurrence in a sample of data does not guarantee dependency. The most well-known sources of inflated co-occurrences without substantial causal links are shared history or contact. For instance, in the Mesoamerican linguistic area, languages frequently display a vigesimal numeral system and they lack switch-reference, traits that distinguish them from neighbouring languages (Campbell, Kaufman & Smith-Stark 1986). A contingency table displaying the number of languages in that region would give the impression that both variables are associated, which will be simply reflecting the fact that those traits have been transmitted together all the way down the genealogical tree or horizontally from other language(s). This confound – known as Galton's problem – applies to any study trying to detect causal connections between traits in languages. Roberts & Winters (2013) demonstrate how pervasive this problem can be by finding co-occurrences between traits with no causal dependencies between them.

These problems can be overcome if the history of contact between languages is taken into account. For example, bidirectional implications can be easily captured by the many regression methods available. Jaeger et al. (2011) recommend a mixed effects model framework so as to be able to account for areal and genealogical dependencies as random effects for that purpose. Another alternative is to use explicit phylogenetic information and map branch lengths to covariance (so languages that diverged more recently in time are expected to have more similar feature values) (Verkerk 2014). The Family Bias method (Bickel 2013) continues the tradition of comparing larger linguistic groupings in a regular regression setting (without any special specification of the covariance between languages) but instead infers the biases of the groupings by assessing the evidence in favour or against one particular typological variant (or set of variants). The literature on the statistical assessment of unidirectional implications is much less restricted, however. Researchers have devised ways of resolving this issue within the frequentist (Everett, Blasi & Roberts 2015) and Bayesian traditions (Daumé III & Campbell 2009).

Another way that co-occurrence probabilities can be distorted, and one that is rarely addressed, involves more complicated causal dependencies. The statistical methods mentioned above become limited when more than two variables are taken into account at a time and indeed, perhaps as an implicit acknowledgement of this difficulty, most typological generalizations are limited to pairs of variables rather than more complex constellations.

Let us see more precisely how complex dependencies might yield spurious dependencies by considering the simplest possible case beyond the two-variable case, which is naturally when there are three variables causally linked in some way. If we regard causal relations graphically as arrows going from the causes to the effects, then this setting will correspond to any of four different possible arrangements depicted in Figure 2.

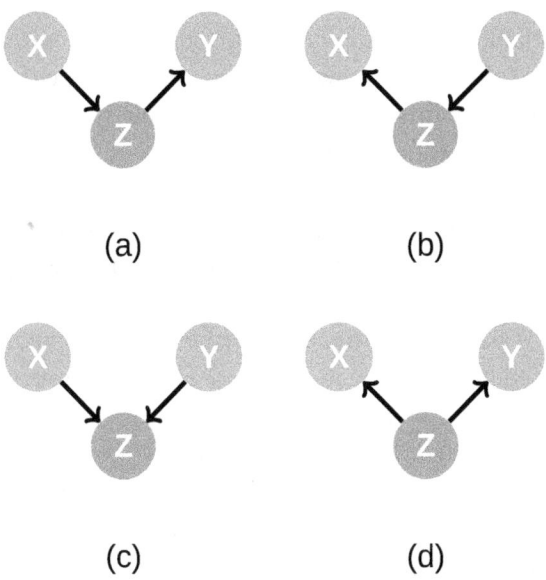

Figure 2: Four possible (non-trivial) ways in which variables X, Y and Z could be causally linked. Arrows represent the flow of causality, so that an arrow pointing from X to Z indicates that changes to X cause changes in Z.

The first two cases (a and b in Figure 2) correspond to Z simply serving as a communicator of the effect of X on Y or vice versa. For instance, it has been suggested that population size and morphological complexity are causally connected via the number of L2 speakers (Lupyan & Dale 2010): the larger the population (X), the more likely it is that the language comes into contact with other languages, increasing the number of L2 speakers (Z) which act upon the language by simplifying the system of its morphological structures (Y).

The third possibility is that Z is causing both X and Y (d in Figure 2), so the observed causal link between the two is an artifact of Z being a common cause.

Damián E. Blasi & Seán G. Roberts

As an example, many languages of the world have noun classes (X) also have applicative voice (Y) (Aronoff & Fudeman 2011). The common cause behind the joint occurrence of these features is that many of these languages come from the Atlantic-Congo family (Z), one of the largest linguistic families.

Finally, it could be that both X and Y contribute jointly to cause Z (c in Figure 2). Languages with isolating morphology (X) will naturally have shorter words in average (Z), and the same is true for languages with tones (Y).

The qualitative Greenbergian implications presented before had a transparent formal counterpart and they can be evaluated statistically with well established methods. However, the discussion and evaluation of dependencies involving three or more variables become increasingly unsuitable without a proper formalization. The probabilistic framework discussed at the beginning finds a justification at this point. In addition to it, we need to briefly review some definitions and concepts from graph theory (see Pearl 2009).

A graph consists of a set of nodes and a set of edges. Directed edges bind two nodes in an asymmetrical fashion – so if A and B are nodes, either A→B or A←B. A sequence of nodes from A to B where each adjacent pair is bound by a directed edge going from the first to the second member is referred to as a path between A and B. A path that starts and finishes in the same node is referred to as a cycle. A directed graph is one in which all edges are directed, and a directed graph with no cycles is called a directed acyclic graph (DAG).

The set of nodes that can be reached through a path from A are A's descendants, and the nodes that are directly connected to A such that their common edge points to A (like B→A) are the parents of A. In DAGs there are no paths which go from a descendant back to one of its parents.

This graphical framework allows a straightforward visualization of causal connections between variables. Variables are represented as nodes and causal relations (of any kind discussed in the binary case) are represented as directed edges, so A→B will be read as "A causes B". The assumption linking this graph representation to the ideas of probabilistic causation discussed before is that of the Markov Causal Condition. If two variables are dependent and one is not a descendant of the other then their dependency can be explained away by appealing to a common ancestor of the pair. Put another way, a variable is only affected by its immediately connected (ancestor) causes.

Embracing this representation of the relations in the data opens up new statistical possibilities. One that partially relies on regression is to use structural equation models (Duncan 2014). Structural equation modelling is a cover term for a number of techniques that allows the testing of more or less well-specified functional dependencies between variables as embedded in DAGs. To take a very basic example (based on a specific case of structural equation modelling called path analysis), suppose that we want to decide between situations (a) and (b) of Figure 2. Assuming that we are in possession of good guesses about what could be the functional dependencies, we then could contrast the model fit (how well the model predicts the observed data) between (a) and (b). The possibilities provided by structural equation modelling include the inclusion of hidden variables and non-parametric functional dependencies.

In cases where uncertainty about the correct model is high, model comparison might not be the best ally. In those cases, it is possible to appeal to the predictions that come "for free" by assuming the Markov Causal Condition along with the DAG. The idea is that the Markov Causal Condition entails a series of conditional dependency statements involving the variables, and that given appropriate conditions it is possible to estimate the most likely underlying causal graph from observational data. There are multiple methods for doing this (Shalizi 2013), a popular efficient and computationally inexpensive method being the PC algorithm (Spirtes, Glymour & Scheines 2000; Kalisch et al. 2012). These techniques are only starting to be explored by researchers in the language sciences (Blasi et al. 2018; Baayen, Milin & Ramscar 2016).

3 Conclusion

The inference of causal dependencies based on surveys of languages has a long history in the field. This methodology faces several complications, like the difficulty of estimating probabilities from counts of languages or the lack of consideration of higher-order dependencies between multiple variables. Methods and formalisms based on probability can address these problems, and help linguists to better test and think about the nature of dependencies in language.

Acknowledgements

We would like to thank the participants of the Dependencies workshop, and in particular Jennifer Culbertson for helpful feedback. SR is supported by an ERC Advanced Grant No. 269484 INTERACT to Stephen Levinson. We thank the Max Planck Society for additional support.

References

Aronoff, Mark & Kirsten Fudeman. 2011. *What is morphology*. Hoboken, New Jersey: John Wiley & Sons.

Baayen, R. Harald, Petar Milin & Michael Ramscar. 2016. Frequency in lexical processing. *Aphasiology* 30 (11). 1174–1220.

Bickel, Balthasar. 2013. Distributional biases in language families. In Balthasar Bickel, Lenore A. Grenoble, David A. Peterson & Alan Timberlake (eds.), *Language typology and historical contingency*, 415–444. Amsterdam: John Benjamins Publishing Company.

Blasi, Damián E., Seán G. Roberts, Marloes Maathuis & Emmanuel Keeulers. 2018. *Inferring causality in lexical properties from observational data.*

Campbell, Lyle, Terrence Kaufman & Thomas C. Smith-Stark. 1986. Meso-America as a linguistic area. *Language* 62(3). 530–570.

Cheng, Patricia W. 1997. From covariation to causation: A causal power theory. *Psychological Review* 104(2). 367.

Comrie, Bernard. 1989. *Language universals and linguistic typology: Syntax and morphology*. Chicago: University of Chicago Press.

Cysouw, Michael. 2010. On the probability distribution of typological frequencies. In Makoto Kanazawa, András Kornai, Marcus Kracht & Hiroyuki Seki (eds.), *The mathematics of language*, 29–35. New York: Springer.

Daumé III, Hal. 2009. Non-parametric Bayesian areal linguistics. In *Proceedings of human language technologies: The 2009 annual conference of the North American chapter of the Association for Computational linguistics*, 593–601. Association for Computational Linguistics.

Daumé III, Hal & Lyle Campbell. 2009. A Bayesian model for discovering typological implications. *arXiv*. preprint arXiv:0907.0785.

Duncan, Otis Dudley. 2014. *Introduction to structural equation models*. Amsterdam: Elsevier.

Eells, Ellery. 1991. *Probabilistic causality*. Vol. 1. New York: Cambridge University Press.

Everett, Caleb, Damián E. Blasi & Seán G. Roberts. 2015. Climate, vocal folds, and tonal languages: Connecting the physiological and geographic dots. *Proceedings of the National Academy of Sciences* 112(5). 1322–1327.

Fitelson, Branden & Christopher Hitchcock. 2011. Probabilistic measures of causal strength. In Phyllis McKay Illari, Federica Russo & Jon Williamson (eds.), *Causality in the sciences*, 600–627. Oxford: Oxford University Press.

Greenberg, Joseph H. (ed.). 1966. *Universals of language*. Cambridge: MIT Press.

Jaeger, T. Florian, Peter Graff, William Croft & Daniel Pontillo. 2011. Mixed effect models for genetic and areal dependencies in linguistic typology. *Linguistic Typology* 15(2). 281–320.

Kalisch, Markus, Martin Mächler, Diego Colombo, Marloes H. Maathuis & Peter Bühlmann. 2012. Causal inference using graphical models with the R package pcalg. *Journal of Statistical Software* 47(11). 1–26.

Lupyan, Gary & Rick Dale. 2010. Language structure is partly determined by social structure. *PloS One* 5(1). e8559.

Nichols, Johanna. 1992. *Linguistic diversity in space and time.* Chigago: University of Chicago Press.

Pearl, Judea. 2009. *Causality.* New York: Cambridge University Press.

Piantadosi, Steven T & Edward Gibson. 2014. Quantitative standards for absolute linguistic universals. *Cognitive Science* 38(4). 736–756.

Roberts, Seán G. & James Winters. 2013. Linguistic diversity and traffic accidents: Lessons from statistical studies of cultural traits. *PloS One* 8(8). e70902.

Shalizi, Cosma Rohilla. 2013. Advanced data analysis from an elementary point of view. http://www.stat.cmu.edu/cshalizi/ADAfaEPoV/13.

Spirtes, Peter, Clark N Glymour & Richard Scheines. 2000. *Causation, prediction, and search.* Cambridge, MA: MIT press.

Verkerk, Annemarie. 2014. The correlation between motion event encoding and path verb lexicon size in the Indo-European language family. *Folia Linguistica Historica* 35. 307–358.

Chapter 10

Real and spurious correlations involving tonal languages

Jeremy Collins
Radboud University, Nijmegen

Why are some languages tonal? Is there a fundamental reason why some languages develop tone and others do not, and and does this have an effect on the way the rest of the language is organized? Tone is important in the context of dependencies, because there is no shortage of hypotheses about what can cause tone and what else tone can cause. For example, tonal languages are found predominantly in warm, humid climates, suggesting that they are culturally adaptive in those environments (Everett, Blasi & Roberts 2015); they are also found in places with low frequencies of two genes microcephalin and ASPM, suggesting that some populations are more likely to use tone than others because of their genetics (Dediu & Ladd 2007). One paper furthermore proposed that phoneme diversity declines with distance from Africa, and number of tones in particular, suggesting a founder effect of migrations, as well as a link with modern population size (Atkinson 2011). As for effects on the rest of the language, SVO word order (Yiu & Matthews 2013) and various other grammatical properties have been suggested to linked functionally with tone, and by Donegan & Stampe (1983) in particular for languages in the Austro-Asiatic family.

At least part of the reason for the large number of correlations proposed in the literature is the visibly skewed geographical distribution of tonal languages (Figure 1). They are predominantly found in Africa and Southeast Asia, immediately suggesting that tone will correlate with a large number of things, from humid climates and SVO languages, to serial verbs, and ancient settlement. The map of ASPM and microcephalin in particular, by Dediu and Ladd's own admission, was the inspiration for their correlation, when they saw that it was similar to the map of tonal languages. But by a similar reasoning, tone can be linked in a spurious way with other things found in those regions, such as acacia trees (Roberts & Winters 2013). It is therefore necessary to work out a way to distinguish which

Jeremy Collins. 2017. Real and spurious correlations involving tonal languages. In N. J. Enfield (ed.), *Dependencies in language*, 129–140. Berlin: Language Science Press. DOI:10.5281/zenodo.573776 of these correlations are real, and which of these are merely accidental consequences of these cultural traits being spatially auto-correlated.

A further major obstacle is the fact that tonal languages are typically not independent. Whole large language families can be tonal, such as Niger-Congo and Sino-Tibetan. The influence of these families in Africa and Southeast Asia has furthermore caused many languages in those regions to become tonal as well, if they were not already due to ancient relatedness with other tonal families (Enfield 2005). If one wants to demonstrate that tone correlates with anything, then one in principle has to use independent data points, which may prove impossible in practice.

I focus in this paper on the correlation proposed by Dediu & Ladd with ASPM and microcephalin, and briefly discuss the correlation proposed by Everett, Blasi & Roberts with humidity, based on my response to their paper (Collins 2016). My assessment of their causal claims will be primarily negative. The reasons I give will be that the evidence for their causal mechanisms are inadequate, and that the methods that they claim control for language family and geographical distance do not work. These points have broader relevance than just for tone, as these affect the way that correlations in general are studied typologically, a point also emphasized by recent work by Ladd, Roberts & Dediu (2015). I end the paper with some broader points illustrating the way that the problem of non-independence in linguistics can take some subtle forms, complicating the search for the genuine dependencies which exist in linguistic systems.

1 Tone and genes

Dediu & Ladd (2007) argue that two genes, ASPM and Microcephalin, may have an effect on the processing of tone. Speakers with particular alleles of these genes are found in regions where tonal languages are. The correlation between these genes and tone is strong (stronger than 97.3% of all gene-language correlations that they tested), and it remains significant in a partial Mantel test controlling for language relatedness and distance between languages. Since these two genes are expressed in the brain, the reason for this may be that these two genes have an effect on speakers' processing of tone, causing some languages to be less likely to develop tone than others, given that there are large differences between populations in the frequency of these genes.

This sounds impressive, until the argument is unpacked. There is nothing about the genes ASPM and Microcephalin which could lead someone to predict any effect on language, much less on a particular property of language such as

10 Real and spurious correlations involving tonal languages

tone. In fact, the reason why the authors decide to focus on those two genes in particular is that these genes are found in the same region as tonal languages. Dediu says, both in their paper and anecdotally in a footnote in his doctoral thesis, that the idea for testing that particular hypothesis came from examining the maps of those two genes which had recently appeared in a few well-known papers (Evans et al. 2005; Mekel-Bobrov et al. 2005), as those two genes have been argued to have undergone recent natural selection because of their high frequency in Eurasian populations, and Robert Ladd suggested that they resemble the distribution of tonal languages (Dediu & Ladd 2007: 192). This particular hypothesis is just one among many resemblances between the distribution of genes and linguistic features that could have been noticed, this one distinguished only by the faint whiff of a plausible causal link – these two genes are involved in the brain, and tone is the type of property which could be affected more than most properties of languages by genetic differences. The authors perhaps did not literally search through all genes and all linguistic features in the hope of finding a meaningful-sounding correlation somewhere, but they might as well have done.

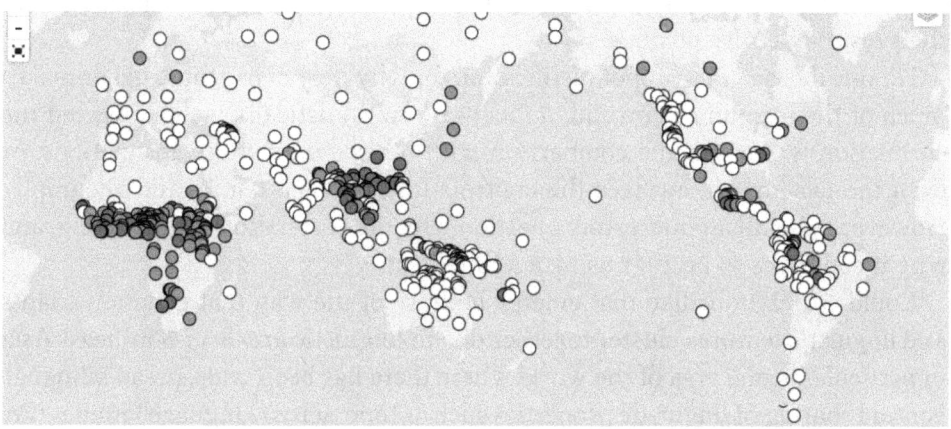

Figure 1: Map of the distribution of complex tonal languages (shown in red), simple tonal languages (pink) and non-tonal languages (white) in WALS (Maddieson 2013).

Picking two genes to focus on because they occur in the same regions as tone, itself a very spatially clustered linguistic feature, automatically makes this correlation better than most randomly selected correlations between genes and linguistic features. This makes the fact that this correlation is in the top 97.3% of gene-feature correlations unimpressive, as all this means is that Dediu and Ladd's ability to spot visual resemblance between two geographical distributions does better than 97.3% of selecting completely randomly chosen geographical distributions.

Jeremy Collins

The two genes *ASPM* and *Microcephalin* had no particular reason to be tested, as their effect on cognition was unclear at the time (Dediu & Ladd 2007; Mekel-Bobrov et al. 2007). If there were an experiment that showed that people with the relevant alleles of *ASPM* or *Microcephalin* were better at tasks involving processing tone, then there would be a reason for studying it. Interestingly, since the publication of Dediu and Ladd's paper in 2007, there was a study by Wong, Chandrasekaran & Zheng (2012) that found that people with the derived allele of *ASPM* were better than those with the ancestral allele at a tone perception task. This would be an important vindication of their choice of these two genes, although a remarkable fluke given that there was nothing else that Dediu and Ladd knew about *ASPM* that could have led them to hypothesise this. However, there are two reasons why Wong, Chandrasekaran & Zheng's study cannot be taken as support for Dediu and Ladd's claim. The first is that the result of their experiment went in the opposite direction to that predicted by Dediu and Ladd; the ancestral allele is the one that is found in regions with tonal languages, not the derived allele. The second reason is that Wong, Chandrasekaran & Zheng's sample only contained thirty-two participants. This makes it quite possible that their result is a false positive.

For me, the lack of a proper justification for why they chose those genes makes much of their argument invalid, no matter how statistically well supported the correlation is, such as the comparison with other gene-feature correlations, or even the fact that it survives the controls for language family and geography. However, it is still an interesting question why the correlation is that strong, and why it continues to be after using a Mantel test.

Could correlations like that emerge because of the way that genetic variants and linguistic features cluster together due to linguistic areality? Southeast Asia in particular is one area of the world where there has been widespread bilingualism and sharing of linguistic properties such as tone across language families (Enfield 2005). To the extent that this was accompanied by gene flow between these populations, a correlation could emerge between tone and particular genetic variants beyond that predicted by language family boundaries and geographical distance. In order to answer this, I looked at mitochondrial DNA haplogroups, in order to see how often a randomly selected haplogroup would correlate with tone (either presence of tone or number of tones) in a Mantel test after controlling for language relatedness and geographical distance. Mitochondrial DNA is a good tracker of human migrations, as it is transmitted to children from their mother, and hence one can use a particular type of mitochondrial DNA (a haplotype) to trace back where ones maternal ancestors have come from. A mitochondrial

10 Real and spurious correlations involving tonal languages

DNA haplogroup can have a historically meaningful distribution, then, which is likely in some cases to correlate with the distribution of tonal languages. There is also the intriguing possibility that if tone was carried by migration of people, such as the spread of Han people in China, that particular maternal lineages may correlate with the presence of tone and illuminate the way that it has spread.

I collected frequencies of mitochondrial DNA haplogroups from 74 populations in Africa and Eurasia, representing 26 different language families. A total of 252 mtDNA haplogrups were used, of all levels of specificity available in the literature (from tables of haplogroup frequencies rather than from the nucleotide sequence data).

Mitochondrial DNA haplogroups range in levels of specificity; for example, a person may belong to haplogroup H1, and this will mean that more generally they will belong to H, and even more generally HV, and so on, back to the haplogroup M and eventually back to L0, which all modern humans belong to. The frequencies of haplogroups were therefore calculated using a family tree of mtDNA: the frequency of H1 in a population contributes to the frequency of H, and so on upwards in the phylogeny, using the phylogeny from van Oven & Kayser (2009).

The conclusion of this analysis is that mitochondrial DNA is a good predictor of the distribution of tonal languages, and remains so after applying statistical controls for relatedness and geographical distance (although I should emphasise that these are not exactly the same as the controls that Dediu and Ladd used). Each haplogroup was tested in a partial Mantel test with number of tones that languages have, controlling for language family (here, pairs of languages are coded as 1 for being in the same family and 0 for being in different families) and geographic distance calculated using the Haversine formula (this does not take landmasses into account or geographical barriers). 26 out of 206 haplogroups correlate with number of tones in this test, meaning that there is a 12% chance that a neutral genetic marker will correlate with number of tones after apparently factoring out historical relationships between languages. This means that their result does not in fact reach conventional significance (i.e. there is a much greater than 5% chance of their result given the null hypothesis). This result is 14% if instead of number of tones languages are simply coded for presence or absence of complex tone (namely having more than two tones), as Dediu and Ladd did.

Overall difference between populations in the frequencies of haplogroups, calculated simply as Manhattan distance of these frequencies, also turns out to correlate with number of tones after controls for language relatedness and geography ($r=0.18$, $p<0.001$). The most impressive claim in their paper, therefore – that after controlling for language history their correlation holds – in fact turns out to be explicable in terms of the way that neutral genetic markers and linguistic features cluster together, perhaps helped by migration between populations.

None of this invalidates the general hypothesis that genes can affect the structure of languages. There is probably genetic variation in linguistic abilities within populations, and when these differences can be between populations too, then one would expect that these can affect language production and what type of linguistic structures catch on in a community. The way to study these, however, is to start from a hypothesis about genes themselves, and then to test the cross-linguistic prediction. There may be variation in places such as China in ability to process tone, just as there are genetic differences in people's ability to process musical pitch; studies of speech disorders may reveal some examples. It is even possible that genes for processing pitch in language may have undergone natural selection, given the communicative importance of intonation in most languages (Cruttenden 1997) and commonalities across languages such as the use of rising intonation for questions and falling intonation for assertions (Dryer 2013).

Work currently being done by Dediu and Moisik on differences in the vocal tract between populations is one example of work on genetic influences on language which begins from a physiological mechanism and makes a cross-linguistic prediction (Dediu, this volume). This type of work may be successful, as it is quite plausible that the morphology of the vocal tract varies between populations and makes certain phonemic distinctions more likely to occur in some populations than others. But the particular case of tone, ASPM and Microcephalin is probably misguided.

2 Tone and climate

Everett, Blasi & Roberts (2015) find a correlation between humidity and complex tone, a correlation that holds up within different families and parts of the world. They suggest that dry air is known to affect the larynx and make precise phonation more difficult, precisely the kind of thing that really could (in principle) affect the way that people use a tonal language.

The number of tones that languages use correlates with humidity within five different global areas (Africa, Eurasia, South America, North America, and the Pacific), and within four different language families (Sino-Tibetan, Austro-Asiatic, Afro-Asiatic, Niger-Congo). This is better statistical support than even for word order universals, which despite having some support when sampling from different macro-areas (Dryer 1992) do not seem to hold consistently within large language families (Dunn et al. 2011).

10 Real and spurious correlations involving tonal languages

In addition, the experimental evidence that they cite showing that dry air has an effect on the larynx raises a host of linguistic questions that are worth exploring anyway, even without this global correlation between dryness and lack of tone. Do speakers of Cantonese alter their use of tone in dryer conditions, for example? This may be a realistic expectation, if the effect of desiccated air on the larynx is as strong as it is reported in experiments. China is a natural testing ground for work of this kind, given that varieties of Chinese vary in their number of tones and in their climatic conditions.

However, as I argue in a response to their paper in the inaugural issue of the *Journal of Language Evolution* 2016, there is an important confound in the correlation between complex tone and humidity. In brief, there are a lot more languages in humid environments than in non-humid environments (the correlation is Pearson's $r=0.31$, $p<0.001$). If tone had developed purely at random in the world's languages, they would still be expected to be found in the more humid places. I show this in a series of simulations in my paper, in which tone develops in a random set of languages and then spreads by language contact to a set of neighbours. In all models, it is very likely (between 50 and 83% depending on the parameters) that tone will correlate with humidity even after using the same controls for language family and the random independent samples test that Everett, Blasi & Roberts employ.

Another finding of Everett, Blasi & Roberts's paper is that number of tones correlates within large language families, such as Sino-Tibetan (Pearson's $r=0.16$, $p<0.01$) and Niger-Congo (Pearson's $r=0.3$, $p<0.001$). However, the major confound here is once again language contact. Sino-Tibetan languages also have fewer tones when they are near to generally non-tonal Indo-European languages, and have more tones when near highly tonal Hmong-Mien languages. Niger-Congo languages similarly lose tones near non-tonal (or low-tonal) families such as Nilo-Saharan and Afro-Asiatic. This matters because speakers of non-tonal languages may be affecting the tonal systems of Niger-Congo and Sino-Tibetan languages. An example is Swahili, which has no tones despite being a Bantu language, most of which have several tones. The reason for this is probably influence from Arabic and its use by Arab traders. A phylogenetic analysis of Sino-Tibetan and Niger-Congo shows that these languages have a strong tendency to lose tones as they move towards non-tonal languages in other families, in accordance with this prediction (Collins 2016).

The causal mechanism is intriguing and worth testing in naturalistic contexts, such as in conversations in different Chinese varieties. However, language contact should be considered a serious confound in the way that it can create a positive global correlation between humidity and complex tone, including after controlling for language family, and even within families.

3 Conclusions

When trying to find dependencies between linguistic traits, one should be aware of various sources of non-independence of data points when testing a correlation. Languages are related to each other by common descent in language families, and hence there needs to be a control for relatedness. But they also influence each other by language contact, and this causes traits such as tone, which spread a long way by contact through languages such as those in Southeast Asia, to form spurious correlations with other traits found in those regions.

With regard to other dependencies discussed in this volume, there are perhaps other unexpected sources of non-independence of data points that need to be taken into account. A particularly subtle form is the historical non-independence of individual linguistic constructions. An example is the way that adpositions often derive from verbs or nouns, and hence correlate in their ordering with verb-object order or genitive-noun order (depending on their source) (Aristar 1991). Prepositions in Mandarin, for example, are thus not historically independent from verbs, as they share a common ancestor. This is a more subtle kind of Galton's problem meaning that the correlation between verb-object ordering and having prepositions in many languages cannot be deduced to be causal, if the word forms for prepositions are in fact derived from verbs. It may be taking it to an extreme to argue that word order correlations are simply due to processes such as grammaticalization, as some people have argued (Aristar 1991), and which is discussed by Cristofaro (2017, in this volume). But it is a surprisingly difficult point to convey to people, who insist that grammaticalization may just be the way that functionally motivated word order correlations can arise. They are missing the point, which is that if they wish to claim a functional motivation, they must first deal with Galton's problem – in this case, in its more subtle form of the common ancestry of constructions, which however is no less real than the common ancestry of whole languages.

This last point in particular stresses the history of individual constructions and properties of languages, for which I think the word "meme" is an appropriate cover term (Dawkins 1976). The way that individual memes can travel between languages and have interconnected ancestries of their own creates problems for inferring causal dependencies. Many of these points are echoed in this volume, as well as in recent work by Enfield such as *Natural Causes of Language* (Enfield

2014). He discusses the fact that behind the illusion of whole languages replicating and dividing into family trees, and behind the illusion of whole linguistic systems, lie instead linguistic replicators which have their own histories but nevertheless need to interact to produce functionally coherent systems. Richard Dawkins makes this point as succinctly as anyone and is arguably its originator, having argued it forcefully for the case of genes building organisms, and then in coining the word "meme" for similar processes acting in cultural evolution. To quote from his foreword to Susan Blackmore's *The Meme Machine* (Blackmore 1999):

"Every gene in a gene pool constitutes part of the environmental background against which other genes are naturally selected, so it's no wonder that natural selection favors genes that 'cooperate' in building these highly integrated and unified machines called organisms. Biologists are sharply divided between those for whom this logic is as clear as daylight, and those (even some very distinguished ones) who just do not understand it – who naively trot out the obvious cooperativeness of genes and the unitariness of organisms as though they somehow count against the 'selfish gene' view of evolution... By analogy with coadapted gene complex, memes, selected against the background of each other, 'cooperate' in mutually supportive memeplexes..."

Although Enfield does not use the word "meme" to describe these replicators, the influence of the idea on this view of language is clear. For me, the additional relevance of the "meme" idea is to think in terms of individual properties of language and the way that they can be transmitted by horizontal transfer, and themselves have interconnected ancestries, as genes can, and these need to be understood in order to where the genuine functional dependencies are.

References

Aristar, Anthony R. 1991. On diachronic sources and synchronic patterns: An investigation into the origin of linguistic universals. *Language* 67. 1–33.

Atkinson, Quentin. 2011. Phonemic diversity supports a serial founder effect model of language expansion from Africa. *Science* 332. 346–349.

Blackmore, Susan. 1999. *The meme machine*. Oxford: Oxford University Press.

Collins, Jeremy. 2016. The role of language contact in creating correlations between humidity and tone. *Journal of Language Evolution* 1(1). 46–52.

Cruttenden, Alan. 1997. *Intonation (2nd edition)*. Cambridge: Cambridge University Press.

Dawkins, Richard. 1976. *The selfish gene*. Oxford: Oxford University Press.

Dediu, Dan & D. Robert Ladd. 2007. Linguistic tone is related to the population frequency of the adaptive haplogroups of two brain size genes, ASPM and microcephalin. *Proceedings of the National Academy of Sciences* 104(26). 10944–9.

Donegan, Patricia & David Stampe. 1983. Rhythm and the holistic organisation of language structure. In M. Marks J. F. Richardson & A. Chukerman (eds.), *Papers from the parasession on the interplay of phonology, morphology, and syntax*, 337–353. Chicago: Chicago Linguistic Society.

Dryer, Matthew S. 1992. The Greenbergian word order correlations. *Language* 68. 81–138.

Dryer, Matthew S. 2013. Polar questions. In Matthew S. Dryer & Martin Haspelmath (eds.), *The world atlas of language structures online*. Leipzig: Max Planck Institute for Evolutionary Anthropology. http://wals.info/chapter/116, accessed 2016-01-26.

Dunn, Michael, Simon Greenhill, Stephen C. Levinson & Russell D. Gray. 2011. Evolved structure of language shows lineage-specific trends in word order universals. *Nature* 473. 79–82.

Enfield, N. J. 2005. Areal linguistics and Mainland Southeast Asia. *Annual Review of Anthropology* 34. 181–206.

Enfield, N. J. 2014. *Natural causes of language: Frames, biases, and cultural transmission.* Berlin: Language Science Press.

Evans, Patrick, Sandra Gilbert, Nitzan Mekel-Bobrov, Eric Vallender, Jeffrey Anderson, Leila Vaez-Azizi, Sarah Tishkoff, Richard Hudson & Bruce Lahn. 2005. Microcephalin, a gene regulating brain size, continues to evolve adaptively in humans. *Science* 309. 1717–1720.

Everett, Caleb, Damián E. Blasi & Seán G. Roberts. 2015. Climate, vocal folds, and tonal languages: Connecting the physiological and geographic dots. *Proceedings of the National Academy of Sciences* 112(5). 1322–1327.

Ladd, D. Robert, Seán G. Roberts & Dan Dediu. 2015. Correlational studies in typological and historical linguistics. *Annual Review of Linguistics* 1. 221–241. DOI:10.1146/annurev-linguist-030514-124819

Maddieson, Ian. 2013. Tone. In Matthew S. Dryer & Martin Haspelmath (eds.), *The world atlas of language structures online*. Leipzig: Max Planck Institute for Evolutionary Anthropology 2013. http://wals.info/chapter/116, accessed 2016-01-26.

Mekel-Bobrov, Nitzan, Sandra L. Gilbert, Patrick D. Evans, Eric J. Vallender, Jeffrey R. Anderson, Richard R. Hudson, Sarah A. Tishkoff & Bruce T. Lahn. 2005.

Ongoing adaptive evolution of ASPM, a brain size determinant in homo sapiens. *Science* 309. 1720–1722.

Mekel-Bobrov, Nitzan, Danielle Posthuma, Sandra L. Gilbert, Penelope Lind, M. Florencia Gosso, Michelle Luciano, Sarah E. Harris, Timothy C. Bates, Tinca J. Polderman, Lawrence J. Whalley, Helen Fox, John M. Starr, Patrick D. Evans, Grant W. Montgomery, Croydon Fernandes, Peter Heutink, Nicholas G. Martin, Dorret I. Boomsma, Ian J. Deary, Margaret J. Wright, Eco J. de Geus & Bruce T. Lahn. 2007. The ongoing adaptive evolution of ASPM and microcephalin is not explained by increased intelligence. *Human Molecular Genetics* 16. 600–608.

Roberts, Seán G. & James Winters. 2013. Linguistic diversity and traffic accidents: Lessons from statistical studies of cultural traits. *PLoS One* 8(8). DOI:10.1371/journal.pone.0070902

van Oven, Mannis & Manfred Kayser. 2009. Updated comprehensive phylogenetic tree of global human mitochondrial DNA variation. *Human Mutation* 30(2). E386-E394.

Wong, Patrick C. M., Bharath Chandrasekaran & Jing Zheng. 2012. The derived allele of ASPM is associated with lexical tone perception. *PLoS ONE* 7(4). e34243. DOI:10.1371/journal.pone.0034243

Yiu, Suki & Stephen Matthews. 2013. Correlations between tonality and word order type. In *The 10th biennial conference of the Association for Linguistic Typology*. Leipzig, Germany.

Chapter 11

What (else) depends on phonology?

Larry M. Hyman
University of California, Berkeley

> To construct phonology so that it mimics syntax is to miss a major result of the work of the last twenty years, namely, that syntax and phonology are essentially different.
>
> (Bromberger & Halle 1989: 69)

1 Is phonology different?

In Hyman (2007) I asked, "Where's phonology in typology?" While phonology turned out to be well represented at the Ardennes workshop and this volume of proceedings, it is typically underrepresented, even ignored by some typologists. I considered three reasons:

(i) Phonology is different (cf. the above Bromberger & Halle quote).

(ii) Phonological typology may seem uninteresting to typologists, particularly if defined as follows:

> "[...] it is possible to classify languages according to the phonemes they contain.... Typology is the study of structural features across languages. Phonological typology involves comparing languages according to the number or type of sounds they contain." (Vajda 2001)

(iii) Phonology is disconnected from the rest (e.g. from morphosyntactic typology).

As evidence that phonology is underrepresented, I noted that there is no coverage in Whaley's (1997) textbook, *Introduction to Typology*. The more recent *Oxford Handbook of Linguistic Typology* (Song 2011) provides confirmation of the above assessment:

Larry M. Hyman. 2017. What (else) depends on phonology? In N. J. Enfield (ed.), *Dependencies in language*, 141–158. Berlin: Language Science Press. DOI:10.5281/zenodo.573784

(i) Phonology is *underrepresented:* there is only one chapter on phonology out of thirty (= 1/30) constitituing 13 out of 665 pages (= 2%)

(ii) Phonology is seen as *different:* Why isn't Chapter 24 entitled "Phonological Typology", parallel with the other chapters?
Chapter 21: Syntactic typology (Lindsay Whaley)
Chapter 22: Morphological typology (Dunstan Brown)
Chapter 23: Semantic typology (Nicholas Evans)
BUT: Chapter 24: Typology of phonological systems (Ian Maddieson)

(iii) Phonology is *ignored:* There is no mention of phonology in Chapter 10 "Implicational Hierarchies" (Greville Corbett), which has sections on syntactic (§3.1), morphosyntactic (§3.2) and lexical (§3.3) hierarchies. As a phonological example the chapter could easily have cited and illustrated the sonority hierarchy (Clements 1990) and the claim that if a lower sonority segment can function as the nucleus of a syllable, then a higher sonority segment in a column to its right also can; see Table 1.

Table 1: The sonority hierarchy: An implicational hierarchy in phonological typology

Obstruent	< Nasal	< Liquid	< Glide	< Vowel	
-	-	-	-	+	syllabic
-	-	-	+	+	vocoid
-	-	+	+	+	approximant
-	+	+	+	+	sonorant
0	1	2	3	4	rank (*degree of sonority*)

There are of course exceptions to the above: *WALS Online* (Dryer & Haspelmath 2013) includes 19 chapters on phonology out of 144 (or 13.2%). There also are several phonological databases and typological projects which are concerned with how phonology interfaces with the rest of grammar, e.g. Bickel, Hildebrandt & Schiering (2009), based on the Autotyp project (Bickel & Nichols 2016). Still, phonology is at best incidental or an afterthought in much of typological work. This stands in marked contrast with the work of Joseph Greenberg, the father of modern linguistic typology, whose foundational work on typology and universals touched on virtually all aspects of phonology, e.g. syllable structure (Greenberg 1962; 1978b), distinctive features (Greenberg, Jenkins & Foss 1967), vowel

11 What (else) depends on phonology?

harmony (Greenberg 1963), nasalized vowels (Greenberg 1966; 1978a), glottalized consonants (Greenberg 1970), word prosody (Greenberg & Kashube 1976). Note also that one full volume out of the four volumes of Greenberg, Ferguson & Moravcsik (1978) was dedicated to phonology!

There are at least two reasons why phonological typology, properly conducted, can be relevant to scholars outside of phonology. First, there are lessons to be learned that are clearest in phonology, e.g. concerning dependencies, the central issue of this volume. Second, there have been claims that grammatical typology can be dependent on phonology. I take these both up in the following two sections.

2 Dependencies require analysis (which requires theory)

It is interesting that Greenberg typically cited phonological examples to make the didactic point that any property found in a language can be stated as an implicans on an absolute universal implicatum:

> We have the unrestricted universal that all languages have oral vowels and the implicational universal that the presence of nasal vowels in a language implies the presence of oral vowels, but not vice-versa. (Greenberg 1966: 509)

> Of course, where an unrestricted universal holds, any statement may figure as implicans. For example, if a language has a case system, it has oral vowels. (Greenberg 1966: 509)

However, phonology teaches us two additional lessons: (i) Dependencies are themselves highly dependent on the level of analysis. (ii) The analysis however varies according to the theory adopted. To illustrate the first point, let us stay with the example of nasality which, in different languages, may be underlyingly contrastive (Table 2).

A problem arises when we attempt to typologize on the basis of languages which have vs. do not have underlying nasal consonants. The class of languages lacking underlying nasal consonants is not coherent, as this includes three different situations: languages like Ebrié (iii) which contrast nasality only on vowels; languages like Barasana (iv) which have nasal prosodies, e.g. /bada/^{N} [mãnã]; languages like Doutai (v) which lack nasality altogether.

While (v) represents an observable ("measurable") fact, assuming that there is also no nasality on the surface, (iii) and (iv) represent linguistic analyses designed

143

Table 2: A typology of nasal contrasts (cf. Cohn 1993; Clements & Osu 2005)

(i)	on consonants only:	/m, n, ŋ/	e.g. Iban
(ii)	on vowels and consonants:	/ĩ, ũ, ã, m, n, ŋ/	e.g. Bambara
(iii)	on vowels only:	/ĩ, ũ, ã/	e.g. Ebrié
(iv)	on whole morphemes:	/CVC/ᴺ	e.g. Barasana
(v)	absent entirely:	-----	e.g. Doutai

to factor out the surface nasality by assigning the oral/nasal contrast either to vowels or to whole morphemes – ignoring the fact that these language have output nasal consonants. To appreciate the fact that languages with contrastive nasality on vowels only (iii) always have surface phonetic nasal consonants, consider the case of Ebrié, a Kwa language of Ivory Coast:

> ... nous considérons que l'ébrié ne possède aucune consonne nasale phonologique et que [m], [n] et [ɲ] sont les allophones respectifs de /ɓ/, /ɗ/ et /y/ [before nasalized vowels] (Dumestre 1970: 25)

In this language, /ɓa, ɗa, ya/ are realized [ɓa, ɗa, ya], while /ɓã, ɗã, yã/ are realized [mã, nã, ɲã]. This analysis is possible because there are no sequences of *[ɓã, ɗã, yã] or *[ma, na, ɲa]. Since contrasts such as /ta/ vs. /tã/ independently require a [+nasal] specification on vowels, the structure-sensitive phonologist cannot resist generalizing: only vowels carry an underlying [+nasal] specification to which a preceding /ɓ, ɗ, y/ assimilate.

The Ebrié example neatly illustrates the fact that there is no language which has SURFACE nasality only on vowels. This raises the question of what level of representation is appropriate for typological purposes: underlying (phonemic) or surface (allophonic)? While Hockett (1963: 24) once noted that "phonemes are not fruitful universals," since they are subject to the individual linguist's interpretation of "the facts", the question is whether the same applies to typological generalizations. As I like to put it, we aim to typologize the linguistic properties, not the linguists. At the Ardennes workshop Martin Haspelmath argued forcefully that observable "surface" properties are the facts and that they should serve as input to typology. If so, we must then address the question of what to do about vowel nasalization in English. As often pointed out, a word like *can't* is often pronounced [kæ̃nt] or even [kæ̃t], in contrast with *cat* [kæt]. The usual assumption is that such variations should be attributed to phonetic implementation

11 What (else) depends on phonology?

(Cohn 1993), i.e. a third level. While this raises the possibility of a different kind of typology based on surface phonetic contrasts, however they may be obtained, thereby blurring the difference between phonetics and phonology, I argue instead for a phonological typology based more strictly on a more structural level of representation. English thereby falls into category (i) in the above typology.[1]

A related question is how we should state the dependency. In an earlier paper I tried to capture the dependency by referring to both levels:

(1) Vocalic Universal #6: A vowel system can be contrastive for nasality only if there are output nasal consonants [i.e. surface phonetic nasal consonants] (Hyman 2008: 99)

To rephrase this: If a vowel system is underlyingly contrastive for nasality, there will always be output nasal consonants, as in Ebrié. However, it appears that this is not general enough: the underlying nasality on vowels may be irrelevant, given systems with prosodic nasality such as Barasana. An alternative is:

(2) Consonantal Universal: A phonological system can be contrastive for nasality only if there are output nasal consonants (i.e. independent of whether the consonant nasality is underlying or derived, and whether nasality is underlyingly segmental or prosodic)

This is true of all four of the systems (i)-(iv) which have contrastive nasality. Thus, the implicans can be either the underlying vowel system or the whole phonological system. We thus are able to relate the dependencies about observable "facts" with our (interesting) analyses of them. The same point can be made concerning vertical vowel systems: Systems such as Kabardian or Marshallese are often analyzed as /ɨ, ə, a/, /ɨ, a/ etc., but always have output [i] and [u] (cf. Vocalic Universal #5 in Hyman 2008: 98).

Above I cited Greenberg's absolute universal "all languages have oral vowels" as a universally available implicatum ("if a language has a case system, it has oral vowels"). What about an implicans that is extremely rare? The velar implosive [ɠ] is very rare in languages:

---

[1] As this volume was going to press I received Kiparsky (2017) which also addresses this question. Concerned with universals and UG, Kiparsky proposes that phonological typology should not be based on the phonemic level, rather what he terms the "lexical level" which contains salient redundancies. At this level Ebrié would have a nasal contrast on both consonants and vowels thereby allowing the universalist to claim that a language which contrasts nasalized vowels also has nasal consonants.

> The velar implosive is a very infrequent sound and... always seems to imply the presence of bilabial, apical, and palatal members of the series. (Greenberg 1970: 128)

What then can be predicted from its presence? Note first that implosives occur in 53 out of the 451 languages in the UPSID database (Maddieson & Precoda 1990). A bilabial implosive occurs in 50 of these 53 languages, while an apical (dental or alveolar) implosive occurs in 42 languages. In stark contrast, a velar implosive occurs in only five of the 53 languages. In Table 3 I attempt to establish dependencies "if ɠ, then X" again to determine the role of analysis in establishing implicational universals.

Table 3: Possible implicational university based on the presence of contrastive /ɠ/

		Chadic	Omotic		East Sudanic	
		Tera	Hamer	Ik	Maasai	Nyangi
other implosive consonants:	if /ɠ/, then /ɓ, ɗ/	✓	✓	✓	✓	✓
basic voiceless consonants:	if /ɠ/, then /p, t, k/	✓	✓	✓	✓	✓
voiced non-implosives?	if /ɠ/, then /b, d, g/	✓	✓	✓	*	*

As seen, if a language has /ɠ/ we can predict that the other two implosives will be present, as well as voiceless stops. While Maasai and Nyangi appear to falsify the implication "if ɓ, ɗ, ɠ, then b, d, g", it can be saved if we re-analyze [ɓ, ɗ, ɠ] as /b, d, g/, which are lacking in the two systems. I would argue against this as a valid move, but it again underscores the problem of level of analysis, which provides us with two different kinds of claims:

(i) a descriptive claim: if a language has [ɓ, ɗ, ɠ], it will have contrastive /b, d, g/

(ii) an analytic claim: if a language has [ɓ, ɗ, ɠ] it will have /b, d, g/ (either contrastively or not)

11 What (else) depends on phonology?

The above summarizes a bit of what we face in phonology. What about grammar depending on phonology?

3 Non-arbitrary ≠ predictive

In this section I begin by considering the empirical bases in establishing a dependency. Specific implicans-implicatum of dependencies are arrived at in a number of ways, combining degrees of inductive observation and deductive reasoning. In this section I consider two types of dependencies which appear to be "non-arbitrary": (i) those which depend on (claimed) absolute universals; (ii) those which depend on historically linked events. To begin with the first, ultimately false claims may at first appear to be based on what the proposer considers to have an external (e.g. physical phonetic) basis:

> "Since sequences containing only pure consonants, such as [kptčsm] or [rʃtlks], cannot be pronounced, all words must include at least one vowel or vowel-like (vocalic, syllabic) sound segment",

> hence:

> "In all languages, all words must include at least one vocalic segment." (Moravcsik 2013: 153)

This statement contains the dependency, "If X is a word, then it contains at least one vocalic segment," which however is false, as seen in the following Bella Coola voiceless obstruent utterance (Nater 1984: 5, cited by Shaw 2002: 1):

(3) xɬp'χʷɬtɬpɬɬs kʷc'
    'then he had had in his possession a bunchberry plant'

In this case there was an extra-linguistic basis to the claim–languages can't have words that are universally unpronounceable. On the other hand, linguists have been known to make arbitrary "universal stabs in the dark" which have no obvious linguistic or extra-linguistic basis, e.g. "No language uses tone to mark case" (Presidential Address, 2004 Annual Linguistic Society of America Meeting, Boston). Stated as a dependency:

(i) If a language has tone, it will not be used to mark case.

(ii) If a language has case, it won't be marked by tone.

Table 4: Case marking by tone in Maasai

	nominative	accusative		nom. vs. acc. tone patterns
class I:	èlòkònyá	èlòkónyá	'head'	L^n-H vs. L-H^n
	èncòmàtá	èncómátá	'horse'	
class II:	èndéròni	èndèróni	'rat'	H on σ_1 vs. σ_2
	ènkólòpà	ènkòlópà	'centipede'	
class III:	òlmérègèsh	òlmérègèsh	'ram'	H on σ_2 & σ_3 vs. on σ_2 only
	òlósówùàn	òlósòwùàn	'buffalo'	
class IV:	òmótònyî	òmótònyî	'bird'	identical tones
	òsínkìrrî	òsínkìrrî	'fish'	

But consider Table 4 from Maasai (Tucker & Mpaayei 1955: 177–184), where the acute (´) marks H(igh) tone, while the grave (`) accent marks L(ow) tone:

In reality, if tone can be a morpheme (which is uncontroversial), it can do anything that a morpheme can do! What innate or functional principle would block tone from marking case?

The above examples reveal a temptation to claim a non-arbitrary relation between certain aspects of grammar and phonology. Recently there has been renewed interest in pursuing a centuries-old "intuition" that certain aspects of syntax and morphology are not only interdependent, but also dependent on phonology. The standard reference is Plank (1998), who attributes the following positions to:

> *Encyclopaedia Brittannica* (1771): "Words tend to be longer than one syllable in transpositive [free word order] languages and to be monosyllabic in analogous [rigid word order] languages." (Plank 1998: 198)

> W. Radloff (1882): "(a) If vowel assimilation is progressive (= vowel harmony), then the morphology will be agglutinative (and indeed suffixing), but not vice versa.... (b) if the morphology is flective, then if there are vowel assimilations they will be regressive (= umlaut), but not vice-versa...." (Plank 1998: 202)

11 What (else) depends on phonology?

> Rev. James Byrne (1885): "Unlimited consonant clustering correlates with VS order, limitations on consonant clustering correlate with SV order." (Plank 1998: 200)

> Georg von der Gabelentz (1901): Languages with anticipatory phonological assimilation should have anticipatory grammatical agreement (e.g. from N to A in an A-N order), while languages with perseverative phonological assimilation should have perseverative grammatical agreement (e.g. from N to A in an N-A order). (my paraphrasing of Plank 1998: 197); also Bally (1944): Séquence Progressive vs. Séquence Anticipatrice (Plank 1998: 211)

Interestingly, Greenberg did not buy into this. Grammar does appear in examples involving the universality of oral vowels, which was didactically exploited as an implicatum to show that any arbitrary implicans follows – grammatical ones are typically cited (Greenberg 1966; 1978a):

(i) If a language has case, it also has oral vowels (repeated from above)

(ii) If a language has sex-based gender, it also has oral vowels

(iii) If a language doesn't have oral vowels, the language doesn't have sex-based gender (or maybe it does)

What this reveals is that there is a world of difference between correlation and causation. Noone would ever claim that the presence of oral vowels has something to do with any of the above grammatical properties. As Plank (1998) put it:

> "Although these implications all happen to be true, their typological value is nil." (Plank 1998: 223)

The last century has seen a proliferation of proposals to distinguish language "types" which identify various phonological properties with grammatical ones, either as non-directional correlations (P↔G) or with one dependent on the other (P→G, G→P), e.g.

- anticipatory vs. progressive languages
- iambic vs. trochaic languages
- stress-timed vs. syllable-timed vs. mora-timed languages

- syllable vs. word languages
- word vs. phrase languages

(See especially proposals of Bally, Skalička, Lehmann, Dressler, Donegan & Stampe, Dauer, Gil, Auer, all in Plank 1998.) As an example, consider the following two languages types from Lehmann (1973 et seq), as summarized by Plank (1998: 208) (Table 5).

Table 5: Lehmann's Holistic Typology of Languages

"think Turkish or Japanese"	"think Germanic"
• dependent-head (OV, AN etc.)	• head-dependent (VO, NA etc.)
• suffixes	• prefixes
• agglutination (exponents = loosely bound affixes)	• flection (exponents = tightly fused with stem)
• no agreement	• agreement
• vowel harmony (progressive, root triggers)	• umlaut (= regressive, suffix triggers)
• few morphophonological rules (mostly progressive)	• many morphophonological rules (mostly regressive)
• syllable structure simple	• syllable structure complex
• pitch accent	• stress accent + unstressed vowel reduction
• mora-counting	• syllable-counting

While such grammar-phonology dependencies have not generally caught on in typological or in phonological circles, there is renewed interest in statistical correlations between phonological properties and OV vs. VO syntax (Nespor, Shukla & Mehler 2011; Tokizaki 2010; Tokizaki & Kuwana 2012) (cf. Cinque 1993) as well as word class, e.g. noun vs. verb, transitive vs. intransitive verbs (Smith 2011; Dingemanse et al. 2015; Fullwood 2014).

Concerning the latter, Fullwood demonstrates a statistical correlation between verb transitivity and stress on English bisyllabic verbs (Table 6). Although the absolute number of verbs having one vs. the other stress patterns is reasonably close (1090 trochaic, 1227 iambic), the smallest group by far are obligatorily intransitive iambic verbs such as *desíst*. Here we can see the consequence of stress to avoid final position–and to especially avoid the "weak" utterance-final position where declarative intonation would normally realize a high to low falling

Table 6: Stress Placement on Verbs in English

	trochaic		iambic	
obligatorily transitive	506	(39%)	804	(61%)
ambitransitive	357	(55%)	293	(45%)
obligatorily intransitive	227	(64%)	130	(36%)

pitch (Hyman 1977: 45). Being utterance-internal is quite different. As Fullwood (2014) puts it:

> Words that frequently occur phrase-finally are more likely to retract stress from their final syllable, while other words that rarely occur in phrase-final position are quite happy to accommodate a final stress. (Fullwood 2014: 130)

Similar proposals have been offered of a relation between word order and stress, but one of causation has not been widely accepted, whether based on universal tendencies or historically linked events.

A case of the latter does comes from Foley & Olson (1985: 50-51), who offer "an interesting list of shared properties", some phonological, some grammatical, among languages with valence-increasing serial verbs, particularly in West Africa and Southeast Asia:

(i) phonemic tone

(ii) many monosyllabic words

(iii) isolating morphological typology

(iv) verb medial word order (SVO)

They go on to explain:

> This cluster of properties is not accidental: they are all interrelated. Phonological attribution causes syncope of segments or syllables, with the result that phonemic tone or complex vowel systems develop to compensate for phonemic distinctions being lost. On the grammatical side, phonological attrition causes gradual loss of the bound morphemes.... At this verbal morphology is lost, a new device for valence adjustment must be found. Verb serialization begins to be used in this function, *provided serial constructions already exist in the language.* (Foley & Olson 1985: 51) [my emphasis]

Foley & Olson suggest that the development of serial verbs proceeds in the following order:

(4) motion/directional verbs > postural verbs > stative/process verbs > valence

Crucially, it is only the last (valence) stage that correlates with the above properties (vs. Crowley 2002 re Oceanic serial verbs which do not meet these criteria). It is the loss of head-marking on verbs (benefactive, instrumental applicatives etc), which was due to the introduction of prosodic size conditions on verb stems in NW Bantu (Hyman 2004), that feeds into verb serialization. Thus there is a *non-arbitrary* relation between the phonological development, the loss of head-marking morphology, and the extended development of an analytical structure with serial verbs.

However, the cause-and-effect is not *predictive*: Neither the synchronic nor diachronic interpretation of these dependencies holds true for all cases:

- synchronic dependency: if valence-marking serial verbs, then tone, tendency towards monosyllabicity, isolating morphology, SVO (but Ijo = SOV)
- diachronic dependency: if serial verbs + phonological attrition, then valence-marking serial verbs, tone etc. (but some serial verb languages do not employ serial verbs to mark valence)

The diachronic alternative for marking benefactives, instruments etc. is with adpositions. Nzadi is a Narrow Bantu language spoken in the Democratic Republic of Congo which has broken down the Bantu agglutinative structure to become analytic and largely monosyllabic. Serial verbs have not been introduced to replace lost verbal suffixes (Crane, Hyman & Tukumu 2011):

(5) a. bɔ   ó   túŋ   ndzɔ sám   ⁺é báàr
         they PAST build house reason of people
         'they built a house for the people'

     b. ndé ó   wɛɛ   ḿbùm tí   ntáp   òté
         he PAST pick fruit   with   branch tree
         'he picked fruit with a stick'

The serial structures '*they built house give people' and '*he take stick pick fruit' are not used in Nzadi, which is spoken outside the West African serial verb zone.

11 What (else) depends on phonology?

"Holistic" typologies such as the one from Lehmann presented above are still only "hopeful" (Plank 1998), based to a large extent on the feeling that clustering of properties across phonology, morphology and syntax is non-arbitrary (e.g. Indo-European and Semitic vs. Uralic and Altaic; West Africa and Southeast Asia vs. Athabaskan, Bantu). But whatever links one can find between the cited properties, these effects are non-predictive. Still, linguists hold strong feelings on such interdependencies, and I'm guilty too. Thus, as my own observation (hope) I offer the following as a concluding proposal.

The highly agglutinative Bantu languages contrast only two tone heights, H and L (often analyzed as privative /H/ vs. Ø). A third M(id) tone height is only present in languages which have broken down the morphology (thereby creating more tonal contrasts on the remaining tone-bearing units). Thus compare the H vs. L agglutinative structure in the Luganda utterance in (6a) with the H vs. M vs. L isolating structure in (6b) of Fe'fe'-Bamileke, a Grassfields Bantu language of Cameroon:

(6) a. Luganda
à-bá-tá-lí-kí-gúl-ír-àgàn-à
AUG-they-NEG-FUT-it-buy-APPL-RECIP-FV

'they who will not buy it for each other' (AUG = augment; FV = inflectional final vowel)

b. Fe'fe'-Bamileke
à kà láh pìɛ náh ncwēe mbʉ̀ʉ̀ hā mūū
he PAST take knife take cut meat give child

'he cut the meat with a knife for the child' (¯ = Mid tone)

The morphological structure of words in polyagglutinative languages like Luganda is highly syntagmatic. This is most compatible with a tone system with privative /H/ vs. Ø, where the Hs are assigned to specific positions. (Although they don't have a M tone, some Bantu languages allow ꜜH, as tonal downstep is also syntagmatic.) A full contrast of /H, M, L/ on every tone-bearing unit would produce a huge number of tone patterns (3 x 3 x 3 etc.), so one should at best expect the /H, M, L/ contrast to occur only on prominent positions (e.g. the root syllable). /H, M, L/ is thus more compatible with languages like Fe'fe'-Bamileke, where words are short, with little morphology. Languages with shorter words often have more paradigmatic contrasts in general (more consonants, vowels–and tones). This may again be non-arbitrary, as the greater paradigmatic contrasts make up for the lost syllables of longer words. But it is not predictive.

Larry M. Hyman

Acknowledgements

I would like to thank Nick Enfield for inviting me to the Ardennes workshop at which I also received several helpful responses. I am particularly indebted to Mark Dingemanse for his detailed review of an earlier version of this paper which has helped me clarify some of the points that I wanted to make.

References

Bally, Charles. 1944. *Linguistique générale et linguistique française.* 2nd edition. Berne: Francke.
Bickel, Balthasar, Kristine Hildebrandt & René Schiering. 2009. The distribution of phonological word domains: A probabilistic typology. In Janet Grijzenhout & Barış Kabak (eds.), *Phonological domains: Universals and deviations*, 47–75. Berlin: Mouton de Gruyter.
Bickel, Balthasar & Johanna Nichols. 2016. *Autotyp.* http://www.autotyp.uzh.ch/.
Bromberger, Sylvain & Morris Halle. 1989. Why phonology is different. *Linguistic Inquiry* 20. 51–70.
Byrne, James. 1885. *General principles of the structure of language.* 2nd edition, 1892. London: Trübner.
Cinque, Guglielmo. 1993. A null theory of phrase and compound stress. *Linguistic Inquiry* 24. 239–294.
Clements, George Nick. 1990. The role of the sonority cycle in core syllabification. In John Kingston & Mary E. Beckman (eds.), *Papers in laboratory phonology I: Between the grammar and physics of speech*, 283–333. Cambridge: Cambridge University Press.
Clements, George Nick & Sylvester Osu. 2005. Nasal harmony in Ikwere, a language with no phonemic nasal consonants. *Journal of African Languages and Linguistics* 26. 165–200.
Cohn, Abigail. 1993. A survey of the phonology of the feature [+nasal]. *Working Papers of the Cornell Phonetics Laboratory* 8. Ithaca: Cornell University, 141–203.
Crane, Thera Marie, Larry M. Hyman & Simon Nsielanga Tukumu. 2011. *A grammar of Nzadi [B865]* (University of California Publications in Linguistics 147). Oakland: University of California Press.
Crowley, Terry. 2002. *Serial verbs in Oceanic: A descriptive typology.* Oxford: Oxford University Press.

Dingemanse, Mark, Damián E. Blasi, Gary Lupyan, Morten H. Christiansen & Padraic Monoghan. 2015. Arbitrariness, iconicity and systematicity in language. *Trends in Cognitive Sciences* 19. 603–615.

Dryer, Matthew S. & Martin Haspelmath (eds.). 2013. *WALS online*. Leipzig: Max Planck Institute for Evolutionary Anthropology. http://wals.info/.

Dumestre, Gaston. 1970. *Atlas linguistique de Côte d'Ivoire*. Abidjan: Institut de Linguistique Appliquée XI, Université d'Abidjan.

Foley, William A. & Mike Olson. 1985. Clausehood and verb serialization. In Johanna Nichols & Anthony C. Woodbury (eds.), *Grammar inside and outside the clause*, 17–60. Cambridge: Cambridge University Press.

Fullwood, Michelle A. 2014. Asymmetric correlations between English verb transitivity and stress. *Proceedings of the 40th Annual Meeting of the Berkeley Linguistic Society* 40. 125–138.

Gabelentz, Georg van der. 1901. *Die Sprachwissenschaft: Ihre Aufgaben, Methoden und bisherigen Ergebnisse. 2nd edition*. Leipzig: Tauchnitz.

Greenberg, Joseph H. 1962. Is the vowel-consonant dichotomy universal? *Word* 18. 73–81.

Greenberg, Joseph H. 1963. Vowel harmony in African languages. *Actes du Second Colloque Internationale de Linguistique Négro-Africaine* 1. Dakar: Université de Dakar, West African Languages Survey, 33–38.

Greenberg, Joseph H. 1966. Synchronic and diachronic universals in phonology. *Language* 42. 508–17.

Greenberg, Joseph H. 1970. Some generalizations concerning glottalic consonants, especially implosives. *International Journal of American Linguistics* 36. 123–45.

Greenberg, Joseph H. 1978a. Diachrony, synchrony and language universals. In Joseph H. Greenberg, Charles A. Ferguson & Edith A. Moravcsik (eds.), *Universals of human language, volume 1*, 61–91. Cambridge, MA: MIT Press.

Greenberg, Joseph H. 1978b. Some generalizations concerning initial and final consonant clusters. *Linguistics* 18. 5–34.

Greenberg, Joseph H., Charles A. Ferguson & Edith A. Moravcsik (eds.). 1978. *Universals of human language*. Stanford: Stanford University Press.

Greenberg, Joseph H., James J. Jenkins & Donald J. Foss. 1967. Phonological distinctive features as cues in learning. *Journal of Experimental Psychology* 77. 200–205.

Greenberg, Joseph H. & Dorothy Kashube. 1976. Word prosodic systems: A preliminary report. *Working Papers in Language Universals* 20. Stanford University, 1–18.

Hockett, Charles F. 1963. The problem of universals in language. In Joseph H. Greenberg (ed.), *Universals of language*, 1–29. Cambridge, MA: MIT Press.

Hyman, Larry M. 1977. The nature of linguistic stress. In Larry M. Hyman (ed.), *Studies in stress and accent* (Southern California Occasional Papers in Linguistics 4), 37–83. Los Angeles: Department of Linguistics, University of Southern California.

Hyman, Larry M. 2004. How to become a Kwa verb. *Journal of West African Languages* 30. 69–88.

Hyman, Larry M. 2007. Where's phonology in typology? *Linguistic Typology* 11. 265–271.

Hyman, Larry M. 2008. Universals in phonology. *The Linguistic Review* 25. 81–135.

Kiparsky, Paul. 2017. Formal and empirical issues in phonological typology. In Larry M. Hyman & Frans Plank (eds.), *Phonological typology*.

Lehmann, Winfred P. 1973. A structural principle of language and its implications. *Language* 49. 47–66.

Maddieson, Ian & Kristin Precoda. 1990. Updating UPSID. *UCLA Working Papers in Phonetics* 74. 104–111.

Moravcsik, Edith. 2013. *Introducing language typology*. New York: Cambridge University Press.

Nater, Hank F. 1984. *The Bella Coola language* (National Museum of Man Mercury Series. Canadian Ethnology Service Paper 92). Ottawa: National Museums of Canada.

Nespor, Marina, Mohinish Shukla & Jacques Mehler. 2011. Stress-timed vs. syllable-timed languages. In Marc van Oostendorp, Colin J. Ewen, Elizabeth Hume & Keren Rice (eds.), *The Blackwell companion to phonology*, Blackwell Reference Online. 31 July 2012. Blackwell Publishing.

Plank, Frans. 1998. The co-variation of phonology with morphology and syntax: A hopeful history. *Linguistic Typology* 2. 195–230.

Radloff, Vasily. 1882. *Vergleichende Grammatik der nördlichen Türksprachen, erster Theil: Phonetik der nördlichen Türksprachen*. Leipzig: Weigel.

Shaw, Patricia. 2002. On the edge: Obstruent clusters in Salish. In *Proceedings of the Workshop on the Structure and Constituency of the Languages of the Americas (WSCLA 7). University of British Columbia Working Papers in Linguistics 10*. Vancouver: University of British Columbia.

Smith, Jennifer L. 2011. Category-specific effects. In, Blackwell Online, 31 July 2012.

Song, Jae Jung (ed.). 2011. *The Oxford handbook of linguistic typology*. Oxford: Oxford University Press.

Tokizaki, Hisao. 2010. Syllable structure, stress location and head-complement order. *Phonological Studies: The Phonological Society of Japan* 13. 135–136.

Tokizaki, Hisao & Yasutomo Kuwana. 2012. Limited consonant clusters in OV languages. In Phil Hoole et al (ed.), *Consonant clusters and structural complexity*, 71–91. Berlin: Mouton de Gruyter.

Tucker, Archibald Norman & J. Tompo Ole Mpaayei. 1955. *A Maasai grammar with vocabulary*. London: Longmans, Green & Company.

Vajda, Edward. 2001. *Test materials dated August 17, 2001.*

Whaley, Lindsay J. 1997. *Introduction to typology*. Thousand Oaks, Cal: Sage.

Chapter 12

Dependencies in phonology: hierarchies and variation

Keren Rice
University of Toronto

1 Introduction

Implicational scales, also often called markedness hierarchies, are proposed in linguistics to account for dependency relationships of the sort "if x, then y," expressing typological generalizations. In general, a markedness hierarchy in phonology involves a family of related linguistic substantive features such as place of articulation and sonority; markedness hierarchies involving non-phonological features are also found, such as the well-known animacy and person hierarchies. In the equation if "x, then y", x is considered to be more marked than y since the presence of y depends on the presence of x.[1] Implicational scales, also often called markedness hierarchies, are proposed in linguistics to account for dependency relationships of the sort "if x, then y," expressing typological generalizations. In general, a markedness hierarchy in phonology involves a family of related linguistic substantive features such as place of articulation and sonority; markedness hierarchies involving non-phonological features are also found, such as the well-known animacy and person hierarchies. In the equation if "x, then y", x is considered to be more marked than y since the presence of y depends on the presence of x.[2]

---

[1] I discuss only one measure of markedness, namely implications. Note that many other factors have been identified with markedness. In general, unmarked is considered more basic, and is described with terms such as natural, normal, general, simple, frequent, optimal, predictable, ubiquitous, and acquired earlier; marked, on the other hand, is described with terms including less natural, less normal, specialized, complex, less frequent, less optimal, unpredictable, parochial, and acquired later. See, for instance, Hume (2011) and Rice (2007).

[2] I discuss only one measure of markedness, namely implications. Note that many other factors have been identified with markedness. In general, unmarked is considered more basic, and is

Keren Rice. 2017. Dependencies in phonology: hierarchies and variation. In N. J. Enfield (ed.), *Dependencies in language*, 159–171. Berlin: Language Science Press. DOI:10.5281/zenodo.573786

There are numerous examples of such hierarchies in phonology. Beckman (1997), for instance, utilizes a vowel height markedness hierarchy to account for the presence of mid vowels in an inventory implying the presence of high and low vowels, but not vice versa (Beckman 1997: 14, drawing on surveys of vowel inventories by Crothers 1978 and Disner 1984), as in (1).

(1)   a.   *Mid >> *High, *Low

This is to be read as follows: mid vowels are more marked than high vowels and low vowels. Hierarchies of this sort are designed to account for a variety of aspects of phonology including inventory structure and asymmetries in terms of processes such as neutralization and assimilation. While they have precedents in other theories, Optimality Theory makes particularly strong use of such hierarchies; see, for instance, Beckman (1997), Lombardi (2002), Hayes & Steriade (2004), and de Lacy (2006), among others. The hierarchies are based on typological findings and expressed with substantive features involving phonetic categories.

In this chapter, I focus on dependencies as they relate to inventory structure and markedness. Perhaps the most extensive recent work on markedness and inventories is found in de Lacy (2006), working within an Optimality Theory framework. De Lacy makes very explicit claims about when unmarked surface forms are predicted, and I draw heavily on his work in the following discussion.

In discussion of diagnostics for markedness, de Lacy notes that inventory structure is a valid diagnostic "to a very limited extent"(2006: 343). More particularly, he says that "If the presence of [α] in a segmental surface inventory implies the presence of [β] but not vice versa, then there is some markedness hierarchy in which [β] is more marked than [α]." He continues with a concrete example based on place of articulation, for which he proposes that dorsal and labial places of articulation are more marked than coronal and glottal places of articulation: "if there is a dorsal and/or labial of a particular manner of articulation in a language, then there will also be a glottal and/or a coronal of the same manner of articulation (as long as no interfering manner-changing processes apply). Consequently, there must be one or more hierarchies in which dorsals and labials are more marked than coronals and glottals." de Lacy (2006: 110) further notes that in the absence of faithfulness constraints (constraints functioning to preserve in-

---

described with terms such as natural, normal, general, simple, frequent, optimal, predictable, ubiquitous, and acquired earlier; marked, on the other hand, is described with terms including less natural, less normal, specialized, complex, less frequent, less optimal, unpredictable, parochial, and acquired later. See, for instance, Hume (2011) and Rice (2007).

12 Dependencies in phonology: hierarchies and variation

put forms) and competing hierarchies, markedness is "decisive in selecting the output form," known in the Optimality Theory literature as the emergence of the unmarked. The emergence of the unmarked refers to situations where a marked structure is generally allowed in a language, but is banned in particular contexts. The emergence of the unmarked is found in epenthesis, where the quality of an epenthetic segment is considered to be unmarked since there is no input correspondent, and in neutralization, as discussed below, among other contexts.

As mentioned above, in this chapter I examine hierarchies with respect to inventory structure, particularly addressing the claim that the presence of a more marked feature in a language implies the presence of a less marked one, determinable on universal grounds. I do this through two lenses. First I consider variation in the realization of a sound within a language, asking why it is that variation between a segment with a more marked feature and one with a less marked feature on the same hierarchy should exist if hierarchies predict that presence of the more marked one implies the presence of the less marked one. Second I examine cross-linguistic aspects of place neutralization in coda position, asking why languages differ in possible places of articulation in a position where no contrasts exist, and where the presence of the least marked is predicted.

I focus in particular on the place of articulation hierarchy, as in (2) (e.g., de Lacy 2006).

(2) Dorsal >> Labial >> Coronal >> Glottal

According to this hierarchy, dorsals are the most marked consonants in terms of place of articulation, and glottals are the least marked. Thus, all other things being equal, one would expect that if there is a dorsal stop present in a language, there will also be a labial stop, and so on. Moreover, in the absence of a contrast, coronals or glottals should arise.

It is important to comment briefly on the notion of all other things being equal. While the place of articulation hierarchy is as in (2), de Lacy notes that both coronals and glottals can pattern as unmarked. He argues that this is due to the fact that while glottals are the least marked on the place of articulation hierarchy, they are more marked than other places of articulation on the sonority hierarchy: relations between features can be different depending upon the hierarchy at issue. It is thus important to examine features that are always in the same markedness relationship with one another; the place features Dorsal, Labial, and Coronal are assumed to be such features, and I focus on these places of articulation, leaving glottals aside. Thus I focus on situations where the only relevant hierarchy is the place of articulation hierarchy. Assuming this, there are very clear predictions: one would expect, both within and between languages, that under equivalent conditions, there would be uniformity. I begin by studying within language variation (§2) and then turn to between language variation (§3).

2 Variation within a language: place of articulation

Many languages are reported to exhibit variation in place of articulation in particular positions. For instance, in some languages there is no contrast in a particular position between coronal and dorsal stops or between coronal and velar nasals. Given the absence of a contrast, one would predict that the less marked place of articulation would be found. However, rather than the unmarked one occurring, in many languages both coronal and dorsal consonants of a particular manner of articulation are in variation with each other even though coronals are less marked than dorsals. In other cases there is no contrast between dorsal and uvular sounds at a manner of articulation and stops of these places of articulation are in variation even though dorsals are considered to be less marked than uvulars. A few examples of languages illustrating such variation are given in (3). In these cases, the variation is not controlled by linguistic factors; there may be social and other factors involved, but these are not mentioned in the literature.

(3)   a.   coronal/dorsal variation San Carlos Apache (Athabaskan) (de Reuse 2006)
[t]~[k] stem-finally
Panare (Cariban): /n/ (Payne & Payne 2013)
[n]~[ŋ] word-finally
     b. dorsal/uvular variation
Sentani (Papuan): /k/ (Cowan 1965)
[k]~[q]~[x]
Qawasqar (Alacalufan) (Maddieson 2011)
uvular~velar stop

As (3) shows, there may be variation in the realization of place of articulation within a language (see section 3 for some examples of variation of place of articulation involving labials).

This kind of variation is unexpected, given the type of fixed substantive markedness hierarchies discussed in §1. Note that while variation might follow as a result of conflicting hierarchies (de Lacy 2006: 344), when all features save the varying one are controlled for, a solution to this problem grounded in conflicting hierarchies does not seem to be appropriate: as discussed earlier, there are no proposed hierarchies where coronal is more marked than dorsal, for instance, and dorsals are generally considered to be less marked than uvulars; in other words, there is no hierarchy where these are reversed. Recognizing this, de Lacy (2006: 341) notes that "The markedness status of freely varying allophones is also unclear: underlyingly marked values do not only vary freely with less-marked ones," and he further writes that "allophonic free variation should not be expected to show markedness effects" since it is due to phonological processes that may either "reduce markedness (e.g. neutralization)" or "inadvertently increase it (e.g. assimilation)" (2006: 342). In the languages given in (3), the variation is found either in a typical neutralization position, or appears to be free. Such variation gives pause, and I examine an alternative account to de Lacy's in §4.

3 Cross-linguistic variation: word-final position (position of neutralization)

Important evidence for markedness hierarchies can be drawn from neutralization, as discussed in Trubetzkoy (1969) and much subsequent work. See Battistella (1990) for a review of literature on neutralization and Rice (2007, 2009) for more in-depth development of the ideas that are summarized in this chapter.

It is again instructive to consider de Lacy's statements about neutralization as a diagnostic for markedness. De Lacy (2006: 342) recognizes the following aspect of neutralization as a relevant markedness diagnostic: "If /α/ and /β/ undergo structurally conditioned neutralization to map to output [α], then there is some markedness hierarchy in which [β] is more marked than [α]." He further notes that not all neutralization presents valid diagnostics for markedness: "If /β/ undergoes neutralization but /α/ does not, then it is not necessarily the case that there is a markedness hierarchy in which /β/ is more marked than /α/" (de Lacy 2006: 340).

One can then look to neutralization positions for evidence for a markedness hierarchy, focusing on cases where there is neutralization between features of the same class (the valid instance noted by de Lacy). Word- and syllable-final positions are well-known sites of neutralization. For instance, neutralization of a laryngeal contrast to voiceless in these positions is very common. In addition, place of articulation neutralization can occur in these positions. Thus, given the place of articulation hierarchy in (2), one would expect to find neutralization to

Keren Rice

either coronal or glottal place of articulation; I again set aside glottal since it enters into the sonority hierarchy as well as the place of articulation hierarchy.

In the following discussion, I distinguish two types of neutralization, passive and active. Passive neutralization is a result of the lexicon: there are simply no lexical contrasts between features on some dimension in a particular position. For instance, with respect to place of articulation, only a single place of articulation is found in some position, with no evidence from alternations for active neutralization. Active neutralization is what the name implies: there is evidence that one place of articulation actively neutralizes to another.

I begin with passive neutralization in word-final position, considering languages with a contrast between labials, coronals, and dorsals in their full inventory. I carried out a detailed survey of languages based on grammars and phonological descriptions, focusing on the places of articulation found in word-final position in stops and in nasals. A sampling of the results of this survey is provided in Table 1 for stops and Table 2 for nasals in word-final position in languages where there is no contrast in place of articulation found in this position.

Table 1: Absence of contrast in place of articulation word-finally: stops

p	t	k	Languages
x			Nimboran (Papuan), Basari (Niger-Congo), Sentani (Papuan), some Spanish (Romance)
	x		Finnish (Finno-Ugric), Alawa (Australia)
		x	Ecuador Quichua (Quechuan), Arekuna (Carib)

Many languages exhibit active neutralization to a single place of articulation in word- or syllable-final position. The expectations are clear: coronals (and glottals) are expected. Again I set aside glottals. Coronals indeed result from active neutralization in a number of languages including Saami (Uralic, Odden 2005) and Miya (Chadic, Schuh 1998). However, labials and dorsals also occur as the sole place of articulation in neutralization positions. Examples of languages are given in (4); some languages are listed twice because variation is reported.

(4) neutralization to Labial: Manam (Austronesian, Lichtenberk 1983), Miya (Afro-Asiatic, Schuh 1998), Buenos Aires Spanish (Romance, Smyth p.c.)
neutralization to Dorsal: Manam (Austronesian, Lichtenberk 1983), some Spanish dialects (syllable-final), Carib of Surinam (Carib; neutralization to [x] in syllable-final position, Hoff 1968), Tlachichilko Tepehua

Table 2: Absence of contrast in place of articulation word-finally: nasals

m	n	ŋ	Languages
x			Sentani (Papuan), some Spanish (Romance), Kilivila (Austronesian), Mussau (Austronesian; [n] in names, borrowings; [ŋ] in one word)
	x		Finnish (Finno-Ugric), Koyukon (Athabaskan), some Spanish (Romance)
		x	Japanese, Selayarese (Austronesian), some Spanish (Romance), Macushi (Cariban)

(Totonacan; neutralization to dorsal in syllable-final position, Watters 1980)

One can conclude that, despite the wide range of evidence that is compatible with the place of articulation hierarchy (and other substantive hierarchies), in fact there are counterexamples where the unmarked does not emerge when it is expected.

In the next section, I examine a possible reason for this: the fixed substantive universal hierarchies cannot provide insight into the non-contrastive kind of variation considered above, either within or between languages, because, in the absence of contrast, substance is not determinate (see, for instance, Rice 2007; 2009; Hall 2011).

4 What is going on?

The substantive generalizations in the hierarchies predict, as de Lacy (2006) emphasizes, that, in the absence of faithfulness constraints (constraints that maintain input independent of its markedness) and competing hierarchies, markedness is "decisive in selecting the output form" (de Lacy 2006: 110). In the types of cases discussed above, faithfulness is not at issue and, given that the outcomes under discussion share in all but place features, competing hierarchies do not offer insight as the places of articulation under consideration do not enter into alternative hierarchies. One can then ask why, despite the predictions of the hierarchy, such variation is found both language-internally and cross-linguistically. In this section I introduce another possibility, that, in the absence of an opposition, substantive hierarchies do not make predictions; rather phonetic naturalness and other factors are at play.

Battistella (1990), in a detailed discussion of semantic markedness, provides interesting insight into the conditions under which it is relevant to talk about markedness. In particular, Battistella notes that marked elements "are characteristically specific and determinate in meaning." Further, he continues, the opposed unmarked elements "are characteristically indeterminate" (Battistella 1990: 27). He concludes that "whenever we have an opposition between two things, one of those things – the unmarked one – will be more broadly defined" (Battistella 1990: 4).

I draw two conclusions from Battistella (1990). First, unmarked elements are more general in interpretation than are marked elements, which have a more specific interpretation. This suggests, for instance, that the unmarked might show more phonetic variation than the marked. Second, and more relevant in a discussion of dependencies, given that markedness is defined with reference to oppositions, it is difficult to know how to understand markedness in the absence of an opposition, where there are simply not two (or more) elements to compare. Battistella focuses on the existence of an opposition between two (or more) features; under such a situation, one can be characterized as unmarked with respect to a particular hierarchy. What about when there is not an opposition?

The variation within languages and the various possible outcomes of neutralization across languages lead us to a different conclusion than that predicted by the markedness hierarchies. Instead of assuming that, all other things being equal, markedness selects the output form, an alternative account is possible: all other things being equal, the substance of the output form is phonologically indeterminate in the absence of an opposition, or a contrast. I will call the first of these the emergence-of-the-unmarked approach and the second the absence-of-an-opposition approach.

The first approach, emergence-of-the-unmarked, predicts substantive uniformity cross-linguistically in the absence of competing hierarchies and faithfulness. The second approach, absence-of-an-opposition, predicts a certain amount of variability cross-linguistically (and language-internally as well). As discussed above, such variability can be captured by the emergence-of-the-unmarked approach through the establishment of different hierarchies where a particular feature is unmarked on one but not on another, with one or the other hierarchy privileged in different languages. However, as noted above, in terms of place of articulation, setting glottals aside, to my knowledge there are no proposals that make, for instance, coronal consonants unmarked on one hierarchy and marked

12 Dependencies in phonology: hierarchies and variation

on another, or labial consonants more marked than coronal consonants on one hierarchy but less marked on another.

The absence-of-an-opposition approach predicts that either a coronal or a labial, for instance, could emerge in a position where there is no contrast. It is not a substantive markedness hierarchy that determines the outcome. Instead, any place of articulation is conceivably possible.

Given this latter approach, some important questions arise, and I briefly consider two of these. First, why have markedness hierarchies been proposed, with considerable empirical support? Another way of putting this is to ask why there are cross-linguistic biases. Second, if the unmarked truly is indeterminate in a universal sense, what factors are involved in determining the actual substance in a language?

The answer to the first of these questions is reasonably straightforward: there are clear biases towards phonetic naturalness, represented in the markedness hierarchies by what is at the unmarked end of the hierarchy. For instance, Maddieson (1984: 39-40) notes the following generalizations with regard to stops. The number following the generalization indicates the percentage or number of languages in the survey that obey the particular generalization.

- All languages have stops. (100%)

- If a language has only one stop series, that series is plain voiceless stops. (49/50 languages – 98.0%)

- If a language has /p/ then it has /k/, and if it has /k/ then it has /*t/ (4 counterexamples in the UPSID sample; '*t' signifies a dental or alveolar stop).

Given these observations, one can make the following predictions.

- Stops are expected to be less marked in manner than other obstruents.

- Plain voiceless stops are expected to be less marked than stops with other laryngeal features.

- Coronal stops are expected to be less marked than stops of other places of articulation.

Maddieson is clear that these are tendencies, or biases, as is well recognized in the literature. What then do we make of the counterexamples?

I will very briefly note some possible contributing factors. First, articulatory and perceptual factors are important in establishing the widespread cross-linguistic uniformity, or biases, and these are well captured by the markedness hierarchies, accounting for the considerable cross-language convergence that we find.

However, other factors are important as well. Diachronic factors can play a role, and in this case unexpected situations might arise (see, for instance Blevins 2004). For instance, Blust (1984) attributes the presence of final /m/ and the absence of other word-final consonants in the Austronesian language Mussau to the loss of a vowel following this consonant (with frequent devoicing but not loss of final vowels following other consonants).

Societal and social factors most likely are also important in shaping what is allowed in the absence of contrast (see, for instance, Guy 2011). Trudgill (2011) identifies a number of societal factors that are involved in what he calls linguistic complexification, focusing on language size, networks, contact, stability, and communally-shared information. For instance, he notes that social isolation often contributes to the existence of both large and small inventories, unusual sound changes, and non-maximally dispersed vowel systems. One might imagine then that there might be a greater tendency to variation and less common outputs of neutralization in closely knit societies with relatively large amounts of shared equilibrium, where, Trudgill notes, less phonetic information is needed for successful communication. Research to establish whether such correlations do exist remains to be done.

5 Conclusion

It is very common to posit dependencies in the form of substantive hierarchies in linguistics. I have not addressed the overall status of such hierarchies in phonology, but have simply asked whether the hierarchies are determinate in the absence of a contrast. I have examined variation in place of articulation within a language and different outcomes of place of articulation neutralization between languages, and found that, all other things being equal, in fact the unmarked is not necessarily found. I conclude that, assuming that the evidence for substantive markedness hierarchies holds overall, they play a role only in the presence of contrasts; in the absence of an opposition, they are not determinate. The frequency of particular phonetic outcomes depends to a large degree on articulatory and perceptual factors, or phonetic naturalness, with diachronic and sociolinguistic factors also playing roles. It is important to understand when dependencies might indeed be a part of shaping a language, and when their existence masks a more nuanced situation.

References

Battistella, Edwin. 1990. *Markedness: The evaluative superstructure of language.* Albany: SUNY Press.

Beckman, Jill. 1997. Positional faithfulness, positional neutralization, and Shona vowel harmony. *Phonology* 14(1). 1–46.

Blevins, Juliette. 2004. *Evolutionary phonology: The emergence of sound patterns.* Cambridge: Cambridge University Press.

Blust, Robert. 1984. A Mussau vocabulary, with phonological notes. *Pacific Linguistics* Series A: Occasional Papers. 159–208.

Cowan, Hendrik Karel Jan. 1965. *Grammar of the Sentani language.* 's-Gravenhage: Martinus Nijhoff.

Crothers, John. 1978. Typology and universals of vowel systems. In Joseph H. Greenberg (ed.), *Universals of human language: Volume 2: Phonology*, 93–152. Stanford: Stanford University Press.

de Lacy, Paul. 2006. *Markedness: Reduction and preservation in phonology.* Cambridge: Cambridge University Press.

de Reuse, Willem J. with the assistance of Phillip Goode. 2006. *A practical grammar of the San Carlos Apache language.* Munich: Lincom Europa.

Disner, Sandra. 1984. Insights on vowel spacing. In Ian Maddieson (ed.), *Patterns of sounds*, 136–155. Cambridge: Cambridge University Press.

Guy, Greg. 2011. Variability. In Marc van Oostendorp, Colin Ewen, Elizabeth Hume & Keren Rice (eds.), *The Blackwell companion to phonology*, 2190–2213. Hoboken: Wiley-Blackwell.

Hall, Daniel Currie. 2011. Phonological contrast and its phonetic enhancement: Dispersedness without dispersion. *Phonology* 28(1). 1–54.

Hayes, Bruce & Donca Steriade. 2004. Introduction: The phonetic bases of phonological markedness. In Bruce Hayes, Robert Kirchner & Donca Steriade (eds.), *Phonetically-based phonology*, 1–55. Cambridge: Cambridge University Press.

Hoff, Bernd. 1968. *The Carib language. Phonology, morphonology, morphology, texts, and word index.* The Hague: Martinus Nijhoff.

Hume, Elizabeth. 2011. Markedness. In Marc van Oostendorp, Colin Ewen, Elizabeth Hume & Keren Rice (eds.), *The Blackwell companion to phonology*, 79–106. Hoboken: Wiley-Blackwell.

Lichtenberk, Frantisek. 1983. *A grammar of Manam.* Honolulu: University of Hawaii Press.

Lombardi, Linda. 2002. Coronal epenthesis and markedness. *Phonology* 19. 219–251.

Maddieson, Ian. 1984. *Patterns of sounds*. Cambridge: Cambridge University Press.

Maddieson, Ian. 2011. Uvular consonants. In Matthew Dryer S. & Martin Haspelmath (eds.), *The world atlas of language structures online*. Munich: Max Planck Digital Library. http://wals.info/chapter/6, accessed 2012-12-28.

Odden, David. 2005. *Introducing phonology*. Cambridge: Cambridge University Press.

Payne, Thomas E. & Doris L. Payne. 2013. *A typological grammar of Panare, a Cariban language of Venezuela*. Leiden: Brill.

Rice, Keren. 2007. Markedness in phonology. In Paul de Lacy (ed.), *The Cambridge handbook of phonology*, 79–97. Cambridge: Cambridge University Press.

Rice, Keren. 2009. Nuancing markedness: Comments on Andrea Calabrese: Prolegomena to a realistic theory of phonology. In Charles Cairns & Eric Raimy (eds.), *Architecture and representations in phonological theory*, 311–321. Cambridge: MIT Press.

Schuh, Russell. 1998. *A grammar of Miya* (University of California Publications in Linguistics 130). Berkeley: University of California Press.

Trubetzkoy, Nikolai S. 1969. *Principles of phonology*. California: University of California Press.

Trudgill, Peter. 2011. *Sociolinguistic typology: Social determinants of linguistic complexity*. Cambridge: Cambridge University Press.

Watters, James. 1980. Aspects of Tlachichilco Tepehua (Totonacan) phonology. *SIL Mexico Workpapers* 4. 85–129.

Chapter 13

Understanding intra-system dependencies: Classifiers in Lao

Sebastian Fedden
The University of Sydney

Greville G. Corbett
University of Surrey

1 Introduction

We are fascinated by the significant but understudied analytic issue of when different linguistic systems (particularly morphosyntactic features) should be recognized in a given language. In the most straightforward instances we can see that two systems are orthogonal (logically independent of each other), and so each should be postulated in an adequate analysis. Thus traditional accounts of languages like Italian, which recognize a number system and a gender system, are fully justified. There are instances which are a little less straightforward. There may be dependencies between different features, for example in German there is neutralization of gender in the plural, but we would still have good grounds for recognizing two systems.

Turning to the specific area of nominal classification, we see that it is certainly an interesting and challenging area of linguistics, but that after a long research tradition we still do not have a clear picture of the different types of classification device that languages employ, much less of their interaction with and dependencies on each other in individual languages. In order to make progress we should undertake analyses of key languages. In some languages we find, arguably, a gender system together with a classifier system, and the interest of the analysis is to determine whether indeed there are two systems of nominal classification or whether the two candidate systems are in fact inter-dependent. In this chapter, however, we undertake a case study which allows us to explore the more difficult yet intriguing issue of dependencies between systems of the same type, that is, between two possible classifier systems. Basing ourselves on Enfield (2004; 2007), we examine the Tai-Kadai language Lao. There are two sets of classifiers, which appear in different constructions. First there is a set of numeral classifiers which are used in contexts of quantification following the numeral. Second, Lao has a set of classifiers consisting of phonologically reduced forms of the numeral classifiers, and appearing as a proclitic before a range of modifiers. Within the broad question of nominal classification, and the even more general issue of recognizing concurrent systems, we are interested in possible dependencies between these two sets of classifiers.

2 Lao

Lao (Enfield 2004; 2007), a Tai-Kadai language spoken by about 15 million people in Laos and Thailand, has two sets of classifiers. The first set consists of more than 80 numeral classifiers (NUM_CL) (Kerr 1972: xxi-xxiii), which appear in contexts of quantification in a construction where the noun comes first, followed by a numeral (or quantifying expression such as how many?, every or each), followed by a classifier. Two typical examples illustrating the use of the numeral classifiers *too3* 'NUM_CL:ANIMATE' and *khan2* 'NUM_CL:VEHICLE', respectively, are given in examples (1) and (2) (Enfield 2007: 120,124). The numbers after Lao words indicate tones.

(1) *kuu3 sùù4 paa3 sòòng3 too3*
1SG.B buy fish two   NUM_CL:ANIMATE
'I bought two fish.'

(2) *kuu3 lak1 lot1   sòòng3 khan2*
1SG.B steal vehicle two   NUM_CL:VEHICLE
'I stole two cars.'

The first singular pronoun *kuu3* is glossed 'B' here to indicate 'bare', that is, semantically unmarked for politeness, as opposed to 'P' ('polite'). When the referent is retrievable from the context, the head noun is often omitted, as in example (3) (Enfield 2007: 139):

(3) *kuu3 sùù4 sòòng3 too3*
1SG.B buy two   NUM_CL:ANIMATE
'I bought two (e.g., fish).'

13 Understanding intra-system dependencies: Classifiers in Lao

Numeral classifiers are virtually obligatory and are only very rarely omitted. Semantically Lao numeral classifiers express distinctions of shape, size, material, texture, measure and social value. Some numeral classifiers have relatively broad semantics, e.g. *too3* 'NUM_CL:ANIMATE' or *phùùn3* 'NUM_CL:CLOTH', whereas others are rather specific, e.g. *qong3* 'NUM_CL:MONKS'. For nouns which do not have a numeral classifier conventionally assigned to them, the noun is used in this construction to classify itself, giving rise to a set of repeaters which is in principle open.

Most numeral classifiers double as nouns in the language, e.g. the numeral classifier *khon2* for people (excluding monks) means 'person' as a noun, and *sên5* for ribbon-shaped things, such as cables and roads, means 'line' as a noun. As is typical of classifier systems, the meaning of the classifier is more general than the meaning of the noun from which the classifier is derived. Another characteristic, also common in numeral classifier languages, is that only a relatively small subset of these 80 classifiers is commonly used in discourse. The most frequent ones in Lao are *khon2* 'person' for humans, *too3* 'body' for animals, but also for trousers and shirts, and *qan3*, which does not double as a noun, for small things.

The second set of classifiers appears in a different construction: first comes the noun, followed by a classifier, followed by a modifier. The set of modifiers includes the general demonstrative *nii4*, the non-proximal demonstrative *nan4*, the numeral *nùng1* 'one', relative clauses and adjectives. Enfield (2007: 137) calls these modifier classifiers (MOD_CL). In principle, all numeral classifiers can appear as modifier classifiers, but in a phonologically reduced proclitic form, which is typically unstressed and shows no tonal contrasts. The following examples illustrate the use of modifier classifiers, with a demonstrative in (4), an adjective in (5) and a relative clause in (6) (Enfield 2007: 139,143). Modifier classifiers are not obligatory with adjectives and relative clauses.

(4) *kuu3 siø=kin3 paa3 toø=nii4*
    1SG.B IRR=eat fish MOD_CL:NON.HUMAN=DEM
    'I'm going to eat this fish.'

(5) *kuu3 siø=kin3 paa3 (toø=)ñaaw2*
    1SG.B IRR=eat fish (MOD_CL:NON.HUMAN=)long
    'I'm going to eat the long fish.'

(6) *khòòj5 kin3 paa3 (toø=)caw4   sùù4*
    1SG.P eat fish (MOD_CL:NON.HUMAN=)2SG.P buy
    'I ate the fish (the one which) you bought.'

In practice, however, almost all modifier classifiers used in discourse come from the following set of three: *phuø*, which has no corresponding numeral classifier, for humans, *toø* (< *too3*) for non-humans and *qanø* (< *qan3*) for inanimates (ø indicates neutralization of tone). Although *toø* 'MOD_CL:NON.HUMAN' and *qanø* 'MOD_CL:INANIMATE' are clearly related to the numeral classifiers *too3* and *qan3*, respectively, their semantics is much more general. The modifier classifier *toø* can in fact be used with any noun with an animal or inanimate referent and *qanø* can be used with any noun with an inanimate referent. Therefore, for inanimates, either modifier classifier is fine. This is illustrated in examples (7) and (8) for the noun *sin5* 'Lao skirt' (which in the numeral classifier system takes *phùùn3* 'NUM_CL:CLOTH'). Semantically, (7) and (8) are equivalent (Enfield 2007: 141). See Carpenter (1986; 1991) for the same phenomenon in Thai.

(7) khòòj5 mak1 sin5   toø=nii4
    1SG.P like Lao.skirt MOD_CL:NON.HUMAN=DEM
    'I like this skirt.'

(8) khòòj5 mak1 sin5   qanø=nii4
    1SG.P like Lao.skirt MOD_CL:INANIMATE=DEM
    'I like this skirt.'

Although the use of a modifier classifier has a unitizing function and strongly implies singular, its use with a numeral other than 'one' is possible; in fact if a noun is modified by both a numeral and a demonstrative the modifier classifier construction is used. This is shown in example (9) (Enfield 2007: 140).

(9) kuu3 siø=kin3 paa3 sòòng3 toø=nii4
    1SG.B IRR=eat fish two   MOD_CL:NON.HUMAN=DEM
    'I'm going to eat these two fish.'

Lao provides a particularly interesting instance of what we are looking for, namely a set of data where we might reasonably consider postulating two systems of the same general type (two systems of classifiers). It is therefore natural to want to compare the two systems. In Table 1 we draw up a matrix which integrates the numeral and modifier classifiers of Lao. The leftmost column gives the classes of nouns and the second column lists the appropriate classifier in the numeral classifier construction. Then, for each numeral classifier, the table specifies which modifier classifiers are possible. For reasons of space we have to restrict the number of numeral classifiers, but this is not a problem since all

13 Understanding intra-system dependencies: Classifiers in Lao

classifiers not covered in Table 1 are for inanimates, which means that *toø*, *qanø* or the phonologically reduced form of the numeral classifier can be used. They all follow the pattern given in the row labelled "etc.".

Table 1: Lao numeral and modifier classifiers

		Modifier classifiers			
Assignment	Numeral classifiers	*phuø* 'human'	*toø* 'non-human'	*qanø* 'inanimate'	Reduced form of numeral classifier
human	*khon2*	yes	no	no	yes
monk	*qong3*	yes	no	no	yes
animal	*too3*	no	yes	no	yes [= *toø*]
small thing	*qan3*	no	yes	yes	yes [= *qanø*]
line	*sên5*	no	yes	yes	yes
lump	*kòòn4*	no	yes	yes	yes
cloth	*phùùn3*	no	yes	yes	yes
etc.	etc.	no	yes	yes	yes

The phonologically reduced form is always an option in the modifier classifier construction. For humans, either *phuø* or *khonø* can be used in the modifier classifier construction. For monks, these are possible but considered disrespectful. For animals, *toø* is used. For inanimates, either *toø* or *qanø* are possible.

In Table 1 we see that for each numeral classifier we can fully predict which modifier classifiers are possible. Given that the modifier classifier system is small and based on general semantic divisions, it is not surprising that it can be predicted from the system with the larger inventory (and hence smaller divisions), i.e. the numeral classifier system.

A good test case which indicates the dependency between the two systems is situations in which different classifiers can be used depending on properties of the referent; here we can examine whether one system is still predictable from the other. This investigation is not intended as a contribution to the semantics of classifier systems, rather our focus is on the dependency or lack of dependency between systems.

We start with the relatively straightforward case of regular polysemy (Apresjan 1974; Nunberg 1996). As we would expect, the noun *mèèw2* 'cat' takes the numeral classifier *too3* 'NUM_CL:ANIMATE' and the modifier classifier *toø* 'MOD_-CL:NON.HUMAN'. The same classification is possible, if the referent is not a real

175

cat but a toy cat. This is an instance of a regular polysemous relation between an animal and a representation of that animal. With an inanimate toy as the referent, the numeral classifier *qan3* 'NUM_CL:SMALL.OBJECT' is also possible, as in (10), which would not be acceptable for living cats. This general fact related to polysemy needs to be specified only once; the fact that it holds true equally of the modifier classifier is fully predictable, as in (11).

(10) mèèw2 saam3 qan3
      cat   three NUM_CL:SMALL.OBJECT
      'three toy cats'

(11) mèèw2 qanø=nii4
      cat   MOD_CL:INANIMATE=DEM
      'this toy cat'

Regular polysemy is the straightforward situation, it does not provide strong support for our case, because we could argue that there are two systems of classifiers, numeral classifiers and modifier classifiers, and regular polysemy is available to each of them; assignment to each of them could operate independently, and the same result would be reached. Thus regular polysemy provides an argument, but hardly a strong argument, for the claim that the systems are in fact inter-dependent.

We therefore move on to cases where a referent has been manipulated out of its normal shape. Even in these situations the systems are parallel. For example, paper normally comes in sheets. In Lao, the noun *cia4* 'paper' takes the numeral classifier *phèèn1* 'NUM_CL:FLAT'. As expected, the modifier classifier for paper is *phèènø* 'MOD_CL:FLAT' (or *toø* 'MOD_CL:NON.HUMAN' or *qanø* 'MOD_CL:INANIMATE', as is possible for all inanimates). While we can use the same classification if the referent is a crumpled sheet of paper, now the numeral classifier *kòòn4* 'NUM_CL:LUMP' is also possible, as in (12), and so is the modifier classifier *kòònø* 'MOD_CL:LUMP', as in (13).

(12) cia4   saam3 kòòn4
      paper three NUM_CL:LUMP
      'three crumpled pieces of paper'

(13) cia4   kòònø=nii4
      paper MOD_CL:LUMP=DEM
      'this crumpled piece of paper'

13 Understanding intra-system dependencies: Classifiers in Lao

Going further, we shall see that there is predictability of the modifier classifier from the numeral classifier even if the referent does not have a normal or expected shape. Take, for example, pieces of putty, which is designed to be modelled into all sorts of shapes, but does not have an inherent shape of its own. In this situation the referent determines classifier use and there is no falling back on an inherent shape when the referent has been manipulated out of that shape. If the referent is a lump of putty the classifiers *kòòn4* 'NUM_CL:LUMP' or *kòònø* 'MOD_CL:LUMP' are used, but not *phèèn1* 'NUM_CL:FLAT' or *phèènø* 'MOD_CL:FLAT'. If the piece of putty is flat the classifiers *phèèn1* 'NUM_CL:FLAT' or *phèènø* 'MOD_-CL:FLAT' are used, but not *kòòn4* 'NUM_CL:LUMP' or *kòònø* 'MOD_CL:LUMP'.

3 Conclusion

Recall that our concern is the analytical issue of recognizing systems with interesting dependencies as opposed to independent concurrent systems. This is a general issue. For instance, turning to a different feature, we note that languages of Australia were frequently analysed as having two different case systems. Goddard (1982) argues convincingly for integrated single systems. This fits these languages more readily into broader typological patterns, and also simplifies the analysis of verbal government in the particular languages. Similarly, Lao has provided a fascinating study. At one level, we might say that there are two systems of classifiers, numeral and modifier classifiers, which appear in different constructions. In terms of the assignment of particular classifiers within those systems, however, we find an interesting dependency. Given the choice of numeral classifier, the appropriate modifier classifier is predictable. This is an argument for dependency between the systems. However, it appears not to be a strong argument. For ordinary uses of nouns, it might be objected that the lexical semantics of the noun are available equally for assigning both types of classifier. Yet this objection (in favour of two concurrent systems) is, perhaps, not fully convincing in those instances where the appropriate classifier cannot be assigned straightforwardly from the lexical semantics of the noun. Then, in cases of regular polysemy, the fact that the choice of modifier classifier seems to "follow" the choice of numeral classifier is also indicative, but again not fully convincing. When finally we look at manipulations of the referent, natural or less so, the fact that even here the choice of modifier classifier follows that of the numeral classifier confirms the interesting dependency between the two systems. Thus the use of the smaller set of forms is predictable given the larger set of forms; this fact prompts us to conclude that Lao has a single integrated system of classifiers.

More generally, where there are potentially two systems in play, as we find in Lao, we need to argue carefully for and against analyses which rest on a dependency between the systems. This is important for typological purposes, and it may also lead to a clearer view of the particular language being investigated.

Acknowledgements

We would like to thank Nick Enfield for providing us with examples and commenting on an earlier version of this chapter. The support of the AHRC (grant: Combining Gender and Classifiers in Natural Language, grant AH/K003194/1) is gratefully acknowledged.

References

Apresjan, Juri. D. 1974. Regular polysemy. *Linguistics* 12.142. 5–32.
Carpenter, Kathie. 1986. Productivity and pragmatics of Thai classifiers. *Berkeley Linguistics Society* 12. 14–25.
Carpenter, Kathie. 1991. Later rather than sooner: Extralinguistic categories in the acquisition of Thai classifiers. *Journal of Child Language* 18. 93–113.
Enfield, N. J. 2004. Nominal classification in Lao: A sketch. *Sprachtypologie und Universalienforschung (STUF)* 57(2/3). 117–143.
Enfield, N. J. 2007. *A grammar of Lao* (Mouton Grammar Library 38). Berlin: Mouton de Gruyter.
Goddard, Cliff. 1982. Case systems and case marking in Australian languages: A new interpretation. *Australian Journal of Linguistics* 2. 167–196.
Kerr, Allen D. 1972. *Lao-English dictionary*. Washington, DC: Catholic University of America Press.
Nunberg, Geoffrey D. 1996. Transfers of meaning. In James Pustejovsky & Branimir Boguraev (eds.), *Lexical semantics: The problem of polysemy*, 109–132. Oxford: Clarendon.

Chapter 14

Structural and semantic dependencies in word class

William A. Foley
The University of Sydney

Is there a dependency between the type of phrase structure that a language has and its inventory of lexical classes? This chapter will argue that there may well be, although not one that is strictly determinative. The claim is that a certain phrase structure pattern, i.e. left-headed and with overt functional categorial heads like determiners and tense-aspect-mood markers, is correlated with an attenuated distinction between nouns and verbs. A striking fact about the languages of the world is a widespread asymmetry between nouns and verbs. It is a salient but remarkable observation that languages often have many more monomorphemic nouns than they do verbs: in Yimas, a language of New Guinea, for instance, there are over 3000 noun roots, but only around 100 verb roots, a skewing commonly found in other languages of the region (Pawley 1994). Even in languages with large inventories of both classes of words, such as English, there is a marked differential in behavior. Basic nouns in English typically have fewer meanings and usages than verbs. The *Webster's New World College Dictionary* (2009), for example, lists seven meanings for the noun *chair*, but no less than seventy for the verb *take*. Furthermore, while the noun *chair* can be used in extended meanings such as *chair a meeting*, there is a clear semantic link between such uses and its basic noun meaning, while with verbs this is commonly not the case; what does *take* contribute when we contrast *to nap* with *to take a nap*?

In most language families around the world the predisposition to distinguish nouns and verbs is strong, and the distinction remains diachronically robust. But in a few, it is a family wide fact that the distinction is not so clear, and very many or most lexemes are flexible, i.e. can be freely used without clear derivational morphology either as a noun or verb. This does not mean a distinction between noun and verbs cannot be recognized; in some languages it may, and perhaps in others, it shouldn't, but that is not my concern here. I am strictly

William A. Foley

concerned with the fact and prevalence of such flexibility and the attenuation of a sharp distinction between them. This will be looked at briefly in this chapter in the Austronesian and Salish language families, for which the status of the noun-verb distinction has long been controversial, and mainly concentrating on the former. What is it about the grammatical organization of Austronesian and Salish languages that leads to a recurring predilection to attenuate the noun-verb contrast? And as this attenuation is relatively rare crosslinguistically, what happens to this structural trait when languages bearing it come into contact with languages with the much more common property of a sharp noun-verb contrast and a different type of phrase structure? This question will be briefly looked at in areas of heavy Austronesian-Papuan language contact in the New Guinea region. Papuan languages across diverse language families exhibit sharp noun-verb distinctions, even sharper than classical languages like Latin, the source of our descriptive grammatical tradition. But it does seem that in Austronesian-Papuan contact situations, the selective pressures of areal features do outweigh inheritance.

Our earliest, more sophisticated grammatical treatment of word classes goes back to the first century BC grammar of Greek by the Alexandrian grammarian Dionysius Thrax, building on the work of Aristotle and the Stoic philosophers before him. He defined the categories of noun and verb and their distinction in the following terms:

- *Ónoma* (noun): a part of speech inflected for case, signifying a person or thing

- *Rhêma* (verb): a part of speech without case inflection, but inflected for tense, person and number, signifying an activity or process performed or undergone

Thrax's definitions are notable for two reasons, and both of these have influenced descriptive grammatical traditions ever since. Note that neither relies on a single criterion, both invoke two, one semantic and the other morphosyntactic. In the hothouse multicultural and multilingual atmosphere of Hellenistic Alexandria, Thrax would have been well aware of the wide differences in grammatical organization across languages, so he knew that a straightforward definition of word classes in semantic terms would not do, as items with very similar meanings could behave very differently in different languages and hence belong to different word classes. Yet he didn't abandon semantic criteria entirely, as he was also aware of the semantic commonality of core members of each word class and the use of this as a heuristic in a first pass at identifying members of a given word class. Still, the semantic criterion on its own wouldn't do, not only because of crosslinguistic differences, but also because the match between the typical meaning of a word class and the meanings of its individual members even in a language like Greek wasn't perfect; there were simply too many exceptions to what would be expected. So he dragged morphosyntactic behavior into use for delineating word class differences, for example, case for nouns and tense for verbs.

In his two pronged approach, Thrax was greatly aided by the grammatical structure of the classical languages; his description was based on Greek. In these languages, the distinction between noun and verb is over-determined; it is virtually impossible to miss it. Consider Table 1, a map of lexical organization in terms of word class membership in Latin.

Table 1: Lexical organization in Latin

(i)	phonology	-a first declension	-ē second conjugation
		↑	↑
(ii)	inflection	DECLENSIONS	CONJUGATIONS
		↑	↑
(iii)	syntax	N + CASE	V + TENSE
		↑	↑
(iv)	semantics	ARGUMENT (thing) +	PREDICATE (event)

The reason, for instance, that the noun-verb distinction was so salient to the Ancient Greek and Latin grammarians is the sharp differentiation in morphological behavior between them in these two languages. Not only do Ancient Greek and Latin have distinct grammatical categories for nouns and verbs due to their syntactic properties (level iii), e.g. case for nouns and tense for verbs, but in addition different noun and verb lexemes belong to distinct inflectional patterns (level ii), declensions for nouns and conjugations for verbs, and these in turn correlate to clear phonological contrasts in their forms (level i) (nouns belong to five phonologically contrastive declensions and verbs to four conjugations). There is overkill in the distinctiveness of these two classes in these languages; grammarians could not fail to notice it. Ancient Greek does have word types that blend the morphosyntactic properties of nouns and verbs, such as participles, gerunds and infinitives, but these are clearly derived secondary forms and do not eclipse the very salient noun-verb distinction in these languages.

William A. Foley

The classical languages with their robust distinction of word classes have provided a largely taken for granted model for thinking about lexical distinctions ever since. Classical languages have provided us with categories of nouns, verbs and adjectives, and linguists have mainly approached language descriptions with these categories in mind (although adjectives have been more controversial) by trying to find analogs of these classical categories in the languages under description, in spite of often very different syntactic properties and inflectional categories. It is almost as if, as Riemer (2010) points out, that knowing baseball and its terminology well, like first base, shortstop, home run etc., we use these familiar categories to describe all ball games: football, volleyball, tennis, basketball, etc. The real question is how much communality there is across languages that permits us to believe that we are talking about the same or even similar categories. In some languages, rather than pervasive difference as attested in Latin and Ancient Greek, what we find is pervasive similarity in the grammatical behavior of lexemes which are prototypically divided into these two word classes, noun and verbs, those which denote objects and those which denote events respectively. Nouns function as arguments, and verbs as predicates. St'át'imcets, a Salish language of British Columbia, is one such language, and as such, is typical of its language family and indeed the languages of its region (Demirdache & Matthewson 1994):

(1) use as a verb/predicate
    a. *qwatsáts-kacw*   event
        leave-2SG.NOM
        'you leave/left'
    b. *smúlhats-kacw*   object
        woman-2SG.NOM
        'you are a woman'

(2) use as noun/argument:
    a. *qwatsáts-∅*   *ti smúlhats-a*   object
        leave-3SG.ABS D woman-D
        'the woman left'
    b. *smúlhats-∅*   *ti qwatsáts-a*   event
        woman-3SG.ABS D leave-D
        'the leaver (one who left) is a woman'

14 Structural and semantic dependencies in word class

When used as verbs, roots occur clause initially and are cliticized by a set of subject and object marking pronominals, here *-(lh) kacw* for 2SG.NOM (St'át'imcets is morphologically split ergative, so first and second person pronouns are inflected on a nominative-accusative basis, while third person exhibits an ergative absolutive pattern; third person absolutive is realized by zero, but the ergative form is *–ás*). When used as nouns, the same lexemes occur in a DP headed by the determiner *ti -a*; arguments are typically realized as DPs in Salish languages. Even more striking is that lexemes of both semantic types can co-occur with such prototypical markers of verbs (going right back to Thrax's definition more than two thousand years ago) as tense clitics like *tu7* PAST and *kelh* FUT:

(3) event

    a. *qwatsáts-∅*   *tu7 kw-s*   *Gertie*
       leave-3SG.ABS PAST D-NOM PN

       'Gertie left'

    b. *qwatsáts-∅*   *kelh kw-s*   *Gertie*
       leave-3SG.ABS FUT D-NOM PN

       'Gertie will leave'

(4) object

    a. *plísmen*   *tu7 kw-s*   *Bill*
       policeman PAST D-NOM PN

       'Bill was a policeman'

    b. *plísmen*   *kelh kw-s*   *Bill*
       policeman FUT D-NOM PN

       'Bill will be a policeman'

I am not claiming that no noun-verb distinction can be found in St'át'imcets and other Salish languages. That depends on wider empirical findings and how one weighs conflicting evidence, and I do not regard this question as settled yet (see the discussion in Beck 2002; Davis & Matthewson 1999; Demirdache & Matthewson 1994; Jelinek & Demers 1994; Kinkade 1983; Kuipers 1968; van Eijk & Hess 1986). What I am simply doing here is exemplifying the pattern of flexibility in the language, and further pointing out that in the survey reported below, over 90% of all its roots exhibited flexibility.

Pretty much the same pattern is found in many Austronesian languages and is also widespread across this vast family, although the rate is variable, as will be reported below. I illustrate here with data from Tagalog, a language with a very high rate of flexibility:

(5) use as a verb/predicate
    a. *um-alis*   *ang lalake*   event
         AV.PERF-leave D   man
         'the man left'
    b. *titser*   *ang lalake*   object
         teacher D   man
         'the man is a teacher'

(6) use as a noun/argument:
    a. *lalake ang um-alis*   event
         man   D   AV.PERF-leave
         'the leaver (one who left) is a man'
    b. *lalake ang titser*   object
         man   D   teacher
         'the teacher is a man'

In Tagalog, both event denoting words like *umalis* 'left' and object denoting words like *titser* 'teacher' function freely as arguments, the usual function of nouns and the reason for their common grammatical categories like case, by being the complements of DPs headed by a set of case marking determiners; the one illustrated in (5) and (6) is *ang*, the nominative determiner. But they both are also equally good predicates, the function associated with verbs; predicates in Tagalog are indicated by their normal initial position in the clause. Predicates are commonly specified for a number of aspectual, voice and other categories by a rich set of affixes. Crucially these are not restricted to only event denoting roots; most object denoting roots also can co-occur with them: *abogado* 'lawyer', *magabogado* 'study to become a lawyer, engage a lawyer'; *tao* 'person', *ma-tao* 'populated'; *manok* 'chicken', *magmanok* 'raise chickens'; *ipis* 'cockroach', *ipis-in* 'be infested with cockroaches'. These cannot be claimed as verbalizing suffixes because they occur also on underived verbs like *mag-linis* 'to clean', *linis-in* 'be cleaned', *ma-nood* 'to watch'.

St'át'imcets and Tagalog share a number of structural traits, and these in fact facilitate the high rate of flexibility in these languages. There may be other structural patterns that some languages may have hit upon to facilitate high rates of

14 Structural and semantic dependencies in word class

flexibility (e.g. Mundari, Evans & Osada 2005), but that found in these two languages is crosslinguistically the most common, even accounting for languages like English. In languages like Latin the functions of arguments and predicates, prototypical uses of nouns and verbs, are built into the word forms themselves, into the inflections they take. But in languages like St'át'imcets, Tagalog and indeed English, this is not the case; rather these functions are indicated syntactically, not morphologically, and commonly phrasally, that is, there are phrasal functional categories like case and determiners to mark argument function and nouns and other functional categories like aspect or tense or agreement or just fixed syntactic constituent structure or perhaps a combination of these to mark predicate function and verbs. Predicate function is indicated by clause initial position and by the possibility of tense or aspect inflection in St'át'imcets and Tagalog, and also by subject agreement clitics in the former. Argument function is marked by being the complement of a determiner head in a DP in both languages (the theoretical model in which these phrase structures are cast is Lexical Functional Grammar; Bresnan 2001; the phrase structure may look different in other frameworks and even more so in dependency based frameworks, but the basic point here about heads being functional categories would still hold):

Figure 1: Favored structures for flexible languages

TAM indicates tense-aspect-mood inflection, IP indicates the projection of these inflections, and X any flexible lexeme. The phrase structure of a basic clause in both languages is identical and is shown in Figure 2.

But there is an interesting contrast as well between St'át'imcets and Tagalog: the direction of derivation, in other words, which of the two meanings, object denoting or event denoting corresponds to the unmarked form. In St'át'imcets it is event denoting, while in Tagalog, it is object denoting. Consider the data in Table 2.

The prefix *s-* in St'át'imcets marks words which are object denoting, but in no sense can it be claimed as a derivational affix that regularly outputs nouns from basic verbs, because probably the majority of object denoting words in the

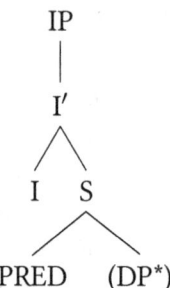

Figure 2: Austronesian/Salish phrase structure

Table 2: Direction of Derivation in St'át'imcets versus Tagalog (St'át'imcets data from Davis & Matthewson 1999).

St'át'imcets	Tagalog
7úqwa 'drink'	inom 'drinking'
s-úqwa 'a beverage'	um-imom 'drink'
núk'w7-am 'help'	tulong 'help'
s-núk'wa7 'friend'	tulung-an 'help someone'
cwil'-em 'seek'	bigay 'gift'
s-cwil'-em 'something sought'	mag-bigay 'give'
náq'w 'steal'	nakaw 'something stolen'
s-náq'w 'something stolen'	mag-nakaw 'steal'

language, derived or not, occur with it: *skuza* 'child', *sqáycw* 'man', *smúlhats* 'woman', *spzúza7* 'bird', *sqaxwá7* 'dog'. The point of the above examples is that in St'át'imcets, the root form has a verb-like event denoting meaning and the noun-like object denoting meaning is derived, but in Tagalog it is the opposite. This is most obviously brought out in the final examples of 'steal', 'something stolen'.

But even in languages with very high rates of flexibility, it is, as we shall see, not universal, and for the classical languages like Latin, the source of our contrasting categories of noun and verb, it is not the case that there is no flexibility (although there are certainly cases of languages with zero flexibility; this is common among the Papuan languages of mainland New Guinea). In Latin, about 10% of the lexemes of basic vocabulary in a survey I carried out with Johanna Nichols, me concentrating on Pacific languages, she on Eurasian and North American

14 Structural and semantic dependencies in word class

languages, turn out to be flexible, close to the mean crosslinguistically that we established for this feature, as in Table 3.

Table 3: Flexible categorization in Latin

		-or third declension	*-ē* second conjugation
(i)	stem form	*calor* 'warmth'	*calēre* 'be warm'
		↑	↑
(ii)	inflection	DECLENSION	CONJUGATION
		↑	↑
(iii)	syntax	N + CASE	V + TENSE
		↑	↑
(iv)	semantics	Subject (*ónoma*) +	PREDICATE (*rhêma*)
		(thing/object)	(event)

To measure rates of flexibility across languages, we drew up a list of nearly 200 basic vocabulary items and then carefully pored over grammars and dictionaries of languages to determine whether each word base was flexible or not. The list of words we used covered a wide range of semantic categories:

- Properties: *heat, cold, length, width, dry, red, black, big, good*
- Experiential states: *fear, anger, shame, hunger, happy, sad*
- Bodily activities: *cry, sweat, sneeze, laugh, sleep, pee, poo*
- Posture: *sit, sit down, stand, stand up, lie, lie down*
- Activities: *run, walk, swim, fly, shout, sing*
- Actions on objects: *eat, bite, tear, hit, cut, open, break, throw*
- Transfer: *give, buy, say, tell*
- Perception: *see, look at, hear, listen to, know, forget*
- Contact: *pour, spill, load, empty, fill*
- Weather: *rain, thunder, lightning*
- Body parts: *ear, eye, hand, tongue, tooth, bone, elbow, hair, blood*
- Environment: *sun, moon, water, fire, sand, earth*

William A. Foley

- Kin: *mother, father, child, sibling, spouse, name*
- Natural kinds: *dog, snake, fish, bird, pig, mouse, louse, ant, tree, leaf*
- Artifacts: *axe, spear, arrow, knife, house, broom, needle, string, clothing*

Flexibility was calculated as follows. A root was counted as inflexible either if 1. it had no derivational processes that shifted it from being object denoting or event denoting, or 2. any derivational affix which had such a shifting function was restricted to that use only and was never used on underived forms which had the same function as the derived form. Consider the following two entries from the corpus for Tagalog:

- 'snake': *ahas* 'snake'
- 'gone': *wala* 'not be, gone, extinct' *mawala* 'to be lost, to vanish, disappear' *mawalan, iwala* 'to lose something' *ikawala* 'to lose, cause one to lose something' *magwala* 'lose something from carelessness' *makawala* 'to miss, let slip by'/ 'to escape' *magpakawala, pakawala* 'to unbind, loosen, let free' *kawalan* 'want, deficiency' *pagkawala* 'disappearance'

ahas 'snake' is not flexible because it has no possible derived forms at all, never mind those which are event denoting. Note that this would not hold for English: *the road snaked its way around the mountain;* for English *snake* would count as flexible. *wala* 'gone, disappear' is also not flexible, because it is an event denoting predicate and all its derived forms, bar the last two, are also event denoting, predicating expressions. The only exceptions are the forms with the "nominalizing" prefix *pagka-, pagkawala* 'disappearance' and the circumfix *ka-...-an, ka-wala-(a)n* 'want, deficiency', but these also fail to qualify the root for flexibility. The prefix *pagka-* has the sole role of deriving event nominalizations and never occurs on underived object denoting words; **pagka-ahas* 'snaking' is impossible (the circumfix *ka-...-an* is more complex, the details of which I cannot go into here; it turns out that it occurs with both object and event denoting roots, see Schachter & Otanes 1972 on its functions). Now consider the following example of a flexible root in Tagalog:

- 'give': *bigay* 'gift' *magbigay/ibigay/bigyan* 'give someone something' *magbigayan* 'to compromise' *mamigay/ipamigay* 'to distribute, give out' *mapagbigayan* 'to accommodate someone in providing something'

The root *bigay* with no affixation at all means 'gift'. When it takes one of the voice affixes, it then takes on the meaning 'give' or some other closely semantically related event type. But these voice affixes cannot be claimed to be deriving a verb from a noun root (see Foley 2008 on this point), because voice is a necessary affixation for *any* event denoting predicating word, not just those seemingly derived from object denoting ones, as the voice affixes on all the event denoting forms for *wala* 'gone' above demonstrate. Hence *bigay* counts as a flexible lexeme, used either as 'gift' or 'give' (in the latter meaning requiring, as all event denoting predicating words do, voice affixation).

I surveyed fourteen Austronesian languages; I report on the data from seven of them in Figure 3:

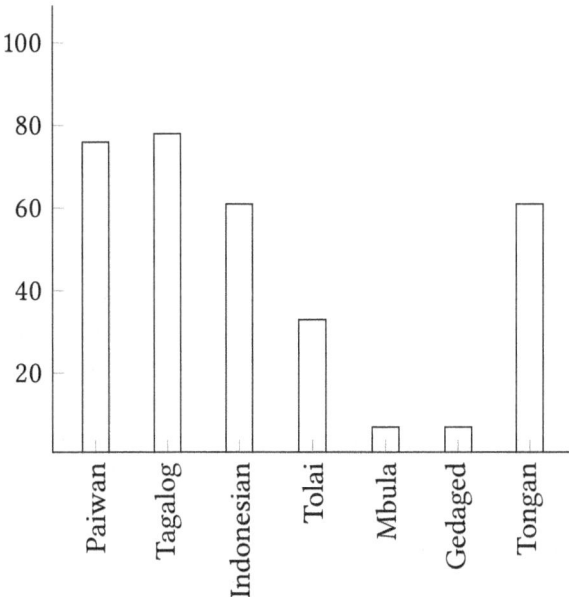

Figure 3: Rates of event/object flexibility of lexical roots between 7 Austronesian languages

Tolai, Mbula and Gedaged are all New Guinea region Austronesian languages of the Oceanic subgroup, and all of them have lower rates of flexibility than their sisters further afield. But even among these three, there is a significant difference in rates of flexibility; it is much lower in Mbula and Gedaged, approaching nil, than in Tolai. There are good sociolinguistic reasons for this. The contact with Papuan languages with their norm of zero flexibility has been much more intense for these two than it has been for Tolai. So intense indeed for Gedaged that its overall typology closely resembles its Papuan neighbors, with verb final clausal word order, postpositions and clause chaining constructions. These data strongly support the claim that flexibility is selected *against* in normal contact situations (those resulting in the genesis of pidgin and ultimately creole languages may be different). The mechanism by which language contact would lead to an increase or decrease in flexibility is not at this point entirely clear; more detailed research is needed. Is it piecemeal lexeme by lexeme as they are borrowed and either adapted or adapted to, importing a flexibility pattern for particular lexical items and then extending that to other items at a later stage through lexical diffusion? Or is it the case that speakers of the importing language abstract a general principle of flexibility or lack thereof from the source language and apply that to different lexical roots in their own language?

The contrastive situation between Tolai and Tongan is also remarkable. Tolai and Tongan like the other two New Guinea languages belong to the same Oceanic subgroup of Austronesian languages, and on archeological grounds, we know that the homeland of the proto-language of this subgroup was somewhere in the Bismarck Archipelago, the region where Tolai is spoken today. The ancestral language of Tongan like that of Tolai, not to mention Mbula and Gedaged, was spoken there. Note that the rate of flexibility of Tongan is the same as that of Indonesian much further to the west and generally closer to that of the languages spoken in the western region of the Austronesian family. The languages of the west belong to a number of different high order subgroups and typically have high rates of flexibility, so on standard assumptions of historical linguistics, we would regard the high rate in Tongan as a retention from its ancestral language. So the question arises why do we find such high retention in Tongan, but not in Tolai? Tolai is in the New Guinea region, but its flexibility rate is much higher than Mbula and Gedaged, and its overall typology is that of a relatively conservative Oceanic language. Its speakers are originally from New Ireland, an island where today almost exclusively Austronesian languages are spoken. That may be the case, but there has been very significant contact with Papuan languages in its history. The genetic data tell the story. The speakers of Austronesian languages originally migrated out of Southeast Asia, so there are certain genetic markers that are closely linked with them. Speakers of Papuan languages, on the other hand, have been in situ in New Guinea for a very long time, at least forty thousand years, so they too are correlated with certain genetic markers. If we compare the Y-chromosomal DNA, which is inherited in the male line, from the father, and mitochondrial DNA, which passes only through the female line, from the mother, for both Tolai and Tongan, we find a very interesting contrast (Table 4, Kayser et al. 2006).

Table 4: Proportion of Asian versus Papuan Y-chromosome and mDNA markers in Tolai-speaking and Tongan-speaking populations

	Tolai		Tongan	
	Asian	Papuan	Asian	Papuan
Y-chromosome DNA	5.3	94.7	41.4	55.2
mitochondrial DNA	29.4	70.6	92.3	7.7

Tolai speakers have been swamped by Papuan genes, an indication of heavy contact through interbreeding. The percentage of Papuan Y-chromosomal DNA in Tolai is particularly high, and this is a signal of a favored cultural pattern of Papuan men marrying into Tolai communities (Tolai society like that of Proto-Oceanic is matrilineal), though many Papuan speaking women also contributed to the Tolai gene pool. For Tongan the percentages of Y-chromosomal DNA is more equally balanced, indicating that the ancestors of Tongan speakers did interbreed with speakers of Papuan languages as they migrated through the New Guinea region on their way to Polynesia, but to a much lesser extent. This is to be expected, as their presence in the New Guinea region could not have lasted more than a few hundred years on current archeological evidence, while the ancestors of today's Tolai speakers have been there for three thousand years. But really remarkable are the percentages for mitochondrial DNA among Tongan speakers; it is almost exclusively of Asian origin. Part of this could be due to founder effects of small populations arriving in Polynesia, but not all. What it does tell us is that very few Papuan women entered the gene pool in the ancestral community. Papuan men commonly interbred with Austronesian women, but the reverse was very uncommon (again the matrilineal basis of early Oceanic society would have had a lot to do with this). This explains the preservation of the high flexibility rate in Tongan from Proto-Oceanic. There is much common wisdom in the term "mother tongue". Children were learning their language mainly from their mothers and other female relatives, and as these were Austronesian speakers and very rarely Papuan speakers, there was much less opportunity for the Papuan pattern to diffuse into ancestral Tongan.

Flexibility rates vary across the Austronesian languages surveyed. And even in languages with very high rates, such as those of the Philippines and Formosa, it is never the case that flexibility is universal; some lexemes strongly resist flexibility. But this is not random. It is tied to specific semantic categories. Consider Figure 4.

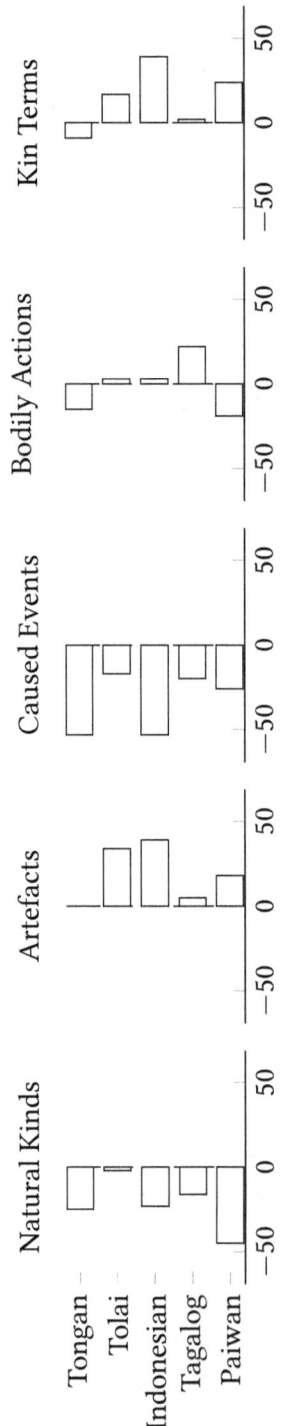

Figure 4: Flexibility Rates across Semantic Types

The central "zero" line below each semantic category heading represents the baseline for each language, that is, the mean rate of flexibility across all categories for that language (Mbula and Gedaged are omitted from this figure because their mean is so low that nothing meaningful can be said about the distribution across categories). Under each semantic category heading, values are given for the degree to which words in that category depart from the language's baseline flexibility value. Note that certain semantic categories are mostly above the baseline, kin terms and particularly artifacts, so that they have higher flexibility rates, while others, natural kinds and especially caused actions are always below the baseline, with lower flexibility rates. This gives us empirical evidence for something we could call "natural ontology". For certain semantic categories, humans are strongly cognitively predisposed to classify the words labeling them as denoting objects or events and thereby further predisposed to only provide them with a grammatical categorization consonant with the expression of an object or an event (Gentner & Boroditsky's 2001 cognitive dominance). In languages with a sharp noun-verb distinction this feeds directly into that grammatical and lexical distinction. But in languages not so organized, the question is more complex. What criterion do we have for saying we have a grammatical and lexical category of noun, if all clear members are restricted to denoting natural kinds? This is just erasing difference, largely due to a theoretical preference for assimilating languages to a shared base structure. I question the desirability of this move. We need to be more careful about the differences between languages before jumping to conclusions about similarities, largely on theoretical preference. If someone were to describe the difference between Latin and languages like St'át'imcets and Tagalog as one "of degree, not of kind", I would ask then empirically what would count as a difference in kind if not the data reported here? Or are our theories so poorly framed that we cannot recognize a difference in kind when we see one? Or even worse, that differences in kind simply don't exist by virtue of theoretical fiat?

References

Beck, David. 2002. *The typology of parts of speech systems: The markedness of adjectives.* New York: Routledge.

Bresnan, Joan. 2001. *Lexical-functional syntax.* Oxford: Blackwell.

Davis, Henry & Lisa Matthewson. 1999. On the functional determination of lexical categories. *Révue québécoise de linguistique* 27. 27–67.

Demirdache, Hamida & Lisa Matthewson. 1994. On the universality of syntactic categories. *Proceedings of the Northeastern Linguistics Society* 16. 79–93.

Evans, Nicholas D. & Toshiki Osada. 2005. Mundari: The myth of a language without word classes. *Linguistic Typology* 9. 351–390.

Foley, William A. 2008. The place of Philippine languages in a typology of voice systems. In P. Austin & S. Musgrave (eds.), *Voice and grammatical relations in Austronesian languages*, 22–44. Stanford: CSLI Publications.

Gentner, Dedre & Lera Boroditsky. 2001. Individuation, relativity and early word learning. In Melissa Bowerman & Steven C. Levinson (eds.), *Language acquisition and conceptual development*, 215–256. Cambridge: Cambridge University Press.

Jelinek, Eloise & Richard Demers. 1994. Predicates and pronominal arguments in Straits Salish. *Language* 70. 697–736.

Kayser, Manfred, Silke Brauer, Richard Cordaux, Amanda Casto, Oscar Lao, Lev A. Zhivotovsky, Claire Moyse-Faurie, Robb B. Rutledge, Wulf Schiefenhoevel, David Gil, Alice A. Lin, Peter A. Underhill, Peter J. Oefner, Ronald J. Trent & Mark Stoneking. 2006. Asian and Melanesian origins of Polynesians: mtDNA and Y chromosome gradients across the Pacific. *Molecular Biology and Evolution* 23(11). 2234–2244.

Kinkade, Dale. 1983. Salish evidence against the universality of 'noun' and 'verb'. *Lingua* 60. 25–40.

Kuipers, Aert Hendrik. 1968. The categories verb-noun and transitive-intransitive in English and Squamish. *Lingua* 21. 610–626.

Pawley, Andrew. 1994. Kalam exponents of lexical and semantic primitives. In C. Goddard & A. Wierzbicka (eds.), *Semantic and lexical universals : Theroy and empirical finding*, 410–439. Amsterdam: John Benjamins.

Riemer, Nick. 2010. *Introducing semantics*. Berkeley: University of California Press.

Schachter, Paul & Fe T. Otanes. 1972. *Tagalog reference grammar*. Berkeley: University of California Press.

van Eijk, Jan & Thom Hess. 1986. Noun and verb in Salishan. *Lingua* 69. 319–331.

Webster's New World College Dictionary. 2009. Boston, MA: Houghton Mifflin Harcourt.

Chapter 15

On the margins of language: Ideophones, interjections and dependencies in linguistic theory

Mark Dingemanse
MPI for Psycholinguistics, Nijmegen

In this chapter I explore some dependencies between form and function in ideophones and interjections, two word classes traditionally considered marginal in linguistics. It is as much about dependencies in language–how different aspects of linguistic structure causally relate to each other–as about dependencies in linguistics: how our theorising may be contingent on preconceived notions of what language is like.

Ideas about language influence how we carry out the scientific tasks of observation and explanation. Observation is the discovery of rules and regularities in language structure. It raises the question of methods. How do we design linguistic inquiry so as to facilitate accurate and meaningful observations? Explanation is the description of observations in causal terms. It raises the question of mechanisms: what entities and processes do we posit to account for the observations? The tools we use for observation and explanation are our methods and theories, which act like optical instruments. They enhance our powers of observation at one level of granularity (at the expense of others), and they bring certain phenomena in focus (defocusing others). Our views of language, including what we consider central and marginal, are shaped and constrained by these tools — and sometimes they may need recalibration.

There are several ways to characterise the margins of language. Here I distinguish between rara and marginalia. Rara are typologically exceptional phenomena which illustrate the fringes of linguistic diversity. Examples are nominal tense or affixation by place of articulation (Wohlgemuth & Cysouw 2010) Marginalia are typologically unexceptional phenomena that many linguists think can be ignored without harm to linguistic inquiry. They are not rare, but linguistic practice assigns them to the margin by consensus (Joseph 1997). Whereas rara can be objectively described as exceptional, marginalia are viewpoint-dependent. One goal of this chapter is to critically examine received notions of marginality by inspecting two supposed marginalia: ideophones and interjections.

1 Ideophones: morphosyntax can depend on mode of representation

Ideophones are words like *gorogoro* 'rolling' and *kibikibi* 'energetic' in Japanese, or *kɛlɛŋkɛlɛŋ* 'glittery' and *saaa* 'cool sensation' in Siwu, a Kwa language of Ghana. They can be defined as marked words that depict sensory imagery: words whose marked forms invite iconic interpretations and evoke sensory meanings. They appear to be uncommon in standard average European languages, which has led some scholars to assume that "the number of pictorial, imitative, or onomatopoetic nonderived words in any language is vanishingly small" (Newmeyer 1992: 758). Typological evidence shows that these words are in fact common across the world's languages and that they number well into the thousands in many of them (Dingemanse & Akita 2016).

Much research on ideophones has focused on their striking forms, with deviant phonotactics and distinctive prosody vying for attention. Their morphosyntactic behaviour has received less consideration, as a common view is that ideophones by definition have no syntax (Childs 1994). However, that simple statement conceals an interesting puzzle. A basic insight of linguistic typology is that lexical classes and their morphosyntactic realisation are best described in language-specific terms (Croft 2001). There is little reason to assume that what we call a "noun" for comparative purposes will show the same morphosyntactic behaviour in unrelated languages. Indeed, precisely because the structural facts can be so different across languages, comparative concepts tend to have a semantic basis (Haspelmath 2010). Ideophones are different. Important aspects of their form and function appear to be predictable across languages.

Ideophones typically display a great degree of syntactic independence. They tend to occur at the edge of the utterance, unburdened by morphology and not deeply embedded in the syntactic structure of the clause. In the Siwu example below, the ideophone *pɔkɔsɔɔ* 'carefully' appears in utterance-final position and is syntactically optional: the utterance would be well-formed without it.

(1) iyɔ nɛ ɔti   kere a-à-|ti   ↑pɔkɔsɔɔɔɔ↑{falsetto} |GESTURE
    so TP sieving just you-FUT-sieve IDPHslow/easy

  'Then you'll just be sieving ↑pɔkɔsɔɔɔɔ↑ [carefully]'
  ((GESTURE: two-handed demonstration of gently jiggling a sieve))

Constructions like this are found in many languages of the world. Why would ideophones show similar patterns of morphosyntactic independence across unrelated languages? A promising explanation is that ideophones in such cases are an instance of showing rather than saying, depictions rather than descriptions. Just as white space separates images from text on a page, so the syntactic freedom of ideophones helps us to see them as depictive performances in otherwise mostly descriptive utterances (Kunene 1965). What we see here is the encounter of two distinct and partly incommensurable methods of communication: the discrete, arbitrary, descriptive system represented by ordinary words, and the gradient, iconic, depictive system represented by ideophones. These two systems place different requirements on the material use of speech, yet both are part of one linearly unfolding speech stream. The morphosyntactic independence of ideophones may be a solution to this linearisation problem.

What kind of evidence could support this proposal? One clue for the depictive nature of ideophones is that they tend to be produced with prosodic foregrounding: features of delivery that make the ideophone stand out from the surrounding material. Thus in the Siwu example above, the ideophone *pɔkɔsɔɔ* 'carefully' is prosodically foregrounded by means of markedly higher pitch (↑) and falsetto phonation. Further underlining their depictive nature, ideophones are also more susceptible to expressive modification than ordinary words, often showing iconic resemblances between form and meaning. Additionally, they are often–as in the example above–produced together with iconic gestures (Nuckolls 1996).

Corpus data can provide a natural laboratory to test the dependency more directly. In many languages, ideophones do in fact participate in sentential syntax to varying degrees. A common enough response is to ignore this: we know that ideophones are supposed to have no syntax, most data appear to confirm this, so we discount the few remaining exceptions. To do so is to accept a preconceived notion of ideophones as marginal. A more interesting question is what happens when ideophones do show greater morphosyntactic integration.

What happens is that we find an inverse relation between prosodic foregrounding and morphosyntactic integration. Ideophones that are more deeply integrated in the structure of the clause lose their prosodic foregrounding. In example 2 from Siwu, the same ideophone *pɔkɔsɔɔ* appears as an adjectival modifier in a noun phrase *ira pɔkɔsɔ-à* 'easy thing'. It carries the adjectival suffix -à and is not foregrounded or expressively modified in any way.

(2) a-bu   sɔ   ira   pɔkɔsɔ-à   i-de ngbe:
    you-think that thing IDPH.easy/slow-ADJ it-be this:Q
    'You think this here is an easy thing?'

Examples like this can be multiplied, and all show the same interaction: syntactic freedom and prosodic foregrounding go hand in hand, and the more integrated the ideophone is, the less likely it is to undergo foregrounding. The interaction works out essentially the same way for ideophones across a wide range of languages (Dingemanse & Akita 2016). The tell-tale signs of depiction that occur when ideophones are morphosyntactically independent all disappear when ideophones lose their freedom and are assimilated to become more like normal words. So the dependency looks like this:

(3) *Morphosyntax can depend on mode of representation.*
The morphosyntactic freedom of ideophones across languages is causally dependent on the fact that ideophones inhabit a depictive mode of representation.

The marked morphosyntactic profile of ideophones receives a unified explanation. Discovering the causal mechanism requires abandoning the assumption that ideophones are always marginal, and accepting that explanations of morphosyntactic behaviour can come from outside morphosyntax. A semiotic account provides the most likely cause, and close attention to corpus data helps solidify it.

2 Interjections: form can depend on interactional ecology

Interjections are words like *Ouch!*, *Oh.* and *Huh?* in English, or *Adjei!* 'Ouch!' *Ah* 'Oh.' and *Ã?* 'Huh?' in Siwu. They can be defined as conventional lexical forms which are monomorphemic and typically constitute an utterance of their own (Wilkins 1992). To the extent that interjections constitute their own utterances, they have little to do with other elements of sentences or with inflectional or derivational morphology, so they could be justifiably called marginal. If we follow scholarly traditions that take the sentence as the main unit of analysis, that might be all there is to say.

Yet utterances, whether they consist of simple interjections or complex sentences, virtually never occur in isolation. They are responsive to prior utterances or elicit responses in turn; and as decades of work in conversation analysis and interactional linguistics have shown, they do so in highly ordered, normatively regulated ways (Schegloff 2007; Selting & Couper-Kuhlen 2001). As every bit of language is ultimately socially transmitted, the structure of conversation forms the evolutionary landscape for linguistic items. How does language adapt to this landscape? What are the constraints and selective pressures it imposes? To make

15 On the margins of language

these questions tractable, it is useful to take one bit of conversational structure and consider its properties in detail.

Consider the interjection English *Huh?*, used when one has not caught what someone just said. This interjection, along with other practices for initiating repair, fulfills an important role in maintaining mutual understanding in the incessant flow of interaction that is at the heart of human social life. At this level of granularity, the interjection is far from marginal — in fact it is right where the action is. Here are two simplified transcripts from conversations recorded in Ghana and Laos. A word equivalent in form and function to English *Huh?* is the central pivot in the sequence, signaling a problem in a prior turn and inviting a redoing in the next. This may seem a trivial operation, especially since we do it so often—but therein lies the crux: without items like this, our conversations would be constantly derailed.

(4) a. Siwu (Kwa, Ghana;)
    A *Mama sɔ ba.*
        'Mama says "come"!'
    B *ã:*
        'Huh?'
    A *Mama sɔ ba.*
        'Mama says "come"!'
b. Lao (Tai-Kadai, Laos; courtesy of Nick Enfield)
    A *nòòj4 bòò1 mii2 sùak4 vaa3 nòòj4*
        'Noi, don't you have any rope, Noi?'
    B **haa2**
        'Huh?'
    A *bòò1 mii2 sùak4 vaa3*
        'Don't you have any rope?'

Comparative work on communicative repair in dozens of spoken languages reveals a striking fact. The interjection occuring in this interactional environment always has a very similar shape: a monosyllable with questioning prosody and all articulators in near-neutral position (Dingemanse, Torreira & Enfield 2013). And this is not the only interjection of this kind. In language after language, a highly effective set of streamlined interjections contributes to the smooth running of the interactional machinery. Other examples of interjections that fulfil important interactional functions and that appear to be strongly similar across languages include *oh* and *ah* (signaling a change in state of knowledge), *mm* (signaling a pass on claiming the conversational floor), and *um/uh* (signaling an upcoming delay in speaking).

It may be tempting to posit that these words are simply instinctive grunts like sighs or sneezes, explaining their cross-linguistic similarity at one blow. However, this proposal merely shifts the question and wrongly assumes that biological adaptation offers a simpler explanation than cultural adaptation. (The survival value of sighs and sneezes is fairly straightforward; much less so for this range of interjections.) A more parsimonious proposal, worked out in detail for *Huh?* in Dingemanse, Torreira & Enfield (2013), is that the interactional environment in which these items occur may provide, for each of them, a distinct set of selective pressures–for minimality, salience, contrast, or other adaptive properties–that squeezes them into their most optimal shape. The resulting paradigm of words may come to have certain universal properties by means of a mechanism of convergent cultural evolution. So the dependency is as follows:

(5) *Form can depend on interactional ecology.* Strong and unexpected similarities in basic discourse interjections across unrelated languages are causally dependent on their appearance in common interactional environments where they are shaped by the same selective pressures.

Interjections are often cast as the blunt monosyllabic fragments of the most primitive and emotional forms of language. Comparative research on social interaction is fast undoing this view, and shows how at least some interjections may be adaptive communicative tools, culturally evolved for the job of keeping our social interactional machinery in good repair.

3 Discussion

About 150 years ago, influential Oxford linguist Max Müller proclaimed of imitative words that "they are the playthings, not the tools, of language", and almost in the same breath pooh-poohed interjections with the slogan "language begins where interjections end" (Müller 1861: 346, 352). Such statements helped shape a scholarly climate in which it is easy to take for granted that we already know where the most important questions about language lie. Yet with linguistics and neighbouring fields constantly finding new sources of data, methods and insights, it is natural every once in a while to take a step back and question received wisdom.

Ideophones and interjections are similar in that they share a degree of syntactic independence, one basis for portraying them as marginal. However, as we have seen, beneath this superficial similarity lie different semiotic functions and distinct causal forces. Ideophones are syntactically independent because they inhabit a mode of representation that is different from the remainder of the speech signal. Their freedom helps foreground their special status as depictive signs. From ideophones we learn that the morphosyntax of linguistic items may depend at least in part on mode of representation. Interjections are syntactically independent because their main business is not carried out within utterances but at other levels of linguistic structure. Their patterning is best analysed in relation to their discursive and interactional context. From interjections we learn that the form of linguistic items may depend at least in part on interactional ecology.

Linguistic discovery is viewpoint-dependent, as are our ideas about what is marginal and what is central in language. The challenges posed by the supposed marginalia discussed here provide some useful pointers for widening our field of view. Ideophones challenge us to take a fresh look at language and consider how it is that our communication system combines multiple modes of representation. Interjections challenge us to extend linguistic inquiry beyond sentence level, and remind us that language is social-interactive at core. Marginalia are not obscure, exotic phenomena that can be safely ignored. They represent opportunities for innovation and invite us to keep pushing the edges of the science of language.

Acknowledgements

I thank Kimi Akita, Nick Enfield and Felix Ameka for being interlocutors on these topics over the last few years. I gratefully acknowledge funding from the Max Planck Society for the Advancement of Science and an NWO Veni grant.

References

Childs, G. Tucker. 1994. African ideophones. In Leanne Hinton, Johanna Nichols & John J. Ohala (eds.), *Sound symbolism*, 178–204. Cambridge: Cambridge University Press.

Croft, William. 2001. *Radical construction grammar*. Oxford: Oxford University Press.

Dingemanse, Mark & Kimi Akita. 2016. An inverse relation between expressiveness and grammatical integration: On the morphosyntactic typology of ideophones, with special reference to Japanese. *Journal of Linguistics* FirstView. 1–32. DOI:10.1017/S002222671600030X

Dingemanse, Mark, Francisco Torreira & N. J. Enfield. 2013. Is 'Huh?' a universal word? Conversational infrastructure and the convergent evolution of linguistic items. *PLOS ONE* 8(11). DOI:10.1371/journal.pone.0078273

Haspelmath, Martin. 2010. Comparative concepts and descriptive categories in crosslinguistic studies. *Language* 86(3). 663–687.

Joseph, Brian D. 1997. On the linguistics of marginality: The centrality of the periphery. *Chicago Linguistic Society* 33. 197–213.

Kunene, Daniel P. 1965. The ideophone in Southern Sotho. *Journal of African Languages* 4. 19–39.

Müller, Max. 1861. *Lectures on the science of language. Vol. 1*. London: Longmans, Green.

Newmeyer, Frederick J. 1992. Iconicity and generative grammar. *Language* 68(4). 756–796.

Nuckolls, Janis B. 1996. *Sounds like life: Sound-symbolic grammar, performance, and cognition in Pastaza Quechua*. New York: Oxford University Press.

Schegloff, Emanuel A. 2007. *Sequence organization in interaction: A primer in conversation analysis*. Cambridge: Cambridge University Press.

Selting, Margret & Elizabeth Couper-Kuhlen (eds.). 2001. *Studies in interactional linguistics*. Amsterdam: John Benjamins.

Wilkins, David P. 1992. Interjections as deictics. *Journal of Pragmatics* 18(2-3). 119–158.

Wohlgemuth, Jan & Michael Cysouw (eds.). 2010. *Rara & Rarissima: Documenting the fringes of linguistic diversity*. Berlin; New York: De Gruyter Mouton.

Name index

Abels, Klaus, 30
Adger, David, 32, 33
Aikhenvald, Alexandra Y., 2
Akita, Kimi, 196, 198
Ambridge, Ben, 90, 111
Anderson, Debora K., 88
Apresjan, Juri. D., 175
Arbib, Michael, 63
Arcuili, Joanne, 85
Aristar, Anthony R., 15, 136
Armstrong, David F., 63
Aronoff, Mark, 64, 65, 73, 124
Asaridou, Salomi, 43
Atkinson, Quentin, 129
Austin, J. L., 3

Baayen, R. Harald, 125
Bailey, Karl G., 55
Baker, Mark, 23, 24, 27
Bally, Charles, 149
Baltaxe, Christiane A. M., 102
Battison, Robbin, 66
Battistella, Edwin, 163, 166
Beck, David, 183
Beckman, Jill, 160
Bernstein, Basil, 78
Bever, Thomas G., 55
Bickel, Balthasar, 23, 122, 142
Bickerton, Derek, 63
Blackmore, Susan, 137
Blasi, Damián E., 43, 45, 122, 125, 129, 130, 134, 135

Blevins, Juliette, 18, 168
Blust, Robert, 168
Blythe, Joe, 4
Bock, J. Kathryn, 53
Bolhuis, Johan, 63
Boroditsky, Lera, 193
Borovsky, Arielle, 56
Botha, Rudolf P., 54
Brentari, Diane, 66
Bresnan, Joan, 185
Brock, Jon, 85, 88
Bromberger, Sylvain, 141
Brown, Penelope, 86
Brunner, Jana, 47
Burling, Robbins, 54
Bush, Jeffrey O., 45
Butcher, Andy, 46
Bybee, Joan, 5, 13, 18
Byrne, James, 149

Caldwell-Harris, Catharine L., 42, 43
Callaghan, Tara C., 86
Campbell, Lyle, 122
Carpenter, Kathie, 174
Carpenter, Malinda, 85–87, 91
Carroll, Sean B., 45
Carstairs-McCarthy, Andrew, 63
Caruana, Nathan, 88
Chandrasekaran, Bharath, 42, 132
Chater, Nick, 46, 53–58
Chatterji, Suniti Kumar, 12
Cheng, Patricia W., 121

Name index

Childs, G. Tucker, 196
Chomsky, Noam, 27, 53, 63
Christiansen, Morten H., 46, 53–58
Christophe, Anne, 72
Cinque, Guglielmo, 30, 150
Clark, Herbert H., 3, 53
Claudi, Ulrike, 13
Clements, George Nick, 142, 144
Cochran, Anne, 101
Cohen, Marcel, 15
Cohn, Abigail, 144, 145
Collins, Jeremy, 130, 135
Comrie, Bernard, 9, 119
Corballis, Michael C., 54, 63
Cornish, Hannah, 25, 41
Couper-Kuhlen, Elizabeth, 198
Cowan, Hendrik Karel Jan, 162
Cowan, Nelson, 54
Cowie, Fiona, 53
Cramon-Taubadel, N. von, 45
Crane, Thera Marie, 152
Cristofaro, Sonia, 13, 16, 18
Croft, William, 5, 9, 17, 26, 196
Crothers, John, 160
Crowley, Terry, 152
Cruse, D. Alan, 5
Cruttenden, Alan, 134
Culbertson, Jennifer, 25, 27, 29, 32, 33
Cyffer, Norbert, 11
Cysouw, Michael, 24, 30, 119, 195

Dachkovsky, Svetlana, 66, 67
Dale, Rick, 123
Darwin, Charles, 63
Dasher, Richard B., 13
Daumé III, Hal, 119, 122
Davis, Henry, 183, 186
Dawkins, Richard, 136

de Lacy, Paul, 101, 160–163, 165
de Reuse, Willem J. with the assistance of Phillip Goode, 162
Debruyne, Frans, 47
Dediu, Dan, 24, 41–45, 47, 56, 129–132
Demers, Richard, 183
Demirdache, Hamida, 182, 183
DePaolis, Rory A., 91
Dickins, Thomas E., 17
Ding, Nai, 54
Dingemanse, Mark, 150, 196, 198–200
Disner, Sandra, 101, 160
Dixon, Michael J., 45
Dixon, R. M. W., 2, 9
Doble, Marion, 102
Donegan, Patricia, 129
Dowman, Mike, 41
Dryer, Matthew S., 24, 26, 27, 30, 31, 43, 113, 134, 142
Dumestre, Gaston, 144
Dunbar, Robin I. M., 54
Duncan, Otis Dudley, 124
Dunn, Michael, 134
Dupoux, Emmanuel, 72

Edelman, Shimon, 56
Edmondson, Jerold A., 102
Eells, Ellery, 120
Elman, Jeffrey L., 56
Emmorey, Karen, 63
Enfield, N. J., 3, 5, 55, 87, 130, 132, 136, 172–174, 199, 200
Evans, Nicholas D., 4, 185
Evans, Patrick, 131
Everett, Caleb, 43, 45, 122, 129, 130, 134, 135

Fay, Nicolas, 25

Name index

Fels, Sidney, 44
Ferguson, Charles A., 143
Fernald, Anne, 56, 91
Ferraro, Vittoria, 55
Ferreira, Fernanda, 55
Ferreira, Victor S., 2
Fitch, W. Tecumseh, 45, 63
Fitelson, Branden, 118, 121
Foley, William A., 103, 151, 152, 189
Foss, Donald J., 142
François, Alexandre, 99, 102
Fuchs, Susanne, 47
Fudeman, Kirsten, 124
Fullwood, Michelle A., 150, 151

Gabelentz, Georg van der, 149
Gentner, Dedre, 193
Gibson, Edward, 24, 119
Giedd, Jay, 45
Gil, David, 43, 78
Givón, Talmy, 68, 73
Gliga, Teodora, 91
Glymour, Clark N, 125
Goddard, Cliff, 177
Goldwater, Sharon, 25
Golinkoff, Roberta, 53
Grace, George W., 78
Green, Jonathan, 89
Greenberg, Joseph H., 2, 9, 14, 23, 24, 53, 113, 119, 142, 143, 146, 149
Griffiths, Thomas L., 41
Guasti, Maria-Theresa, 72
Guy, Greg, 168

Haberl, Katharina, 87
Hale, Kenneth L., 2
Hall, Daniel Currie, 165
Halle, Morris, 141

Haspelmath, Martin, 9, 23, 43, 142, 196
Hasson, Uri, 54
Hauser, Marc, 63
Hawkins, John, 113
Hawkins, John A., 23, 27, 53
Hayes, Bruce, 160
Healy, Christina, 66, 67
Heine, Bernd, 13, 14, 57
Hess, Thom, 183
Hildebrandt, Kristine, 142
Hirsh-Pasek, Kathy, 53
Hitchcock, Christopher, 118, 121
Hockett, Charles F., 65, 68, 144
Hoff, Bernd, 164
Honey, Christopher J., 54
Hudson Kam, Carla, 28
Hume, Elizabeth, 159, 160
Hurford, James, 41, 56
Hurtado, Nereyda, 91
Hyman, Larry M., 141, 145, 151, 152
Hünnemeyer, Friederike, 13

Ibbotson, Paul, 91
Iemmolo, Giorgio, 12
Illari, Phyllis McKay, 39
Israel, Assaf, 71

Jackendoff, Ray, 53, 63, 68, 75, 78
Jaeger, T. Florian, 122
Jelinek, Eloise, 183
Jenkins, James J., 142
Jiang, Rulang, 45
Johnson, Mark, 25
Johnson, Robert E., 66
Jones, Emily J.H., 89
Joseph, Brian D., 195
Jusczyk, Peter, 72

Name index

Kakati, Banikanta, 12
Kalisch, Markus, 125
Karmiloff-Smith, Annette, 90
Kashube, Dorothy, 143
Kaufman, Terrence, 122
Kayser, Manfred, 133, 190
Kellogg, S. H., 2
Kemmerer, David, 63
Keren-Portnoy, Temar, 91
Kerr, Allen D., 172
Kinkade, Dale, 183
Kiparsky, Paul, 145
Kirby, Simon, 25, 41, 56
Klein, Wolfgang, 78
Kolodny, Oren, 56
Kuipers, Aert Hendrik, 183
Kunene, Daniel P., 197
Kuteva, Tania, 57
Kutsch Lojenga, Constance, 11
Kuwana, Yasutomo, 150

Ladd, D. Robert, 24, 41–43, 45, 129–132
Ladefoged, Peter, 101
Lammert, Adam, 45
Lass, Roger, 2
Legendre, Géraldine, 27, 29, 32, 33
Lehmann, Winfred P., 150
Lepic, Ryan, 71
Leslau, Wolf, 15
Levinson, Steven C., 47, 87
Lichtenberk, Frantisek, 164
Liddell, Scott K., 66
Lieberman, Phillip, 54
Lieven, Elena, 86, 90, 91, 111
Lightfoot, David, 24
Lillo-Martin, Diane, 66
Liszkowski, Ulf, 86
Liu, Fan, 45

Lloyd, John E., 44
Lombardi, Linda, 160
Lotem, Arnon, 56
Lupyan, Gary, 123
Luuk, Erkki, 110

MacNeilage, Peter F., 63
Maddieson, Ian, 41, 43, 101, 131, 146, 162, 167
Malt, Barbara C., 3
Mandel, Mark, 66
Matthews, Stephen, 129
Matthewson, Lisa, 182, 183, 186
McCauley, Stewart M., 55, 56
McCloskey, James, 23
McMahon, April M. S., 17
Mehler, Jacques, 72, 150
Meir, Irit, 64, 65, 71, 73, 78
Mekel-Bobrov, Nitzan, 131, 132
Merlan, Francesca, 97, 103, 110, 111
Milin, Petar, 125
Miller, George Armitage, 54
Mithun, Marianne, 13
Moisik, Scott R., 44
Moll, Henrick, 87
Moravcsik, Edith, 147
Moravcsik, Edith A., 143
Moreton, Elliott, 25
Mossé, Fernand, 11
Mpaayei, J. Tompo Ole, 148
Müller, Max, 200

Nagell, Katherine, 86, 87
Narayanan, Shrikanth, 45
Nater, Hank F., 147
Neeleman, Ad, 30
Nespor, Marina, 66–68, 72, 73, 150
Newmeyer, Frederick J., 23, 63, 196
Newport, Elissa L., 28, 29

Name index

Nichols, Johanna, 9, 119, 142
Nitz, Eike, 11
Noens, Ilse, 87
Norbury, Courtenay, 88
Nordhoff, Sebastian, 11
Nuckolls, Janis B., 197
Nunberg, Geoffrey D., 175

Odden, David, 164
Olson, Mike, 151, 152
Osada, Toshiki, 185
Osu, Sylvester, 144
Otanes, Fe T., 188
Over, Harriet, 91
Ozonoff, Sally, 89
Özyürek, Aslı, 2
O'Grady, William, 53

Padden, Carol, 64, 71, 73
Pagliuca, William, 13
Pater, Joe, 25
Patson, Nikole D., 55
Pawley, Andrew, 97, 179
Payne, Doris L., 162
Payne, Thomas E., 162
Pearl, Judea, 39, 124
Perdue, Clive, 78
Perfors, Amy, 56
Perkins, Revere, 13
Perrier, Pascal, 47
Pfau, Roland, 66
Piantadosi, Steven T, 24, 119
Pickering, Martin J., 2
Pine, Julian, 90
Pinker, Steven, 53, 68
Plank, Frans, 148–150, 153
Praveen, B. N., 45
Precoda, Kristin, 146
Prizant, Barry M., 87

Proctor, Michael, 45

Quer, Josep, 66

Radloff, Vasily, 148
Ramscar, Michael, 125
Remez, Robert E., 54
Rice, Keren, 159, 160, 165
Riemer, Nick, 182
Roberts, Jacqueline, 88
Roberts, Seán G., 24, 42, 43, 45, 122, 129, 130, 134, 135
Rumsey, Alan, 97, 103, 110, 111
Ruskin, Ellen, 88
Russo, Federica, 39

Samek-Lodovici, Vieri, 30
Sandler, Wendy, 63–67, 70–77
Sapir, Edward, 12
Schachter, Paul, 188
Schegloff, Emanuel A., 198
Scheines, Richard, 125
Schiering, René, 142
Schuh, Russell, 164
Scott-Phillips, Thomas C., 17
Seiler, Walter, 14
Selkirk, Elizabeth, 68, 73
Selting, Margret, 198
Shalizi, Cosma Rohilla, 125
Shaw, Patricia, 147
Sherman, Donald, 2
Shukla, Mohinish, 150
Sidnell, Jack, 3
Sigman, Marian, 88, 89
Siller, Michael, 88, 89
Simon, Herbert A., 4
Simpson, Jane, 4
Singleton, Jenny L., 28
Smith, Adam, 4

Name index

Smith, Jennifer L., 150
Smith, Kenny, 25, 41, 56
Smith-Stark, Thomas C., 122
Smolensky, Paul, 25, 27, 29, 32, 33
Song, Jae Jung, 141
Spirtes, Peter, 125
Stampe, David, 129
Stavness, Ian, 44
Steddy, Sam, 30
Steinbach, Markus, 66
Stephens, Greg J., 54
Steriade, Donca, 160
Stokoe, William C., 63, 66
Stoll, Sabine, 86
Studdert-Kennedy, Michael, 54

Taylor, Walter G., 54
Tenenbaum, Joshua B., 56
Thomason, Sarah Grey, 2
Thompson, D'Arcy Wentworth, 5
Tokizaki, Hisao, 150
Tomasello, Michael, 2, 56, 85–87, 91
Torreira, Francisco, 199, 200
Traill, Anthony, 44
Traugott, Elizabeth C., 13
Traunmüller, Hartmut, 44
Travis, Lisa, 27
Trubetzkoy, Nikolai S., 163
Trudgill, Peter, 168
Tucker, Archibald Norman, 148
Tukumu, Simon Nsielanga, 152

Vajda, Edward, 141
van Eijk, Jan, 183
van Oven, Mannis, 133
Verkerk, Annemarie, 122
Vihman, Marilyn M., 91
Vogel, Irene, 68, 72, 73

Wan, Ming Wai, 89
Wang, William S., 56
Warren, Richard M., 54
Watters, James, 165
West, Stuart A., 17
Wetherby, Amy, 87
Whaley, Lindsay J., 141
Wilbur, Ronnie B., 68
Wilcox, Sherman E., 63
Wilkins, David P., 198
Williamson, Jon, 39
Wilson, Colin, 25
Winters, James, 122, 129
Wittenberg, Eva, 75, 78
Wohlgemuth, Jan, 195
Woll, Bencie, 66
Wong, Patrick C. M., 42, 132
Wonnacott, Elizabeth, 41, 56
Wray, Alison, 78

Yip, Moira, 41
Yiu, Suki, 129
You, M., 45

Zelditch, Miriam Leah, 47
Zheng, Jing, 42, 132
Ziwo, Lama, 102

Language index

Afro-Asiatic, 134, 135, 164
Al-Sayyid Bedouin Sign Language, 65
Alacalufan, 162
Alawa, 164
Altaic, 153
Amharic, 15
Ancient Greek, 181, 182
Arabic, 76, 135
Arekuna, 164
Assamese, 12
Athabaskan, 153, 162, 165
Atlantic-Congo, 124
Australian, 113, 177
Austro-Asiatic, 129, 134
Austronesian, 102, 164, 165, 168, 180, 183, 186, 189–191

Bambara, 144
Bantu, 43, 135, 152, 153
Barasana, 143–145
Basari, 164
Bella Coola, 147
Bengali, 12
Berber, 40

Cantonese, 135
Carib, 164
Cariban, 162, 165
Chadic, 164
Chinese, 135
Cushitic, 43

Dahalo, 43
Doutai, 143, 144

Ebrié, 143–145
Ecuador Quichua, 164
Ekari, 102
English, 10, 27, 29, 32, 33, 76, 91, 99, 144, 145, 150, 179, 185, 188, 198
Enita, 104–107, 109, 111
Estonian, 2

Fe'fe'-Bamileke, 153
Finnish, 164, 165
Finno-Ugric, 164, 165

Gedaged, 189, 190, 193
German, 171
Germanic, 150
Greek, 180, 181

Hadza, 43
Hindi, 2
Hiw, 102
Hmong-Mien, 135

Iban, 144
Ijo, 152
Imonda, 13, 14
Indo-European, 135, 153
Indonesian, 190, 192
Israeli Sign Language, 66, 67, 76
Italian, 171

Language index

Japanese, 150, 165, 196

Kabardian, 145
Kanuri, 11
Khoekhoe, 40
Khoisan, 14, 43
Kikuyu, 33
Kilivila, 165
Kimi, 201
Kopia, 104
Koy, 103
Koyukon, 165
Ku Waru, 97–104, 109, 110, 112, 113
Kwa, 144, 196, 199
Kxa, 43
Kxoe, 14

Laghuu, 102
Lao, 172–178, 199
Latin, 180–182, 185, 186, 193
Luganda, 153

Maasai, 146, 148
Macushi, 165
Manam, 164
Mandarin, 136
Marshallese, 145
Mbula, 189, 190, 193
Miya, 164
Mussau, 165, 168
Músa, 11

Ngiti, 11
Niger-Congo, 130, 134, 135, 164
Nilo-Saharan, 135
Nimboran, 164
Num, 26–28, 30–34
Nyangi, 146
Nzadi, 152

Oceanic, 152, 189–191

Paiwan, 192
Panare, 162
Papuan, 97, 102, 103, 162, 164, 165, 180, 186, 189–191

Qawasqar, 162
Quechuan, 164

Romance, 164, 165

Saami, 164
Salish, 180, 182, 183, 186
San Carlos Apache, 162
Sandawe, 43
Selayarese, 165
Semitic, 153
Sentani, 162, 164, 165
Sinhala, 11
Sino-Tibetan, 130, 134, 135
Siwu, 196–199
Soti, 104
Southern Paiute, 12
Spanish, 164, 165
    Buenos Aires Spanish, 164
St'át'imcets, 182–186, 193
Swahili, 135

Tagalog, 184–186, 188, 192, 193
Tai-Kadai, 172, 199
Thai, 3, 174
Tibeto-Burman, 102
Tlachichilko Tepehua, 164
Tok Pisin, 99–101
Tolai, 189–192
Tongan, 190, 191
Totonacan, 165
Trans-New Guinea, 97, 102
Tu, 43, 44

Language index

Turkish, 150

Uralic, 153, 164

Wapi, 105

Xhosa, 43

Yimas, 179

Zulu, 43

!Xóõ, 44

Subject index

absolute universals, 147
acoustics, 44, 47, 54
acquisition, 1, 53–56, 111, 112
affective meanings, 43
African languages, 129, 151
agglutination, 153
alignment, 182
archeology, 190
areal relations, 26
arguments, 110, 182, 185
artificial language learning, 25, 26, 28, 29, 34
ASPM, 130, 131
Austin's ladder, 3
Autism Spectrum Disorder, 85, 87–90
automacity, 72
autonomous syntax, 65, 73, 90

baby talk register, 100, 102, 111, 112
biases, 5, 25, 27–30, 33, 55
    soft, 33
    weak, 41, 42, 45
bilingualism, 132
biological adaptation, 199
biological inheritance, 86, 90
biomechanical modelling, 44
borrowing, 43, 44

causal strength, 117, 121
causality, 1, 3, 117, 118
causal chains, 45

children's speech, 104, 109
chunk-and-pass processing, 54, 55
classifiers, 71, 171–173
clicks, 43, 44
climate, 41, 43, 134
Co-occurrence patterns, 14
cognition, 5, 117, 119
comparative typology, 101, 112
compensation, 47
complementizers, 75
computer models, 41, 42, 47
concurrent systems, 171, 172, 177
conditionals, 75
constituent order, 24, 34, 120, 129
constructional diffusion, 56
context dependent, 13
context-driven, 12
conventionalization, 4, 5, 65, 72
conversational analysis, 198
coreference, 76
corpus data, 197
cultural adaptation, 129, 199
cultural evolution, 23, 45, 56

depiction, 3, 197, 198
derivation, 185, 188
derived alleles, 41, 42
diachrony, 4, 5, 10, 11, 16–19, 152, 168, 179
Dirichlet process, 119
discourse, 4, 76

Subject index

discrete infinity, 63
docility principle, 4
domain-general, 25
domain-specific, 24, 25
duality of patterning, 65
dynamic phenomena, 41

ease of articulation, 71
echolalia, 88, 91
economy principle, 9
embedding, 76
emerging languages, 70
enchrony, 4
erosion, 56
    phonological, 16
esoteric code, 78
European languages, 196
evolutionary biology, 17, 19

faithfulness constraints, 165
Family Bias method, 122
familylect, 71
founder effects, 191
functional principles, 9, 10, 16, 17, 136, 148
functional typology, 23, 34
functionalism, 117

Galton's problem, 136
garden-path effects, 55
gender, 14, 18, 171
genealogical signal, 41
generative linguistics, 23, 24, 33, 34, 53, 90
genetics, 4, 26, 41, 45, 190
gesture, 3, 197
goal oriented vs source oriented, 16
grammar of the body, 64, 66, 76
grammar-phonology dependencies, 148

grammaticalization, 13, 18, 56, 136
graph theory, 124

haplogroup, 132
harmonic vs. non-harmonic, 26, 28, 29
Haversine formula, 133
historical linguistics, 16, 117
historical relations, 118
holophrases, 63
human language faculty, 23, 24, 33, 117
human vs. inanimate, 65, 73

iconicity, 71, 72, 197
ideophones, 195–198, 200
implicational scales, 159
implicational universals, 9, 10, 14, 16, 18, 19, 23, 30, 119, 124, 143
    bidirectional, 119, 121, 122
    bidirectional vs. unidirectional, 119
    unidirectional, 119, 121, 122
implosives, 145
inference, 4, 12, 16
inter-individual differences, 45, 47
inter-population differences, 47
interactional ecology, 200
interactional linguistics, 65, 198
interjections, 195, 196, 198–200
intonation, 67, 72
inventory structure, 160
invisible hand processes, 4
isolating languages, 124
iterated learning, 41

joint attention, 86, 88, 89
juxtaposition, 104

L2 speakers, 123

Subject index

language acquisition, 90
language change, 1, 56, 119
language contact, 41, 122, 135, 136, 180, 189, 190
language development, 85, 87
language evolution, 53, 54, 56, 63, 64
learnability, 27, 34
lexeme formation, 71
lexical classes, 179, 182
    flexibility, 179, 183, 184, 186, 188–191, 193
lexical diffusion, 56
linguistic complexity, 70
local dependencies, 55
loss vs. maintainence, 17

machine learning, 119
manner of articulation, 160
Mantel testing, 130, 132, 133
marginalia, 195, 198, 200
markedness, 112, 160, 161, 165, 166
    hierarchies, 101, 159, 162, 163, 167
    semantic, 166
Markov Causal Condition, 124
Maximum Entropy, 25
meaningful vs. meaningless, 65
meme, 136, 137
mental universals, 24
Meso-American languages, 122
microcephalin, 130, 131
mini-linguist, 55
mitochondrial DNA, 132, 133, 190
mixed effects model framework, 122
modifier classifiers, 173–175, 177
morphological complexity, 123
musical protolanguage, 63

nasal consonants, 143, 145
nasal vowels, 143

natural ontology, 193
neutralization, 163
nominal classifications, 171
nominal word order, 26
noun-verb distinction, 179, 181, 183, 193
now-or-never bottleneck, 54–57
number, 171
numeral classifiers, 172–175, 177

ontogeny, 4
optimality theory, 160
oral vowels, 143, 145, 149
overt marking, 9, 13, 14, 16, 17

Pacific languages, 186
parent-child interaction, 89, 90
parentheticals, 75
pattern congruity, 97, 113
perception, 41, 42, 44
phonation, 3
phonetic naturalness, 167
phonological changes, 10, 11
phonology, 65, 66, 97, 141
phrasal stress, 72
phrasal verb constructions, 97, 102, 105, 109–111
phrase structure, 179, 185
phylogeny, 122, 133, 135
Pidgins, 68
pitch, 3, 41
place neutralization, 161, 163
place of articulation, 160, 162
    hierarchy, 161, 163
polysemy, 175–177
poverty-of-the-stimulus, 32
predicates, 110, 185
prediction, 55, 56, 152
prepositional languages, 15, 120

Subject index

preverbal infants, 87
Probabilistic Harmonic Grammar, 25
probabilistic models, 25, 45, 47
probability, 118, 121
probable languages, 117
processing, 53–55, 57
processing ease, 18
production, 41, 42, 44, 55
prosodic nasality, 145
prosodic organization, 64
prosody, 197, 198
prosody vs. syntax, 65, 68
proximate vs. ultimate, 17

rara, 195
reduction, 56
regression methods, 122
regularization, 28–30
repair, 199
restricted code, 78
rhythm, 72

sampling models, 119
scope, 30, 32, 33
semantic bleaching, 56
serial verb constructions, 97, 103, 105,
      109–111, 129, 151, 152
shared information, 67, 78
shared intentionality, 85–88
sign languages, 63, 66
    established, 66, 67, 70, 71, 76
    new, 63, 64
simplicity vs. complexity, 97, 112
Southeast Asian languages, 129, 151
statistical learning abilities, 91
statistical vs. absolute, 24
stress, 150
structural congruity, 97, 113
Structural equation modelling, 124

subordination, 68, 75
surface properties, 144
syllables, 63
synchrony, 3, 5, 18, 68, 152
syntactic recursion, 63
syntactic relations, 73
syntacticization, 56
syntax, 63, 73, 97, 185, 196–198, 200

time adverbials, 75
timescales, 1, 53, 56
tone, 3, 41–43, 129, 130, 132–134
tonogenesis, 41
topic, 11, 12, 67, 76
transmission, 5, 17, 122
    cultural, 41, 42, 47
    genealogical, 122
    horizontal, 122, 132, 137
    social, 198
typological universals, 24, 26, 32, 34
typology, 9, 18, 23, 24, 33, 34, 101, 112,
      117, 119, 141, 159, 160, 177

universal grammar, 90
universals, 112, 143
usage properties, 119

variation, 161, 162
    inter-language, 163, 166
    intra-language, 162, 166
vowel height, 159

Williams syndrome, 90
word order, 65, 73
words vs. phonology, 68

Y-chromosomal DNA, 190

zero marking, 13, 16
zero vs. overt marking, 10

www.ingramcontent.com/pod-product-compliance
Lightning Source LLC
Chambersburg PA
CBHW081203170426
43197CB00018B/2912